father tongue, mother land

ADVANCE PRAISE FOR THE BOOK

'Never before have I read such an insightful and comprehensive historical account of Indian languages as Peggy Mohan's, lighting up the subterranean pathways of language continuities over vast time spans. It offers an entirely original and thoughtful re-reading of India's cultural and linguistic past'—**Ganesh Devy, chief editor, *People's Linguistic Survey of India***

'As expected, this book is both serious and entertaining, appealing to academics as well as laymen readers like me. *Father Tongue* is quite appropriate as a title, and should tickle the curiosity of readers'—**Sumanta Banerjee, journalist and writer**

'Continuing to speak to the ordinary critical reader, *Father Tongue, Motherland* fleshes out the details in the map of languages and peoples in India's past—right up to the colour and texture of the soil in which the trees and bushes of our time are rooted. Challenging the nineteenth-century picture of how the ingredients of old languages go into the growth of new languages, this book shows just how the visible work done by air and sunlight complements the quiet underground dynamics of soil, water and nutrients, to give languages a spectacularly new look'—**Probal Dasgupta, former professor of linguistics, Indian Statistical Institute, Kolkata and honorary member, Linguistic Society of America**

'The theory of the blending of the races is applied to the emergence of new languages in this page-turner. *Father Tongue, Motherland: The Birth of Language in South Asia* by Peggy Mohan transcends its genre and becomes accessible to readers who have never wanted to do linguistics. Humorous and sarcastic, it tickles linguists and others. Written in a lucid and conversational style, the book will reach out to various readers about the genesis of languages'—**Anvita Abbi, adjunct professor, Department of Linguistics, Simon Fraser University, Vancouver, B.C., Canada, B.B. Borkar Chair, Goa University, and former professor and chair, Centre for Linguistics, Jawaharlal Nehru University, New Delhi**

'Peggy Mohan's *Father Tongue, Motherland* is a compelling sequel to her seminal *Wanderers, Kings, Merchants* (2021). It is a refreshing uniformitarian sociohistorical account of how modern East Indian languages, in particular, are consequences of layers of population movements and language contacts that produced either language shifts concurrent with substrate influence or significant superstrate influence on structures of some populations' heritage languages. The numerous comparisons between the evolution of the languages the author discusses and that of especially creoles are absolutely insightful. The lucid prose makes the book a more enjoyable read for genealogical linguists, including creolists, ready to revisit "creole exceptionalism" or the Stammbaum representations of language families, including what they mean'—**Salikoko S. Mufwene, Edward Carson Waller Distinguished Service Professor of Linguistics. University of Chicago, and founding editor, Cambridge Approaches to Language Contact**

'Peggy Mohan's book *Father Tongue, Motherland: The Birth of Language in South Asia* continues her earlier research on the origins of Indian languages and breaks new ground. The book explores prehistory with fresh insights into migration patterns, now corroborated by genetic evidence showing that most incoming migrants were males who married local women. This created a fascinating linguistic dynamic between the father's language, the mother's language and their children's language acquisition patterns. Using this framework, Mohan examines the linguistic landscape across multiple regions—the Deccan plateau, the Dravidian south and along India's northern rim. Perhaps her most significant contribution is her analysis of the "Language X" phenomenon—ancient linguistic features in northern Indian languages that cannot be traced to any known language family. Through this innovative approach, Mohan offers new perspectives on India's linguistic prehistory'—**Madhav M. Deshpande, Professor Emeritus, Sanskrit and linguistics, University of Michigan, Ann Arbor, Michigan, USA; senior fellow, Oxford Centre for Hindu Studies and adjunct professor, National Institute of Advanced Studies, Bengaluru, India**

father tongue, mother land

The Birth of Language in South Asia

PEGGY MOHAN

PENGUIN
ALLEN
LANE

An imprint of Penguin Random House

ALLEN LANE

Allen Lane is an imprint of the Penguin Random House group of companies
whose addresses can be found at global.penguinrandomhouse.com

Published by Penguin Random House India Pvt. Ltd
4th Floor, Capital Tower 1, MG Road,
Gurugram 122 002, Haryana, India

Penguin
Random House
India

First published in Allen Lane by Penguin Random House India 2025

10 9 8 7 6 5 4 3 2 1

ISBN 9780670099740

Typeset in Adobe Caslon Pro by Manipal Technologies Limited, Manipal
Printed at Thomson Press India Ltd, New Delhi

www.penguin.co.in

To Dinesh

The oft-repeated phrase 'unity in diversity' most aptly describes South Asia's modern population, the unity coming from its maternal heritage, the diversity from its paternal.[1]

~

বাঙলা ভাষার বিচারেও দেখা যায়—এটি দাঁড়িয়ে আছে খেরওয়াল গোষ্ঠীর ভাষার কাঠামোর উপর।

Bāŋlā bhāṣār bicāreo dekhā jāy—eṭi dāṛiye āche Kherwāl goṣṭhīr bhāṣār kāṭhāmor upar.

Analysis of the Bengali language shows clearly that it has been built on the structure of the Kherwal (Santal) language.[2]

Contents

1. The Road Within 1
2. The Deccan as a Twilight Zone 26
3. The Taming of the Ergative Dragon 59
4. In Search of 'Language X' 95
5. Across the Sangam 157
6. The Dravidian Dreamtime 220
7. A Chimera on the Northern Rim 253
8. The Return of the Tiramisu Bear 275

A Note on Spelling 295
Acknowledgements 299
Bibliography 301
Notes 317
Index 345

1

The Road Within

The road within without a right or wrong . . .

The Silence of a Candle, Paul Winter

One morning, as I sat with a crossword puzzle, a song floated up into my mind, a song by Simon and Garfunkel composed in honour of Frank Lloyd Wright.[1] I was not really listening to the tune, and only a little to the words that merely underlined the song's message. What blew me away was the chord structure. The bass notes and chords tracked out in gentle retreat, from time to time stepping back up on to higher ground to catch a last glimpse into an amazing life, bathing the song in the shadowless light that comes after the sun itself has set. How wonderful, I thought, to be able to capture this sense of loss and write a requiem for an architect in the architecture of a song, treating the melody as something like a coat of paint, almost an afterthought.

As a linguist, I look at languages in much the same way. I do note the vocabulary and the writing system, but I see words and script symbols as something ephemeral, always ready to change, while the bass notes and chord structure in the sound system and grammar are the more eternal parts of the song. It is a bit like a raga. Two songs might have similar tunes, but if the raga notes and the inner architecture of note combinations differ, they are not the same song.

~

In my earlier book, *Wanderers, Kings, Merchants*, we had wondered if the modern Indo-Aryan languages of South Asia, with a grammatical structure that went back to a time before Sanskrit but vocabulary that was related to Sanskrit, might be not simply hybrids but creoles. That was a delicious almost heretical thought: weren't creoles the languages that had come up in slave plantation societies, where small numbers of European planters lived among huge numbers of African slaves? Could the creole model be extricated from the Caribbean setting and applied to languages in South Asia from an era when there had been no Europeans and no slave plantations?

Creoles seemed to have a unique backstory. They were supposed to have started out as pidgins, which were ad hoc attempts to deal with a situation of chaos, where even among African slaves, it seems, from the same part of West Africa, communication was impossible. Creoles were said to have emerged when young children took that disordered and inconsistent input and fashioned it into a first language. But had anything like that ever happened in South Asia? Had there ever been the sort of chaos back in medieval times where huge numbers of people were thrown together with no language in common?

What we had been told, in South Asia, was another story, that the first new languages to emerge when settlers came into contact with local people were not pidgins, but prakrits. There was no talk of chaos in these encounters: just local people who learnt to communicate with the settlers, but whose way of speaking was . . . different. The Indo-Aryan languages we saw as likely creoles came up much, much later.

What was the real story behind all these mixed languages?

~

As a child in Trinidad, West Indies, I grew up speaking Trinidadian Creole English* as my first language. This creole is not as remote from Standard English as other Caribbean creoles like Jamaican Creole English, which non-Jamaicans often find impossible to follow. I once took my husband and his brother and sister to a play in Jamaica and ended up having to translate every single line of the dialogue, since they could not understand anything at all. In Trinidadian Creole English, for example, 'that's my book' is *daiz mih book*, but in Jamaican it could well be *a fi-mi bwuk-dat*. Trinidadian Creole English is much more like English, and every time I look it seems to have edged even closer, so much so that my cousins now tell me that I sound old-fashioned, and are surprised to hear the sort of Creole I can dredge up when I have to speak to old villagers. Trinidadian Creole English now shares almost all its vocabulary with Standard English, and most of the remaining words are so easy for an outsider to

* Upper-case 'C' in Creole is used here because it is part of the name of the language. Whenever the word is used to mean a type of mixed language, a lower-case 'c' is used: creole.

grasp that we envy Jamaicans the warm hug of seclusion they get from their creole.

So it is no surprise that the schooling system when I was a child did not see this creole as a separate language from English. It was seen, rather, as nothing more than 'mistakes' that our teachers needed to correct for us to be transformed into perfect English speakers.

But my friends and I, sitting at our desks in school, did not think it was going so well. Like Bhojpuri speakers in India who have no trouble understanding spoken and written Hindi, while still being foxed at the idea that its nouns and verbs have genders, we understood our teachers easily, but were tongue-tied when we had to stand up and speak, and our copybooks were full of red ink, especially on the endings of our verbs, where the teacher had found 'mistakes', what we called 'green verbs': *I does go* (I go), *I did go* or *I had go* (I had gone), *I had-was to-go* (I was supposed to go), or even *I goes* (I go), with a final *s*. 'Green verbs' were not obvious creolisms like *ah go go'* (I will go), or *mi ent go* (I didn't go). They were meant to be English, but they didn't make it all the way. It was only when I was fourteen that I looked up one bright day and realized that I was ready to stand up in class and speak comfortably in English.[2]

Trinidadian Creole English is a good compass to hold on to for the journey into language evolution in the Indian subcontinent. It forces you to look past words into the architecture of language to see how outward resemblances and similarities in words can lead you astray, because the elite languages of India's medieval era, the prakrits,* which were essentially based on Sanskrit, have radically different grammars

* Upper-case 'P' is used when referring to the name of a language, like Māgadhan Prakrit. Whenever the word is used to mean a type of language, lower-case 'p' is used: prakrit.

from the modern Indo-Aryan languages. To say 'in the house' in Sanskrit, you would use the locative case of the word for house: *gr̥he*. In modern Hindi, you would use a postposition, *mẽ,* a separate word that comes after the word for house: *ghar mẽ*, because Hindi doesn't have cases like Sanskrit and the prakrits. So even though the Sanskrit word *gr̥ha* looks a lot like Hindi *ghar*, there is a huge difference in the architecture of the sentences they occur in.

What do we mean by a 'prakrit'? What is this local variety of English in Trinidad and other one-time British colonies that doesn't do anything *wrong*, in terms of English grammar, but which still has its own flavour?

The most familiar example of a prakrit that comes to my mind is Indian English. Not the version that bends the rules of English to come up with *you* ***must be knowing*** *my father*, or ***are you having*** *a pencil* (which would not be okay even in Hindi: **mere pitā-ji ko* ***jān rahe honge***[3] simply doesn't work). What I mean here is the Indian English most of us write all the time. You couldn't point to anything grammatically wrong with it, but you know that some of those turns of phrase would not appear in a book published outside India. They are uniquely Indian.

A friend once sent me a manuscript of a novel she had written and asked me for my comments. As I read it on my computer, I began to see, first in the dialogue, words that were a bit too ... precise, too literary, to sound like spoken English. I changed *'Why are you sweating* ***profusely****?'* to *'You are sweating* ***like anything****!'*, an observation, no longer a question. I changed '*she* ***concurred***' to '*she* ***agreed***'. The small, neat lawn looked ***incongruous*** (no: *out of place*). Or old-fashioned words like *weep* (cry) and *wed* (marry). I asked her if I could edit her manuscript on track changes, as I was beginning to see a bigger pattern in the differences between her usage and Standard English. It was a win-win situation: she would get a first edit, and I would get prakrit data I had only had a vague sense of up to then.

What I expected to find was overuse of the passive, *it was required*, instead of the more active *I needed*, or expressions like *it is with me*, an avoidance of the English verb *have*, which doesn't exist in Indian languages. I even expected a lot of *while saying so* or *having sat down*, which are inspired by Indian languages, which prefer to nest actions into *having eaten he went home*, rather than stringing them out as in English *he ate and then went home*. Even these would count as conforming to the rules of English grammar, though still with an Indian flavour. But when I looked again at the manuscript, that was not what I found.

What I found was something old, something that went back to a time before Sanskrit, and I wondered if it could have been a feature of the vanished languages of the Indus Valley: a love of nouns. One could feel *the* ***advent*** *of winter* (*that winter was coming*). ***Progress*** *was preliminary* (*things were in their early stages*). *Even with a Western* ***upbringing*** (*even though he had grown up in the US*). *This* ***journey*** *I decided to undertake* (*I was the one who decided to come here)*. He looked at her *to assess her* ***state*** (*to see if she was really up to going on a bike ride*). *The* ***knowledge*** *of past* ***intimacy*** (*because they had been so close in the past*). She could not *pinpoint the* ***cause*** *of her* ***disquiet*** (*make out what was bothering her*). She needed a man *for* ***identity*** *and* ***protection*** (*to define and protect her)*. He would save her from *the* ***confines*** *of this place* (from *being stuck here)*. There was a sense *of* ***loss*** *and* ***finality*** (of *things coming to an end)*.

None of it was in any way wrong. Just different. It was *Indian* English.

When we speak of a prakrit, we are thinking of precisely *this* sort of difference from, say, Sanskrit. Something that gives a local flavour which, when you add a local accent, would strike a purist as 'different' enough for them to see prakrit speakers as 'not us'.

Why would Sanskrit speakers be so irked by the prakrits that they could not bring themselves to see them as essentially the same family as Sanskrit, the way we go through material written in English without being spooked by localisms that come up in international English? At a guess, I would say that it has to do with the obsessively *oral* nature of Sanskrit, such that the first impression made by 'texts' would be the accent of the speaker. So much of our interaction in English these days is in written form as many of us prefer to send an email or a short WhatsApp message instead of making a phone call. As a result, it can come as a surprise when we finally meet people we know only through written 'chats', or hear their voices on WhatsApp audio recordings if they are, say, driving and not in a position to type out their responses.

All of a sudden, these Internet friends turn into voices that change the sounds we are expecting to hear, using *saṁdhi* rules, or sound assimilation rules, from languages that are not ours. Think of how *śrimati* becomes '*srimadi*', *empathy* becomes '*yum-patti*', or *Shakespeare* comes out as '*sex-peer*' in the mouths of fluent English speakers from other parts of India. These things reveal something more than strange *saṁdhis*. We see that these friends did not 'go to English-medium schools' as 'we' did. Just as prakrit speakers were not actually from those Brahman *śākhās*, or families, that preserved the Rig Veda. These are the sort of things that Sanskrit purists were obsessed with because there wasn't much else that set the early prakrits apart from Sanskrit. They were Sanskrit's close cousins. In written text, most of these differences in accent would have sunk out of sight below sea level.

That is a far cry from the sort of difference between a Caribbean creole and English or French. Or a modern north Indian language and Sanskrit. In Caribbean creoles and north Indian languages, there is a sense of a different operating system, a different 'architecture', even if speakers are not aware of how far their languages have drifted away from English and Sanskrit.[4]

If modern Indian languages are actually creoles, current theory would insist that they must have started out as pidgins, in an atmosphere of primordial chaos. This is the one sticking point that has prevented us from seeing north Indian languages as creoles and unifying the discussion of mixed languages in different parts of the world. Caribbean creoles are supposed to have started out as pidgins, which went on to become creoles, the native languages of children whose parents came to the Caribbean as African slaves. But modern north Indian languages could not have started out as pidgins: because no matter how hard we look, we see no sign of social disruption, of groups of people suddenly uprooted and thrown together with no language in common, and no need for any pidgin, in medieval India. On the contrary, India's modern languages could have taken shape gradually, slowly displacing earlier local vernaculars over a period of centuries.

What if the pidgin-creole model itself is wrong? What if pidgins and primordial chaos are not actually a part of the process that made creoles? This thought is exciting because it is a rare moment when we in India get to use our own languages to challenge linguistic theory and posit one that is better. In this book, I aim to turn the whole model of language change on its head and arrive at another that makes more intuitive sense, one that better explains what happened in our land as well as in other parts of the world where languages met and merged.

~

Creoles are mixed languages that came up in the Caribbean during the time of slavery when Africans were forcibly transported as labour to the Caribbean sugar estates or to the cotton fields in North America. These new languages had vocabularies drawn from English and European languages like French, Dutch and Portuguese, the official languages of the different islands and mainland territories with slave plantations, but their grammars retained features from the West African languages that the Africans had spoken earlier. There were creoles in the Gullah Islands off South Carolina and Louisiana, in the United States, Mauritius and the Seychelles in the Indian Ocean, and even in Hawaii, in the Pacific Ocean.[5] These creoles were not made to facilitate communication between Europeans and their labour: Europeans to this day have their old languages. But in the Caribbean, Africans were left with only the creoles as community languages, as their old languages were lost. Creoles, in short, were mixed languages made by Africans for Africans, even if others did learn and use them.

In pidgin-creole theory, the European parent was just a sperm donor, providing only the words for the new language, and the African parent the 'mother', actually incubating the new life form and supplying the grammar into which all the new words fit.

This was exactly the sort of layered mixture that had excited me about the Indo-Aryan languages spoken in the north of the Indian subcontinent. These languages too had words drawn from local prakrits, medieval languages of power close to

Sanskrit, which is why they were called 'Indo-Aryan' languages. But their grammar had a number of features that had nothing to do with the Indo-Aryan family, looking instead like things that had survived from the older languages of the area.[6] Sanskrit and the prakrits did not have separate words placed after nouns to mean 'in', 'of', 'to' or 'from', like Indian languages do now, but a case system—*kārakas*—where the noun *bālaka*, 'child', inflected to become *bālakaḥ, bālakau, bālakāḥ; bālakam, bālakau, bālakān; bālakena, bālakābhyām, bālakaiḥ* . . . a different set of endings for each separate class of noun. For example, if we ignore the *saṁdhi* rules when words are strung together, *bālakaḥ gacchati* means 'the child goes', where the child is the subject. And *bālakaṁ paśyāmi* means 'I see the child' where the child is the object. And *bālakasya pustakaṁ* means 'the child's book', where the child is in the genitive (or possessive) case.

These endings made the nouns singular, dual or plural, and also the subject of the sentence, the object, an 'instrumental', an indirect object, ablative, possessive, locative or vocative, eight cases in all. In Sanskrit, the case marker would also change depending on the class of the noun it went with. The instrumental case marker is *ena* for *bālaka* (*bālakena likhita*, 'written by the child'), *-nā* with *muni*, 'sage' (*muninā likhita*, 'written by the sage'), *-rā* with *netā*, 'leader' (*netrā likhita*, 'written by the leader'), and *-vā* with *vadhū*, 'bride' (*vadhvā likhita*, 'written by the bride').

The Sanskrit word for 'in the house' is *gṛhe*, where *-e* is a locative case ending. In Hindi *gṛhe* is *ghar mẽ*, where a separate word, *mẽ*, now means 'in', exactly the way that *vīṭṭ-il* means 'in the house' in Tamil and Malayalam, Dravidian languages spoken in the south of India, where *-il* means 'in'. Postpositions like *mẽ* are now the norm in all the Indo-Aryan languages of north India, making these languages more like Dravidian languages of south India, in this respect, than like Sanskrit and the prakrits. It is as if the same forces that had mixed West African and European languages in the Caribbean had also been at work in the subcontinent, much earlier, and without any help from the Europeans. The Indo-Aryan languages look exactly like creoles.

~

But there were problems. The first stumbling block that kept us from exploring this resemblance was the way creoles were tightly bound up not with a *process*, but with the slave estates themselves. We simply couldn't wrest the model away to apply it to other situations with mixed languages that looked amazingly like creoles. It was like a force field around a piece of private property, shooing away linguists working on any other mixed languages. Creoles were *only* about colonial planters who were White and the 'little people', who were not. 'Little people' is a term I used in my earlier book, *Wanderers, Kings, Merchants* to mean ordinary people—in this case, African slaves—who had no option but to adapt to changes brought by powerful outsiders like the slave traders and the colonial planters. But all of us who had studied Latin, French and Spanish, or Sanskrit, the prakrits and the modern north Indian languages, could feel the buzz of something familiar at work in how they must have come into being, a scent of creoles. It was impossible to imagine that the forces that created the plantation creoles could be in any way different from those that had made the modern mixed languages of Europe and the Indian subcontinent. We will get to this later in this chapter.

The other thing that made no sense was: If these pidgins had come up separately on estates that were isolated from each other, how was it that the creoles that emerged on each island had a sameness to them? There is such a thing as Trinidadian Creole English, or Jamaican Creole English, or Barbadian, or Guyanese, transcending the particular estate a family had been bound to, and taking in the entire territory. And not only creoles: even the Bhojpuri spoken centuries later by Indian migrant labour to some of the same sugar estates seemed to have easily bypassed the formidable estate gates and evolved into a language shared by all the Indian migrants in the territory, one with very little local variation. Whatever fusion was going on did not have its origin in separate moments of conception on estates that were as hermetically sealed off from each other as modern prisons would be.

But the biggest problem with the model, which did not square with what we knew of medieval India, or indeed southern Europe, was that creoles were not a thing in themselves. They came with one piece of extra baggage: pidgins. Creoles were supposed to have started out as pidgins, so the story went, in an atmosphere of chaos when West Africans were first transported as slaves to the Caribbean sugar plantations. But try as we might, we just could not find a period of chaos, or any sign of a pidgin, in the Indian subcontinent or in southern Europe at the time when the modern languages we know were making their appearance.

Pidgins are stripped-down codes, unstable and 'no one's mother tongue', though some pidgins do stabilize over time.[7] According to the pidgin-creole model, the first adult Africans on Caribbean slave estates would have had no option but to communicate with each other using a pidgin that took all its words from the language of the 'masters'. But when these early Africans had children, and the children found themselves with only the pidgin as input for establishing a first language—as their parents supposedly had no African language to pass on—they were able to impose a system on it, drawing on their innate ability to listen and configure it all into a first language that did all that a first language was supposed to do. Creoles, according to this model, were languages made by the first generation of African children on the estates, and because they were able to impose a system on all the disordered input, they ended up creating stable natural languages. The route from stable West African languages to stable Caribbean creoles that preserved features of a West African substratum, the inner architecture of the little people's languages, transited through a time of chaos and a sketchy unstable pidgin.

But how, I wondered, could you say that the old languages had vanished into thin air if their grammars were to miraculously come back to life a generation later in creoles made by the children? If the children were going by their inborn linguistic ability, and nothing else, why did the innards of the new languages they made call to mind old African languages they had never heard? Wasn't the pidgin supposed to be a watershed moment, a tabula rasa, with everything that came after it a fresh start?

It had to go back to the idea of a pidgin, I thought, and the certainty that the creoles had started out from pidgins, or (according to one theory) from a single proto-pidgin that got tweaked.[8] It had to be a European man, during the time of slavery, who was struck by what the Africans were speaking, with fewer word endings than in European languages and words that sounded like a garbled version of the words in his language, deciding that these must be pidgin forms of European languages. Could that be how it had happened? Is that how the word pidgin had got attached to creoles? I decided to check my suspicions by delving into the literature to find out whether that man who thought he heard a pidgin had really existed.

But when I found a piece in the *Encyclopedia Britannica* titled 'Creole Languages' by Salikoko Mufwene, professor of linguistics and veteran creolist at the University of Chicago, I saw that I was wrong.[9] Mufwene is the only creolist I know who looks not only at language data but also at the historical record to make sure that he has the story right. Yes, there had been a gentleman back in 1685, the French explorer Michel Jajolet, sieur de la Courbe, who had mentioned a Portuguese-based language spoken in Senegal, but he had called it a *creole*, not a pidgin. Mufwene, however, went on to give a different timeline for how the idea of a pidgin found its way into the discussion of creoles:

> Since the 1930s some linguists have claimed that creoles emerged from pidgins, languages with very reduced vocabularies and grammars that are typically seen where otherwise mutually unintelligible groups come together intermittently. That hypothesis is controversial, in part because the plantations on which creole languages emerged started as small homestead communities in which non-European slaves, European indentured labourers, and European masters lived fairly intimately. Typically, all three of these groups spoke similarly until a colony shifted from subsistence to plantation agriculture and institutionalized segregation. The hypothesis proposed by several creolists in the 1970s and '80s—namely, that creoles emerged abruptly—has also been contested by those who posit a gradual development during the transition to a plantation economy.[10]

The Spanish-based language, Pay̆ol, spoken in Trinidad by the descendants of Africans brought to small cocoa plantations in the 1500s, when Trinidad was a Spanish colony, is very much like the European Spanish of those times. It is not at all simplified, as it includes complex features like the subjunctive, and some of its vocabulary harks back to a time when Spanish and Portuguese had not yet fully separated. In a sentence fragment that I remember hearing from an old man in Maracas, *cuando venga la noich*, 'when night comes', *venga* is the subjunctive form of the verb 'to come'. The word *noich*, 'night', is the same word as in Brazilian Portuguese (where it is spelt *noite*), and 'now' in Pañol is *agora*, like it is in Portuguese, not *ahora* as in modern Spanish. This subjunctive, *venga*, to express a future that is imaginary, is something very Spanish. Pañol is not a creole. It is just a good example of how Africans on small homestead farms spoke what Mufwene calls *varieties* of European languages.

According to Mufwene, even early traders on the African coast did not use a pidgin for communication with Europeans. 'Such transactions,' he says, 'could not have taken place in a broken language. Colonial history actually appears to have relied on interpreters from the beginning all the way to the early twentieth century . . . Newitt (2010) is very clear about the role played by the *Lançados* and *Tangomaos* (self-exiled European traders who escaped jail sentences and religious persecution) and their children from unions with African women, in serving as go-betweens, along with the *Pombeiros* (African merchants), in the slave trade.'[11] And as for creoles, 'most creoles probably emerged in the eighteenth century, though some creolists claim that they emerged in the seventeenth century already.'

~

To put all this in Indian-friendly terms: there was, in the heyday of the slave trade, a strong tradition of prakrits along the coast of West Africa,[12] with a class of local people who learnt the languages of Europeans very well (though undoubtedly with a local accent), along with a huge hinterland of little people who were completely outside the loop, continuing their lives in older local languages. This scenario would be utterly familiar to anyone who read about the Vedic migration to the subcontinent in my earlier book, *Wanderers, Kings, Merchants*: a male-driven migration of settlers arriving one fine day from lands to the north without their own womenfolk, and going on to have children with local women, creating a new bilingual generation that knew both its mother tongue as well as its 'father tongue', Sanskrit. Some boys would have learnt Sanskrit well enough to carry on the tradition of Vedic composition. But others, along with their mothers and sisters, and a few local men with an eye on the main chance, managed to get close, but not quite close enough. What they spoke were called prakrits, varieties of Sanskrit that followed the same grammar, but had a strong local flavour.

By the medieval era, these prakrits had grown into regional languages of power, differing mostly in accent and local details from Sanskrit in the same way as the Portuguese, English and French spoken by the interpreters in West Africa would have differed from the language spoken by the metropolitan elites.

The Indo-Aryan languages on the subcontinent, the actual mixtures, did not come up right away. There were many centuries when the older local languages, some of them probably linked to the vanished Indus Valley languages, must have lived alongside the Indo-Aryan prakrits (just as the indigenous West African languages carry on to this day separate from the elite prakrit varieties of English and French in West Africa). It was only in the tenth to twelfth centuries that we began to see signs in the Indian subcontinent of these mixed languages in the written record, with features of the old local languages spoken by the early mothers and their community tucked into their grammar. Over the centuries, however, these mixed languages completely replaced the older languages of the northwest, which survive only in the substratum features that we use as we speak without giving them a thought.[13]

~

Pidgins are not the ancestors of creoles, but it isn't as though they don't exist at all. They do. Nigerian Pidgin English is an example of an 'expanded pidgin'. I remember one afternoon listening to a performer on YouTube and wondering where he could be from. He wasn't Jamaican, or Guyanese, or even Tobagonian: but going by the way he spoke he had to be one of 'us', Trinidadian. But somehow he wasn't, quite. Then he turned to someone off stage and shouted 'Babatunde!', and the penny dropped. Babatunde is a Yoruba boy's name that means 'Grandfather returns', and it is given to the first grandson born after an old man dies. He was Nigerian.

Mufwene says that 'there is a neat ecological complementary division between creoles and pidgins: the creoles that have informed our theorizing typically emerged in plantation settlement colonies, whereas pidgins emerged in trade colonies or on whaling ships.'[14] The difference between creoles and pidgins, then, according to Mufwene, is not in their actual structure, but in their histories.

~

Where does that leave us, looking for a model to help us understand how languages mix in the Indian subcontinent?

Well, for one thing, the force field around the term 'creole' has been switched off. 'Creole Exceptionalism', the idea that creoles and pidgins are a special case, and not language mixtures that could appear in places other than colonial plantations, has been laid to rest.

Could the Indo-Aryan languages really be creoles? They did not come to life on plantations in settlement colonies, in an atmosphere of racial apartheid, though our little people, the ones who spoke the old languages, did live within a formidable caste system that kept them segregated from the ones at the top, with women the most isolated of all. But Creole Exceptionalism is dead. Now creoles as an idea have to be about something more than an anecdotal tale of settlement colonies and their plantations. We have to dig deeper to find out what creoles are in a more systematic way. And this trail leads us through the thorny issue of what makes a pidgin so different from a creole to what recent genetic research tells us about early settlement in the Indian subcontinent[15] and its impact on how our languages came to be mixed.

In all sorts of ways, our modern Indo-Aryan languages call to mind creoles. They too came to life between the tenth and twelfth centuries from a multitude of little people making a transition to a world designed and ruled by an elite that was connected across the entire north of the subcontinent. And like the plantation creoles, these Indo-Aryan languages erased the earlier languages of the region[16] in a way that Nigerian Pidgin English has still not been able to do. The indigenous languages of Nigeria are alive and well.

Creoles and expanded pidgins are startlingly alike, except for the fact that the expanded pidgins seem to be able to live alongside older languages without erasing them, while creoles essentially replace them as the native language of a new community. In fact, one of the main descriptors of pidgins is that they are 'no one's mother tongue'. Why is it that pidgins do not go on to be 'mother tongues'? Why is it that pidgins do not have offspring, while the creole situation is quintessentially about a mixed language becoming a 'mother tongue'?

The answer to this question takes us back to where all the pidgins began: in trading communities and on whaling ships. These were worlds of *men* stepping out of their normal environment for short-term encounters with the big global world of the Market. These are the same sort of male migrants we have seen throughout history, male explorers on journeys without their womenfolk and families. They came, they connected, and then they vanished. Any offspring they might have had would have been back in their original homes, speaking the old languages, or from encounters with local women who were not part of the male world they ventured into from time to time.

The first migrants to the subcontinent, the early hunter-gatherers who arrived from Africa 65,000 years ago, according to geneticists tracking the first migrants out of Africa, were a mix of men and women, wandering and spreading slowly rather than purposefully 'migrating'. But subsequent migrants here were almost always men, explorers, and if they hadn't stayed and settled and found wives locally, theirs would have been the same sterile pidgin story, because men by themselves do not have children. Even in Trinidad, Indians as a *community* date back to the 1870s, and not earlier, even though Indian migration started in 1849, because the first migrants were all men. If any of these men had survived the plantations and had children with local women, these children would not have perpetuated an Indian culture but would have melted into the Afro-Caribbean world of their mothers. It was only when

Indian women began coming as migrants to Trinidad and having children, by the 1870s, that a community could survive and grow, with a language, Bhojpuri, spoken not near the port of Calcutta, but deep inland, in eastern Uttar Pradesh, the area where migrants were recruited from after the 1860s until the end of the migration in 1919.[17]

The difference between pidgins and creoles, then, is that pidgins are 'sterile', unable to generate a community of native speakers, as they are a male phenomenon, and something by their very nature, temporary. Pidgin speakers are men who never 'left' their original homes. They did, in between trips, go back to their families and their old languages and continue their 'real' lives. Or they became extinct without offspring (to speak of) on the high seas.

Emanuel Drechsel, a linguist who lives in Hawaii, tells of an early pidgin, Maritime Polynesian Pidgin (MPP), spoken by sailors who plied the routes all the way from New Zealand to the Canadian west coast.[18] What is interesting about MPP is that it came up before Europeans came to the Pacific, making it a very local pidgin. Drechsel thinks this pidgin may have been the model for what eventually came up as Hawaiian Pidgin English on the sugar estates of Hawaii. The Hawaiian sugar estates were unlike the colonial plantations in the Caribbean and the Indian Ocean in that their labour force was made up not of slaves (men and women) but of contract labourers, who would almost all have been men, just the right conditions for a pidgin to emerge.[19] These contract labourers lived separately in different 'houses', with their families brought from home. According to Mufwene, in Hawaii what came up on the plantations was indeed a pidgin, while the more durable Hawaiian Creole English, which had native speakers, emerged in the city.

This is important for us to understand how things happened in medieval India, which had no plantation system as the settler colonies had. What it tells us is that *cities* too are the sort of places where families settle and mix, and where creoles could arise. In the Indian subcontinent, the tenth to twelfth centuries was a time of urbanization and a shift in focus from Brahmans and kings to traders and craftsmen, when we began to see signs of the modern Indo-Aryan languages appearing in secular written documents.[20]

The Caribbean plantations, much more than the small homestead farms that preceded them, would have been worlds that included a number of African women, many more than before, newcomers fresh from West Africa who came into contact with the prakrit forms of European languages spoken by African men already there. So while the plantation system was strongly associated with the emergence of creoles, the real reason for this was that large plantations needed *women*, as they found it cost-effective to maintain the pool of labour by natural increase, children born on the plantations, instead of depending only on a constant supply of adult men from Africa. Women are not natural migrants; there is a reason why the overwhelming majority of the migrants in the world, human or animal, are male. But the transition to a plantation economy created a demand for women, and the slave traders had to be incentivized to get as many women as possible, especially as there was strong opposition to the slave trade (which ended in the British Empire in 1807, though slavery itself went on for a long while after). If those African women hadn't come, all those boatloads of men crossing the Atlantic would have done no better than the pidgin-speaking men on the whaling ships, and we would have ended up without any creoles.

The women in medieval India, like the African women on the Caribbean plantations, had children and nurtured them through their early years, ensuring that any mixed languages that came up would have a new generation to pass on to in the new urban environment. So in that sense children *were* important in the formation of creoles, but not for the almost magical reasons we had once thought. It was not settler colonies and plantations per se that decided whether there would be a creole and not a pidgin, but the presence or absence of *women* able to incubate a new life form. Women were the key to it all. And the Indo-Aryan languages are creoles too, because they are also, as the witches in Shakespeare's Macbeth might have said, 'of woman born'.

~

But was 'mother', as in 'mother tongue', the full story? Or was it just that in male-driven migrations mothers tended to be local, and in that case were part of the larger local environment? Look at my own story as a 'Tiramisu bear'. When my parents met and married in Canada, my father was indeed a 'male migrant' and my mother a 'local female'. But a few years later, he brought her back to live in Trinidad, after which she was no longer 'local'. She was the foreigner. And I was born and raised in a large Indian joint family in a small town in rural Trinidad. There, I spent most of my time with my Trinidadian cousins, grandmother, aunts, uncles and neighbours. As a result, Trinidadian Creole English became my first language: *not* my mother's Canadian English. Creole, for me, was not a choice of 'father' tongue over 'mother' tongue, but a way of bonding with Trinidad and other children my age, rather than a Canada that was unreal to me.

So when we say that the hybrid children of male settlers first learnt their 'mother' tongues, we need to remember that those mothers were part of a huge local ecosystem, even if they also had a major role in early child care. And we also need to remember that nuclear families, where young children are cared for almost totally by their parents, would have been quite rare in the sorts of societies we are talking of here.

The model that emerges from this begins with an encounter between male settlers and various local people, which generates a prakrit, a language variety close to the language of the explorers but with a local 'accent' and other local touches. The speakers of this prakrit are a small group of local men who come into contact with the settler group, and the local women who have children with the settlers, creating a new bilingual generation. In the early Vedic families of the Indus Valley, the wives and children of the Vedic men, and a few elite local men, would have had enough access to native speakers of Sanskrit to speak a closely related version with a strong local accent: a prakrit.[21] And in the trading outposts of West Africa, and the early homestead farms of the New World, Africans would have lived close enough to White traders and White planters to speak a prakrit based on English, French, Dutch, Portuguese or Spanish.

This prakrit phase would not be about language mixture. This early stage would only be about a few little people mastering a close approximation of the language of the settlers.

The mixing stage comes later. Conditions change, and there is a surge in the number of little people, men and women, speakers of the older local languages, in contact with earlier ones from their group who speak the prakrit. This is when we begin to see features of the local languages getting tucked into the grammar of new languages that are full of words from local prakrits, and stabilized and passed on via a new generation of children as the native languages of new communities.

Going by the millennia that elapsed between the emergence of the early prakrits and the first signs of the modern north Indian languages, between the tenth and twelfth centuries, it is possible that the mixing stage begins more gradually than we once thought. This is what Mufwene also found in West Africa: a long period with only a few local 'interpreters' who speak prakrits of the European languages and little people speaking as they always did, and a later period where creoles emerge on huge plantations across the Atlantic. It also seems that there isn't the dramatic binary of all the vocabulary coming from one parent, and all the grammar from the other. Some of the grammar of the little people's languages finds its way into the creoles, but not all of it. And not just words but even grammatical features can cross over into creoles from the *lexifier* language that was only supposed to give the vocabulary.[22] The process is more ambidextrous than it seemed at first.

We also seem to have been wrong about the timeline: most creoles did not begin as varieties that were grammatically close to the little people's languages, and then sanskritize their way gradually towards the languages of the elites. Some of the least European features in creoles seem to have come in later, as more of the little people got into the game. What appeared first were the most prakrit-like forms of the creoles, while the varieties of the creole with the most features drawn from the local substratum languages are the last to appear.[23]

The best way to know if a model is accurate is to test it out on something you can see, a situation where all the ingredients are present because it is happening before you. And there is exactly this sort of contact scenario in India, in the borderlands between the Dravidian south of India and a language from the north, Urdu, that came to the royal courts of the Deccan during the Deccan Sultanate. In the Deccan plateau region of south India, there is a hybrid language called *Dakkhini*—a word that comes from Deccan—which has features of Urdu as well as Telugu, Kannada and Marathi. In the next chapter, we will turn our lens on the story of Dakkhini, and on other mixed languages spoken in this twilight zone between the north and the south, and see if they fit our model. Only after we have tested the model on a situation that we *can* see in the clear light of day, can we trust it to guide us back into the darkness of the remote past, shining a light on the inner architecture of our languages to give us a glimpse of how they looked and lived when they were young.

2

The Deccan as a Twilight Zone

Sounds of hope to light my way

The Silence of a Candle, Paul Winter

Every year in early summer, back in the 1950s, a swarm of colourful visitors would descend upon the town of Aligarh in Uttar Pradesh, filling up all the hostel rooms at Aligarh Muslim University (AMU) and spilling out to occupy the homes of locals who lived close by. These were Muslim girls from Hyderabad, in the Deccan, who had had their education not in schools but at home, and who had come to sit for their final high school exams. Aligarh was a safe place for Hyderabadi parents to send their unworldly girls, full of family friends to board with and rooms to stay in in the AMU hostels, which had just been vacated for the summer. AMU was also a rare institution in that it allowed private candidates to register for final school exams.

They wore bright headscarves and dupattas and spoke fast in their lilting Hyderabadi dialect that fascinated the locals, who said they could 'almost' understand what these girls were saying. Things like '*mereku nakko*' for 'I don't want it'. Or '*kaiku?*' for 'why?'

This is Dakkhini, a language some call Hyderabadi Urdu, but it is different enough from the Urdu of north India for the people of Aligarh to have seen it as another language altogether. In the expression *mereku nakko*, 'I don't want this', *mereku* means, literally, 'to me' (like the colloquial Delhi Hindi *mere-ko*) and *nakko* means, simply, 'no', a Marathi word there in Hyderabadi Dakkhini because much of what is now Maharashtra was once part of a more open-ended Deccan. But most glaringly missing from this sentence is the verb, *honā*, which would normally mean 'to be', but which here would translate as 'to be required'. The verb 'to be', in present-tense sentences like these, is left out in Dravidian languages. Dakkhini here is behaving like a south Indian language, not a north Indian language. And yet its words are close enough to north Indian Urdu words that people hearing it in Aligarh could follow the gist of what the girls were saying.

For someone like me, born and raised in Trinidad, this story is full of déjà vu. I can easily identify with these Dakkhini-speaking girls transported into Urdu-speaking Aligarh. When I was in school in the 1950s and 1960s, I spoke not English but Creole with my friends and steered clear of the Standard English I would hear all the time from my Canadian mother and the almost-English my Trinidadian father would speak. Yes, the day would come when I would make the shift to Standard English, and so would most of my friends. But while we were together, all of us girls spoke to each other only in

Creole, a language that was full of English words, but whose grammar all too often 'behaved' as if it came from a headspace that was something other than Standard English.

Is Dakkhini a creole? This was a question that struck me when K.V. Subbarao, a retired professor of linguistics at Delhi University and a native speaker of Telugu, mentioned in passing that Dakkhini was full of 'calques' from Telugu, a Dravidian language spoken in the Deccan region of India. Calques are phrases that sound as if they were first thought in one language and then translated literally into another. Think of the Indian English sentence *it is with me only*. It feels like a literal translation of *mere pās hī hai* in Hindi, with the emphatic *hī* translating as *only*, neatly avoiding the English verb 'to have', which does not exist in Indian languages.

It is with me only is a calque that does not go against the rules of English grammar, even if it sounds a bit exotic to speakers of Standard English. But the Telugu calques you find in Dakkhini are more ruthless, more oblivious of standard Urdu grammar. They are like the West African features we saw in the previous chapter in the grammars of Caribbean creoles, which pushed their way past English and French and blazed a trail of their own.

~

Urdu did not begin its life in the south of India,[1] nor, for that matter, did it start out in Aligarh. It first came up as a dialect of Delhi, and it must have been well established as a local vernacular by 1206, the year the Central Asians arrived and set up the Delhi Sultanate, because early Urdu was in every sense an Indian language. It has always, for example, had retroflexion, that quasi-genetic tag that marks a language as South Asian: *dānt* (tooth) and *ḍāṇṭ* (a scolding) are two separate words in Urdu, because the first has *t* and *d* (which are dental) while the other has *ṭ* and *ḍ* (which are retroflex).[2] Persian, however, like Standard English, has only one *t* and one *d*. In its early days, this language was not yet called Urdu: it was called Dehlavi, or even Hindi, and what we see of it in the poetry of Amir Khusro, writing in Delhi in the latter half of the thirteenth century, is so close to modern Hindi that it could have been written only yesterday.[3]

Map 1: Early Dakkhini terrain, overlapping Marathi, Telugu and Kannada areas

It took barely a century for this dialect to start spreading south. Between 1308 and 1311 Alauddin Khilji, the Sultan of Delhi, sent his armies across the Vindhyas to conquer the south of India, and by 1327 Sultan Muhammad bin Tughluq was able to shift his capital from Delhi to Daulatabad, which is now in Maharashtra, but which was then part of the larger Deccan region that extended as far south as the River Krishna. With him went a retinue of nobles, administrators and soldiers, as well as others from around Delhi willing to join the migration. By 1347, when the Deccan region became an independent Muslim state under the Bahmani Sultanate,[4] adventurers were already pouring in in large numbers from as far afield as Turkic Central Asia, Ethiopia and Iran, almost all of them men migrating without their womenfolk, and happy to settle down with local wives. This was the same pattern we have seen in all the other major migrations in the subcontinent: an early era of mixed families, even among the rulers, with wives who started out as speakers of the local language and the menfolk as speakers of the languages they brought with them. The language of the court was Persian, as it was in the north, but Dehlavi,[5] the first northern vernacular to arrive with the Sultanate forces in the Deccan, quickly put down local roots and took on features of Marathi, Kannada and Telugu, and came to be known as Dakhni, Dakni, Dakkhini or Dakkani. From its shape-shifting name, sometimes with the second-to-last vowel missing as per north Indian *saṁdhi* rules, or a south Indian *kk*, or a south Indian unaspirated *k* in place of 'kh', it was clear that this language was going to be a mixed bag.[6]

Dakkhini soon became the native language of the Muslim community that sprang up in the Deccan. Not all these Muslims traced their roots back to men who came from the north. Many local people too, speakers of Marathi, Kannada,

Telugu and Tamil, converted to Islam. These were men who brought their wives and children with them to join the new community. As they took on the new language brought by the northerners, they held on to the sounds and grammar of the older languages of south India they had lived with for as long as they could remember, fusing these two parental strands into a new linguistic life form.

~

When I look at a language to determine whether it is mixed, I choose a few features, areas of the grammar where the two parent languages are not compatible. What I expect to find in the mixed language is that the earlier local language (the maternal stream) will prevail in shaping the grammar, and the newcomer language (the paternal stream) will donate the vocabulary. That is a neat hypothesis, but over time I have seen that it is never quite that simple: there are many instances in India, and elsewhere in the world, of grammatical structure leaking from the paternal side across the fault line.[7] Nevertheless, it is a clear explicit formula for choosing areas of grammar to use as a test.

I once tried, years ago, to think of an area of Kannada grammar that would be a problem for a Marathi speaker, something he would have no instinct for. The first thing that came to mind was relative clauses. *The knife you used to cut the fruit is very sharp.*[8]

Standard Marathi uses a north Indian-style correlative construction, starting with *which* and the next clause repeating *which* in the form of *it*:

which knife you used to cut the fruit, it is very sharp

Dravidian languages would construct this sentence differently:

> *you-knife-with-fruit-cut-use [nominalizer] [relative linker] very sharp*[9]

I was certain that native Marathi speakers would not be able to wrap their brains around this tightly nested Dravidian structure unless they were truly fluent in Kannada. Would the obverse also be true? Would native speakers of Telugu confronted with a north Indian language like Dehlavi in the early days of the Deccan Sultanate prefer to stick with their Telugu way of making relative clauses?

Harbir Kaur Arora, a native speaker of Dakkhini from Hyderabad, looks at precisely this sort of question in her PhD dissertation, titled *Syntactic Convergence: The Case of Dakkhini Hindi-Urdu.* She examines a number of sentences in Dakkhini that are framed differently from their equivalents in standard Hindi-Urdu, but which line up perfectly with the equivalent sentences in Telugu:

Dakkhini:	*kaun*	*bolā-**<u>ki</u>***	*us-ku*	*ich*[10]	*pūchho*
Telugu:	*ewaru*	*annāru-**<u>o</u>***	*wāḍni*	—	*aḍugu*
	Who	said-***<u>ki</u>/<u>o</u>***	to-him	(emph)	ask
	'Ask (the person) who said it'[11]				

The Dakkhini -***<u>ki</u>***, which looks outwardly like a north Indian word, is actually a calque that stands for the Telugu -***<u>o</u>***. Arora calls it a 'relative linker'.[12] Now here is the same sentence in north Indian Hindi-Urdu:

Hindi-Urdu	*us-ko*	*pūchho*	*jisne*	*yeh*	*kahā*
	to-him	ask	who	this	said
	'Ask (the person) who said it'				

The order of the clauses in north Indian Hindi-Urdu is a complete reversal of the order in the Dakkhini and Telugu sentences. Also missing in the north Indian example is the very south Indian -***ki*** (-***o*** in Telugu), Arora's 'relative linker', which comes at the end of the clause that begins with a *k*-word.

This pattern, and sameness between Dakkhini and Telugu, appears again when it is an 'embedded interrogative clause', or an actual question ('who came?') stuck into the sentence as though it thought it was a relative clause:

Dakkhini:	*kaun*	*āyā-**ki***	*mere-ku*	*naĩ mālum*
Telugu:	*ewaru*	*waccāru-**o**nā-ku*		*teliyadu*
	Who	came-***ki***/***o***	to-me	(is)not known
	'I don't know who came'			

K.V. Subbarao goes so far as to say that whenever languages are in contact in the north-south borderlands, and speakers of Dravidian languages find themselves having to make sentences with relative clauses (in Dakkhini, Marathi or Konkani), they will always fall back on the model of Telugu or Kannada, and use something based on the Dravidian ***o***:[13]

> A question expression is used as a relative pronoun, as there are no relative pronouns as such in all these languages.
>
> A relative complementizer occurs to the right of the embedded clause that links the subordinate clause with the matrix clause.[14]

Or, to put this into simple language, in any mixed borderland language, the first part of the sentence will begin with a *k* word, based on a question word in a northern language, and will be separated from the second part of the sentence by a word, *ki* in Dakkhini, that does the same work as the ***o*** that you get in all the Dravidian languages. Subbarao goes on to give the examples of Karnataka Saraswat Konkani (Mangalore Konkani) and Saurashtran Gujarati, which both make relative clause sentences in this way, with Konkani using the same 'relative linker' *ki* as in Dakkhini, and Saurashtran Gujarati using *gi*.[15]

This does not answer the question I began this exploration with: 'What area of Kannada grammar would be a problem for a Marathi speaker?' I asked my Marathi-speaking friends, and they did not know or were not sure. But the flipped version of this question, 'How would a Kannada speaker handle a relative clause in Marathi?' gave me the answer I was looking for, the one that gave the full flavour of the north-south borderlands: with a *k* word to start, and a 'relative linker' like ***ki*** (meaning ***o***) at the end of that clause. There is a characteristic way the twilight zone mixes northern and Dravidian relative clauses, keeping the essence of the Dravidian marker ***o*** but dressing it up in the *k* colours of the north.

This sort of reversal is not limited to relative clauses. There are other situations in Dakkhini where clause order is 'flipped', following a Dravidian model. For example, there are sentences with ***bol ke***, where Hindi-Urdu *bol ke*, 'having spoken', has, like -***ki***, been turned into a 'linker':

Rām ātā	***bol ke***	*bolā*	*pan*	*naĩ āyā*,
Ram would come	***bol ke***	he said,	but	he didn't come[16]

'Ram said that he would come, but he didn't come.'

This is totally in line with Marathi, where the equivalent word for ***bol ke*** is *mhaṇun*, and it isn't even seen as a Dravidian touch. It is just normal Marathi.

But could things ever be that simple? Was Dakkhini always like this, in lockstep with Telugu? No. Arora does mention that early Dakkhini texts show relative clauses that look more like the correlatives you get in northern Hindi-Urdu, with the *jo . . . vo* pattern:

> At this stage, we do not come across the relative construction formed on the Dravidian pattern with the interrogative [*k*-] pronoun. The development of the Dravidian type of relative construction seems to be occurring much later . . . there is no evidence in the [early] literary texts showing the occurrence of the [Dravidian or hybrid] relatives.[17]

What do we make of this? Was the very Telugu-flavoured Dakkhini left out of early literature? Or was there actually an early stage of Dakkhini, linked to a literate elite, which was closer to northern Hindi-Urdu? We are, after all, talking about evolution, and looking at Dakkhini to see if it validates our model: of an early 'variety' of the language of the migrants, spoken by their half-local children and elite local men, followed, later, by a much more radical mixture when the little people of the region, the earlier people who found their lives radically changed by the entry of powerful new migrants, adopted it as a first language.

We will get more deeply into this issue later, when we turn our gaze on the history of this language, and how exactly the community came into being.

But the iconic feature that demarcates the north from the south and the west from the east in the subcontinent is *ergativity*. This is an areal feature found all over the northwest, with minor variations, in the languages of Pakistan (Punjabi, Sindhi, Balochi, Pashto) and in all the languages and dialects of Rajasthan, Gujarat and Maharashtra, Madhya Pradesh and all of the Hindi family as far east as the Ganga-Jamuna confluence. In languages with ergativity (or rather, *split* ergativity, as it is only found in the past tense) past tense sentences don't have *I saw*, or *I ate*, like English or the languages of the east and the south. There is a twist, where the subject becomes just an 'agent' and the object the thing that 'agrees' with the verb: *(by me) food-eaten* or *(by me) picture-seen*. And since ergative languages tend to be the ones in South Asia with grammatical gender,[18] this 'agreement' between the 'object' and the verb comes as a gender agreement. In Hindi-Urdu these are the sentences where you get the *-ne* in the past tense that is so daunting to learners from the east and the south:

mai-ne	*khānā*	*khāyā*
by-me	food	eaten

In this sentence the verb *khāyā* (eaten) is marked as masculine, even if the eater is female, because the word *khānā* (food) is masculine. In fact, 'eaten' is the best translation, because it is instantly clear that only the 'food' can be eaten. 'I' am not the thing being eaten. *Eaten* is behaving more like an adjective than a finite verb. What would a language like Dakkhini, in the north-south borderlands, make of ergativity?

Dakkhini speakers are well aware of this strange gender-bender thing in the Urdu that northerners speak, and it finds its way into some of their best humour. I couldn't possibly put it better than this joke from Sajjad Shahid, an engineer by training and the Secretary of the Centre for Deccan Studies in

Hyderabad, whom I just had to meet in person. He has written about the language and the history of the Deccan in detail and with insight.

A northern man asks a Hyderabadi man:

Āp-ne namāz paṛhī? (Did you say your *namāz*?)[19]

The Hyderabadi man, foxed, retorts:

Tū paṛhī ki naike, (Whether **you** said yours or not)
Apan to paṛh liyā! (**I** said mine!)

This is a joke that simply does not translate into English! The northern man has used an ergative construction with the past tense, so the verb *paṛh**ī*** must have a feminine ending, as it must agree with the noun *namāz*, which is feminine, and not the man doing the *namāz*.

In good Dakkhini what the northern man *should* have said was: *Āp namāz paṛhe?*[20] With the verb agreeing with *āp* and masculine, like the man he was talking to.

So *paṛhī* makes no sense to the Hyderabadi gentleman. How can the verb ending be feminine, ***ī***, if he, the subject of the sentence, is so obviously a man? Can't this northerner tell that he is speaking to a man? Or worse: is the northerner not a man himself? So when our Hyderabadi gentleman replies, he uses a feminine verb form, *paṛh**ī***, to taunt the northerner, insinuating that this guy might not actually be male, and ends his retort with a masculine verb form to refer to himself, *paṛh liy**ā***, and no ergative markers.

Dakkhini, like a good south Indian language, does not have ergativity.

But it clearly has natural gender: we can see from this joke that living things that are male or female need masculine or feminine endings on verbs. But what about inanimate nouns? Do they have grammatical gender like in northern Hindi-Urdu? I put this question to Arora on WhatsApp.

Yes, she replied. All nouns have a gender in Dakkhini:

*bacchā gir**ā***	the boy fell	(masculine)
*bacchī gir**ī***	the girl fell	(feminine)
*patthar gir**ā***	the stone fell	(masculine)
*diwāl gir**ī***	the wall fell	(feminine)

This gender, she adds, requires agreement with adjectives too:

*uno ek acch**ā** bacch**ā** ai*	he is a good boy
*uno ek acch**ī** bacch**ī** ai*	she is a good girl
*darwāz**ā** ūnch**ā** ai*	the door is high (*darwāzā*: masculine)
*diwāl ūnch**ī** ai*	the wall is high (*diwāl*: feminine)

So Dakkhini does not have ergativity, but it does have grammatical gender, not only on verb endings, but on adjectives too. Up to now, ergativity and grammatical gender have always gone hand in hand in our subcontinent. The old languages without ergativity, in the east and in the south, also do not have grammatical gender. Now here comes a hybrid, with gender but no ergativity. We are truly in a twilight zone!

In fact, gender is not a totally resolved issue in Dakkhini. When I did a workshop at the Maulana Azad National Urdu University in Hyderabad, the professor, Shagufta Shaheen, mentioned something that was bothering her: she found herself using only masculine verb forms in her Dakkhini to refer to herself, though with feminine nouns she used the feminine form of adjectives. And this, she said, was not just her: she knew a number of other women who did this too. This is eerily similar to Dravidian languages, where gender in verbs is only in the third person, he/she/it, and never the first person 'I'. Is that why she and her friends never use the feminine form of the verb when they refer to themselves? It isn't that they do not think they are female, but because 'I' is supposed to use the default gender, which is masculine.

Gender is one of those things that one doesn't expect will make it into hybrid languages if it is not in the languages of the little people that form the substratum. Telugu does not have grammatical gender. But here it is in Dakkhini. This is not the first time we are seeing grammatical gender in languages that otherwise feel like creoles. The Romance languages of southern Europe. The Indo-Aryan languages up in the northwest of the subcontinent. It is as if there is a pecking order: features, like gender, that can slip across the gap into hybrids from their lexifier languages that supply the vocabulary, and features like ergativity that cannot.

Why did I push Arora to tell me if there was agreement in Dakkhini between nouns and adjectives too, besides the masculine and feminine verb endings? Because there is some equally enigmatic evidence from another borderland region, the east-west tectonic divide of north India. Bhojpuri, the westernmost of the Māgadhan languages, seems to be picking up a bit of gender, but only in its verb marking. During a seminar at BITS-Pilani Hyderabad[21] when I was listing the languages of India with no grammatical gender, I sweepingly included my own ancestral language, Bhojpuri, in that list. According to my data from the language we took from India to the Caribbean in the 1860s, there wasn't any. Bhojpuri lined up with Bangla, Odia and Assamese as being devoid of grammatical gender.

Then a student raised his hand politely and told me that there *was* gender in Bhojpuri. He was a Bhojpuriya too,[22] from Bihar, and for him, in 2023, verbs in Bhojpuri were marked for gender. I asked him to tell me more.

He listed a few contrasting pairs:

*laik**ā** jāt**ā***	the boy goes (**masc**)
*laik**ī** jātiyā*	the girl goes (**fem**)
*bābā sūtal bāṛ**an***	father is (**masc**) asleep
*maiyā sūtal bāṛ**ī***	mother is (**fem**) asleep

Boys and girls and fathers and mothers have natural gender, I said. What about inanimate objects? Do they have this sort of gender agreement with verbs in your Bhojpuri?

No, he thought. Inanimate nouns didn't seem to have gender:

chhātā gir gail	the umbrella fell (**masc**?)
fōn bājtā	the phone rings (**masc**?)

But umbrella and phone are masculine in Hindi anyway. What about feminine nouns?

*relgāṛī āwat**iyā***	the train comes (**fem**)

This was probably the 'impact of Hindi', he mused, *relgāṛī* being seen as feminine.[23] He wasn't ready to say that the gender in Bhojpuri went beyond natural gender. Only living things that could actually be male or female had gender, he insisted.

And only verb endings had gender agreement: adjectives did not change their endings to show gender:

acchā ādmī (good man)
acchā aurat (good woman)

Is grammatical gender—a contrast that affects all the nouns in a language, including nouns that don't yet exist—not something formidable? Could natural gender (the kind we find in Tamil verbs[24]) be where it all begins? Is Bhojpuri now following a path similar to the one that Tamil, Telugu and Kannada chose to take?[25]

We will think about this again in Chapter 4, when we look at the languages in the northwest of India that all have gender, the languages where the Indus Valley Civilization (IVC) once flourished, and in its large periphery. Was it actually easy for them to get comfortable with the grammatical gender that must have come to them from Sanskrit and the prakrits?

~

Let us pause now and recap the timeline of the new creole model we are testing.

After the first migrants, almost all male, arrive in a new land and marry local women, their half-local children along with some elite local men pick up a close approximation of the migrant men's language, with a local accent and a few other local touches, but essentially no change in the grammar. Later on, little people from the region join the community and soon a version of the language emerges with a number of grammatical features from the local language/s they spoke before. In this creole variety, while the grammar tends to be strongly influenced by the earlier local language/s and the vocabulary contributed by the migrants, this is not a hard and fast rule. It is not impossible for grammatical features from the language of the migrants to slip into the new hybrid. These are two distinct stages in the life of the hybrid. The first stage is the close approximation of the migrants' original language, the prakrit stage. Later, a radically mixed creole variety may (or may not) emerge as a separate development.

This new model is sharply different from the pidgin-creole model. Here there is no pidgin at all, and the variety close to the language of the migrants is the one that appears first. (In the old pidgin-creole model the first thing to appear is supposed to be a pidgin, followed soon by a creole that has native speakers. The variety closest to the language of the original migrants, the *acrolect*, is supposed to emerge last, as creole features are gradually 'lost'.)

~

Dakkhini is not a neat homogeneous language, the way it might have seemed when we were looking at the grammar a few moments ago. It is easy to walk around in Hyderabad and *not* notice that it is different from the Urdu of north India, because speakers of Dakkhini are able to tune their speech to suit northerners when they have to. Many educated speakers of Dakkhini know northern Urdu quite well. After all, the literary Urdu we know in the north did start out in the Deccan, with poets like Zatalli who came from Narnaul, near Delhi, in the early 1700s breaking with the tradition of writing ghazals only in Persian in order to reach out to a larger audience.[26] These poets wrote their ghazals in the Dehlavi dialect they had brought with them when they came to Hyderabad, not in Dakkhini. But centuries before literary Urdu made its first appearance in the Deccan, there were already local writers writing in Dakkhini.

Sajjad Shahid and Shagufta Shaheen, in their article titled 'The Unique Literary Traditions of Dakhnī', say that it is Sufi mystics who first promoted the development of a 'common language' in the region. Sufiism,

> [G]ained popularity due to its inherent mass appeal right from the time of its first introduction into Indian society . . . It spread rapidly across north India following the permanent settlement of Delhi by Muslims. Among the many Sufi orders active in the country, the "extraordinary success of the Chīshtī order was due to the fact that it knew better how to adapt itself to the practices and customs of the country in which it had come to settle" . . . The founder of this order, Khwājā Muinuddin Chīshtī (*Sultan-é Hind, Gharīb Nawāz* 1141-1236) arrived in India in 1190 and after a brief stay in Lahore, settled down in Ajmer.[27]

The last few decades of the fourteenth century saw a 'remarkable coming together of diverse mystic traditions in the Deccan with some of the primary teachings of the Bhakti cult, especially those pertaining to social ideas, being greatly influenced by Islamic mysticism . . . These developments, promoting syncretism in the Deccan, were instrumental in promotion of a shared idiom . . . and ensured the development of Dakhnī language'[28] as the most common and effective medium of propagating Sufiism in the Deccan. As Dehlavi did in the north, this common language, Dakkhini, first gained popularity through its usage by the Sufis who had migrated to the Deccan.

In fact, the Sufis' presence in the Deccan '*predates* incursions of Sultanate forces into peninsular India *by more than a century*'.[29] This leads Shahid and Shaheen to conclude that what grew into Dakkhini evolved first through early contact in the Punjab and Sindh and reached the Deccan directly from there, not via Delhi and the Sultanate forces. The Sufis had stolen a march on the eventual rulers of the region. From the very beginning, the Dakkhini spoken by the elite and the Dakkhini adapted by the local people who converted to Islam to join the new community were . . . separate.

The first samples of written Dakkhini are from Khwaja Syed Mohammed Hussaini, better known by his two pen names Gésudarāz and Banda Nawāz, who arrived in the Deccan in 1390. Syed Ubaidur Rahman in his book, *Peaceful Expansion of Islam in India*, mentions 'Sayyid Muhammad Gesu Daraz' having converted Hindu weavers to Islam in the Bombay Presidency region before the existence of the Sultanate.[30] Gésudarāz was known for saying that God had given him the talent for 'explaining his secrets'.[31] In his verse, he used simple everyday language, and his imagery was drawn from the most homespun situations:

Pānī mẽ namak ḍāl mazā dékhtā vasé,
Jab ghul gayā namak tō namak bōlnā kīsé;
Yũ khōī Khudi apnī Khuda sāt Mohammed,
Jab ghul gaī Khudi tō Khuda bīn na kōī dīsé.[32]

Put some salt in water, look at all the fun,
When the salt dissolves, its days as salt are done.
This way you lose your Khudi in Khuda, Mohammed,
When Self goes no one takes God from you, no one.[33]

Note the play on words between *Khudi* (the self) and *Khuda* (God), and the image of salt dissolving in water, something any villager would relate to. The idea is original; Gésudarāz had no problem resorting to an unconventional metaphor to convey 'God's secrets'. Just think of how much he was ready to tinker with the Islam of the Qur'an just to connect with his new followers!

~

Let us stop a moment and think about this verse. It is in a north Indian dialect of those times, and it does seem to be aimed at the little people of the Deccan. But this kind of Dakkhini makes us seriously doubt that this verse could originally have been 'thought' in Telugu. While this variety may see itself as a 'common language' and may indeed have connected with the little people before the Sultanate forces arrived, there isn't anything particularly local about it.

Harbir Arora did warn that some of the more local features in Dakkhini took a while to come into the literature. But past tenses without ergativity seem to have appeared early, as we see in this example from Kuraishi Bidari, written in 1520, where *-ne*, the ergative marker, is missing:

so is śahar ke daur mẽ bīdar mukām
yõ ***śāyar kiyā*** *nazm dakkhinī tamām*[34]

In this town, there is a place called Bidar
There **a poet composed** verse all in Dakkhini.

But she also gives the example of the famous early Dakkhini poet Wajahi, writing in 1645, who used the term Hindavi as well as Dakkhini. Here, except for *usku*, his language does not look different from northern Hindi-Urdu. His relative clauses have a northern feel to them (*jise . . . so*), as does his use of *hai* (instead of *ai*).

jise fārsī kā nā kuch gyān hai
so dakkhini zabā̃ usku āsā̃ hai[35]

For the one with no knowledge of Farsi
For him the Dakkhini language is easy

~

Is this the early variety of Dakkhini predicted by our new model? The one spoken by elites, which never strayed too far from the language of the first Sultanate migrants? Or is it just a neutral variety that appeared in writing, but maybe not in speech? Seeing as the elites in the Deccan never seemed to have a problem understanding or speaking northern Hindi-Urdu, and that we have no way of going back in time to hear them speak among themselves in the 1300s, 1400s, 1500s and 1600s, we cannot say for certain. But it does look as if there was, and still is, a less local variety of Dakkhini floating around the Deccan that has always been part of the repertoire of the literate class.

The most interesting challenge to our model comes from the assertion that something like Dakkhini had reached the Deccan a full century *before* the arrival of the Sultanate forces. That would maintain a separation in time between the coming of an elite Dakkhini variety and of the more radically mixed creole, but not the separation we were thinking of. It raises the question of whether mixed creole varieties can only appear *after* an elite local variety is up and running. How much later must that be? Couldn't an elite local variety and a mixed creole come up at the same time? Could a mixed creole not start to emerge even before new elites arrive, if it came separately with Sufis who settled down with the little people? Would Sufis and their message be enough, by itself, to bring about enough change to generate a new language? Or would it take nothing less than women and children, families, making a permanent change to join a new community? What is important here in the model: that the elite approximation, the 'prakrit', come up *before* the little people's more mixed variety, or that the two processes be separate?

Or was there actually a time gap in the Deccan? Did the language the Sufis brought with them take time to put down roots and 'go native'? When did the spoken Dakkhini that has a strong Telugu flavour first appear? When did the little people of the Deccan convert to Islam and become a Dakkhini-speaking community?

~

There is not much written about the little people of the Deccan and their decision to become Muslim. But there is a feeling that the bulk of the conversion happened fast, and without any great sense of trauma. Almost all of the material about it seems to be written by outsiders looking in, with no instinct for what could have been going on in the minds of the people making such a life-changing decision. There are reports of entire castes converting together from Hinduism,[36] and there is always a suggestion that, while there could have been many reasons, it was mostly due to lower castes wanting to escape the caste system and being attracted to Islam because of the equality it offered.

But as I moved around in Hyderabad, there were other clues from the past winking at me all the time. The sight of Hussain Sagar, with the world's tallest monolith of the Buddha standing in the middle like a guardian over the city. The island in Nagarjunasagar Lake with its museum full of excavated relics from an earlier Buddhist civilization in the Deccan. A mall by the name of 'Lumbini' in Banjara Hills. There has always been a neat match between the parts of the subcontinent that have large Muslim populations now and regions that were strongly Buddhist in earlier times. Bengal. Kashmir. Kerala. And the Deccan.

About the demise of Buddhism in India, the *Encyclopedia Britannica* says that with 'the collapse of the Pala dynasty [in Bengal] in the 12th century, Indian Buddhism suffered yet another setback from which it did not recover'.[37] In the last centuries of Buddhism, many monks and scholars fled abroad with their texts (and many of the texts they took with them have had to be transliterated *back* into Devanagari so that modern Indian scholars could read them). And ordinary Buddhists, the little people who remained in the subcontinent, were reabsorbed into Hinduism and the Hindu caste system, but nowhere near the top. It cannot have been as smooth and happy a return as many scholars in India, all upper caste, would like to claim.

Many of these groups of converted Buddhists would have been curious enough about exploring other options to be receptive to the Sufis who came as early as the twelfth century promoting Islam. In Bengal there is the word *nerey*, an abusive term used by Hindus to refer to those 'double-tonsured' people who had converted earlier from Hinduism to Buddhism, and then off again to Islam after a brief return to being Hindus in between.[38]

~

What would these little people have been thinking as they listened to the Sufis in a Golden Age when orthodoxy was already being challenged by movements like Bhakti, a time of change when new local languages were raising their heads above sea level and making their mark on the written record?[39] This is something I can easily imagine.

My own family is part of a community that converted from Hinduism to Christianity in the Caribbean in the late 1800s. At the centre of this movement were craftsmen and their families, eager to embrace the possibilities offered by education and the schools being set up by Canadian missionaries. It was a matter of pride that they never *took* anything from the church: they contributed a small portion of their wages even when they were still indentured labourers on the sugar estates. When I asked my great-grandfather why his father had become Christian, he said that it was because of the 'caste system'. But that made no sense to me: we had not given up our earlier caste trade. We were still goldsmiths. But there was a difference.

My great-grandfather had a long-term plan. He and his brothers remained goldsmiths, but my father's generation would study metallurgy at university, or chemistry, or dentistry or optics. Only then would we get to venture further, away from 'safe' professions allied to goldsmithing into brahmanical fields like linguistics, for example.

Poor Muslim families in India seem to have taken note of this as a good strategy. We have all seen how many of the young men who work as electricians, mechanics and in tech setting up and maintaining our Internet connections and working with the gadgetry side of film and television seem to be Muslim. In *Wanderers, Kings, Merchants* I tell of one of my students, also from a Muslim craftsman family, who went to Jama Masjid to make a film on old calligraphers, and found himself surrounded by their grandsons who were fascinated, not by their grandfathers' skill, but by his camera.[40] There seems to be an overlap between being from an artisan family, a curiosity about gadgetry and tech, and the flexibility that would lead such a family to change its identity. Become Buddhist. Or

Muslim. These are precisely the sort of people who make new languages. These are the ones who think like . . . migrants.

In migration studies, there is the concept of a 'voluntary migrant'. This is an idea that aims to explain the difference in fortunes between, say, middle-class Jamaicans who migrated to the United States (Black people making a secondary migration) and Black Americans who are on average poorer and much less entitled than the Jamaican migrants even today. It makes a distinction between people who migrate in anticipation of a better life and know how to take advantage of new opportunities, and those taken abroad by force, as happened to a large number of Africans during the slave trade, whose descendants are still at the mercy of the system that changed their ancestors' lives.

Most people, or castes, who convert do not do so in helpless obedience, or they would not remain 'converted' for long. Old beliefs that never died would quickly resurface when the new pressure to conform goes away. The craftsmen's and traders' castes in India, who would have been an incipient middle class, have a strong overlap with castes that were once Buddhist. According to Basham, 'a money economy only existed in India from the days of the Buddha'.[41] Gail Omvedt, in her book *Buddhism in India*, tells of great monastic caves in the Western Ghats which . . .

> . . . reveal the mercantile nature of the Satavahana society; the caves marked trade routes and show both the link with Rome and a local monetized economy. The donors, shown through their signatures or occasionally in statues, are a remarkable group. They include foreigners (Greeks), bankers, wealthy merchants, and also a perfume-vendor, a carpenter, braziers, a blacksmith, flower-vendors, ploughmen and householder-farmers. (In contrast, the

> monuments sponsored by the northern Kushanas at about the same time had many more kings and nobles). Many women were shown making or sharing in donations, including nuns (who thus apparently held property!). Often the craftsmen were organized in powerful guilds, which themselves made donations, took money on interest and entered into other financial agreements with rulers.[42]

The Satavahanas were a dynasty that ruled in the Deccan region from the third century BCE to the third century CE. While the rulers were Hindu, they built Buddhist and Jain temples, and their traders and craftsmen were often Buddhist. If these Buddhists were pushed back into Hinduism after the fall of Buddhism, and assigned to low castes, they would probably not have been so invested in their old Hindu identity that they were averse to exploring the Islam offered by the Sufis and the Sultanate. So while all converts to Islam in the Deccan might not have had a Buddhist past, many probably shared a class background with the people of the region who would have been Buddhist in earlier times.

That might explain the lack of trauma in the conversions, and, in the absence of concrete evidence about the time of conversion, suggests that it might have been quite early, maybe even around the same time as the Deccan Sultanates were taking shape.

~

Hyderabad is not the only part of the Deccan where there is this sort of north-south interlanguage. Dakkhini is also the language of Muslim communities in parts of Karnataka and Tamil Nadu. In fact, in Tamil Nadu, there are, besides Muslim groups speaking Dakkhini, Muslim groups that have only Tamil as their ethnic language. The difference between the two is that Dakkhini speakers trace back to the Deccan Sultanates, while the Tamil-speaking Muslims are part of the coastal spread of Islam that started with Arab merchants who had been trading all over the Indian Ocean littoral, and setting up local families in the Malabar region, long before Islam came into existence. When Islam emerged in the seventh century CE, those Arab traders became Muslim, and their families in India converted too, making them the first Muslim community in India. Because their connection with Islam was via Arabic, they do not say *Ramzān* in the Persian way as Dakkhini speakers and north Indians do for the name of the holy month of fasting, but *Ramaḷān*: *ḷ* is a Tamil/Malayalam variant of *ḍ*, between vowels, and it replaces *D* in Arabic *RamaDan*, with its deep pharyngeal d-sound.[43]

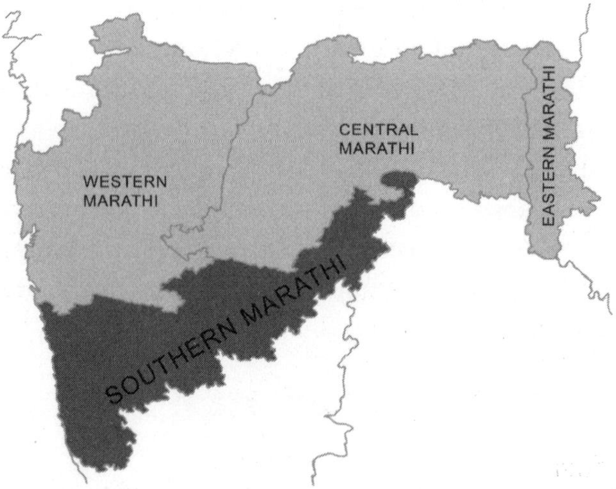

Map 2: The ergative boundary between the Indus Valley Periphery and the south, part-way through Marathi territory

But there is more going on in this twilight zone between north and south, much more. Once you head west into the zone where Marathi from the north meets Kannada from the south, you begin to see a kind of language mixture familiar to us from Dakkhini, but this time not linked to any conversion to Islam. Chinmay Dharurkar, a linguist and native speaker of Marathi, in an article in the Wire,[44] says that 'Marathi in south-eastern Maharashtra differs from other regions of the state, although all varieties have been shepherded together under the linguistic state of Maharashtra and a broad category called the Marathi language.' One of his first examples of 'misunderstandings' that come with this takes us right back in the direction of our Dakkhini joke about ergativity:

pora khālli? Did the children eat?

Speakers of Marathi from the central or western parts of Maharashtra might be 'perplexed as to what is being asked . . . "*Pora khālli*" may leave them shocked [as to] whether the children have been eaten,' Dharurkar writes. In southern Marathi, as in Dakkhini, one key northern feature that seems to be missing is . . . ergativity.

But it goes even further: 'South-eastern Marathi and north-eastern Kannada are more thickly related to each other than they are to their so-called respective standardized varieties. It is in this sense that these varieties are a world in themselves . . . The grammatical and linguistic cohesion of this kind, in fact, shows how the Deccan is a culturally cohesive area, though it may have been politically fractured and reconstituted.'[45] In other words, southern Marathi and northern Kannada are in many ways in sync. 'Until 1956, south-eastern Maharashtra, north-eastern Karnataka and Telangana constituted the Hyderabad-

Deccan state, and the three major languages of Marathi, Kannada and Telugu lived a culturally syncretic life here, as these languages still do.'[46] In some of their morphology—the building blocks that make up their words—the two often line up grammatically in ways that differ from standard Marathi and standard Kannada.[47]

This recalls the 1960s Kupwar study by John Gumperz and Robert Wilson, which went so far as to claim that the languages of the area—Marathi, Kannada, Telugu and 'Urdu'—had become so in line with each other that they were morph-for-morph translatable from one to the other: they seemed to have a single grammar with only superficial vocabulary differences.[48] Kupwar is a small town in northern Karnataka where Gumperz and Wilson, two American linguists, had stumbled on the kind of convergence and mixing of language families that one expected to find only in creoles, and had gone to the first major conference on pidgin and creole languages at the University of the West Indies in Jamaica, in 1968, to report this amazing find. But their referring to Dakkhini as 'Urdu' just because it was Muslims speaking it smacked of a less-than-careful approach. There was something else going on in Kupwar.

Sonal Kulkarni-Joshi, a professor of linguistics at Pune University who has been working on the languages of the borderlands and reviewing the Kupwar study, takes a more nuanced position. She is not convinced that there is any single grammar in Kupwar and 'morph-for-morph intertranslatability' between the four languages. She instead sees a lot of variation, depending on who is speaking, and whether they are speaking their own ethnic language. She also wonders if it could not have been, instead, a case of 'divergence', not convergence: of one original language branching out into several different directions, the grammar being in place before the vocabulary replacements.[49] What an exciting (and counter-intuitive) thought! And a caution that the neat present-day linguistic division of India could be blinding us to a far more complex and connected history if only we knew where to start.

But do southern Marathi and northern Kannada both have gender? Grammatical gender? I paused and sent off a WhatsApp message to Dharurkar to ask him. It would be significant if the two differed in this important respect.

They do differ, he replied. Southern Marathi has full grammatical gender, like all the rest of Marathi: nouns are masculine, feminine and neuter (Marathi, like Sanskrit, has three grammatical genders). But northern Kannada does not have anything like this: all it has is the standard Dravidian spread of natural gender in the third-person pronoun, *he*, *she* and *it*, but no masculine or feminine inanimate nouns, and no adjectives having masculine and feminine endings when they go with nouns. When northern Kannada speakers have to use Marathi, they just lump all nouns together and treat them as neuter. Clearly, it depends on who exactly is speaking the 'southern Marathi'. There are native speakers of 'southern Marathi' in the borderlands who have the full grammatical gender of Marathi, though without ergativity: exactly the same as you find in Dakkhini. Native speakers of southern Marathi line up with Dakkhini to complete a twilight zone between the north and the south, with grammatical gender (two in Dakkhini, and three in southern Marathi), but no ergativity.

If we put together all that we have just seen about Dakkhini, southern Marathi, and what Subbarao says about varieties of Konkani and Saurashtran Gujarati being a part of the picture, we have a twilight zone that stretches all the way across India from the east coast to the west coast, each region on the arc of contact responding in its own way to the same pressure:

the need of people who live together to get past north-south barriers and be in a single conversation.

~

The model of change that we have been exploring and refining essentially works to capture how Dakkhini came into being. It was a two-part process. First the earliest migrant men from the north—nobles, administrators and part of the Sultanate forces—married local women and had children who spoke a close approximation (a prakrit version) of the dialect their fathers had brought with them from Delhi, with some local turns of phrases and a bit of a local accent. After infancy these children went on to learn Persian, the language of literacy and of the royal court.

The Dakkhini with the strong Telugu flavour that we looked at earlier in this chapter came up separately from the variety that the elites were calling 'Dakhni'. Crucial to the emergence of this mixed version was the discontinuity in the lives of the local families that had converted to Islam and became more urban as they moved to join the new community. These were people who had previously been speakers of Telugu and who adopted Dakkhini as their language, bringing in a Telugu 'operating system', which they passed on to their children. All this while, the lives of these poorer local converts were reasonably separate from those of the elite Muslims, whose male ancestors had come from the north.

It is hard to imagine that the little people of the Deccan converted to Islam *before* the Deccan Sultanate had come into existence, even if they had been listening to the Sufis for a long time before that. Conversion is, after all, a formal change, not the gist of an idea taking root inside your head one fine day after listening to inspiring discourse. Conversion to Islam means a change of identity, getting a new name, joining a new group and trying to switch to the language of that group. There has to be an administration in place to record that change, to enrol you, so to speak, in the group.

This means that while the two varieties of Dakkhini had separate origins, the more mixed variety could only emerge after the Deccan Sultanate was in place, with its cities to which the new converts moved. But there is nothing to suggest that there was a gap in time. The mixed variety of Dakkhini could have come up at essentially the same time as the prakrit version spoken by the elite. Or it could just as well have come up much later, if the little people had not been so rapidly assimilated through a singular event like conversion. They could have continued as Hindus, and speakers of Telugu, for a long time, even indefinitely: the way it happened in the Karnataka-Maharashtra borderlands, where there is still much variation depending on whether the speaker is, at heart, a Kannadiga or a Maharashtrian.

The mixed Dakkhini did not come up *because* there was an elite prakrit variety there before it. It came up because something else happened that changed the environment: a large group of little people converting together. Later, the two varieties came together as a single language when elite children began to pick up the Dakkhini that was spoken by the little people.

In this chapter, we have seen a situation eerily parallel to the story of early Sanskrit that I sketched out in my earlier book, *Wanderers, Kings, Merchants*. It is the story of a powerful migrant group entering new territory, settling down and marrying local women. It is also, separately, the story of the little people of the area, suddenly finding a new environment and new options, and approaching the new elite language, bringing with them the mindset of their old language and creating a creole variety. We already know, from the previous chapter, that there was a possibility of grammatical features 'leaking' into the new mixed creole from the language of the first migrants, the one that we expect to supply only the vocabulary.

And in this respect, Dakkhini does not disappoint. Dakkhini has reasonably well-established grammatical gender, even though Telugu, its substratum language, does not. This flies in the face of all our experience, and our expectations of simplification, because when we see Bengalis learning Hindi, or English speakers learning French, we get the impression that grammatical gender is arbitrary and *difficult*. How, then, does it find its way into a mixed language like Dakkhini? Could it be that some kinds of new languages are more receptive to grammatical gender than others? Or that some features, like ergativity, find it harder to travel across porous borders than others like gender?

Ergativity is a beast we will have to come to terms with before we proceed to reconstruct the vanished language of old Harappa. What are the antecedents of this feature in the Indus Valley area, and how might these have played a role in leading our new languages, and indeed the old prakrits and Sanskrit too, to the split ergativity that characterizes the way we express past time?

In the next chapter, we will think about this, using our now tested model to clear away the undergrowth around this feature, smoothening our way before we embark on our onward journey into the remote past.

3

The Taming of the Ergative Dragon

To free myself from darkness . . .

The Silence of a Candle, Paul Winter

Before we set out to think about Language X, the unknown language of the Indus Valley Civilization that lies at the base of the modern languages of the northwest, there is a beast we need to befriend, a dragon that sits atop a huge boulder we must pass in order to gain access to the spaces below. This is a creature we will meet again and again as we search out the histories of the languages in our subcontinent, so we need to get comfortable with it before we proceed.[1] This dragon goes by the name of ergativity.

In most of the world's languages, sentences have subjects, objects and verbs. In the sentence 'I see the cat', 'I' is the subject, the one doing the seeing, and 'the cat' is the object, the thing that is being seen. The verb agrees with the subject, 'I': it is not 'sees', but 'see', to agree with 'I'.

But there are other languages, ergative languages, where instead of a subject there is an 'agent', which has a marker that translates as 'by'. In languages with full ergativity, this happens in all tenses: *by-me food eaten* for the past, *by-me food eat* (or something like that) for the present. It is actually not a complicated system: in many of these languages, verbs agree with both 'agents' and 'objects' in all tenses. Ergativity is essentially a matter of sticking an agent marker, 'by', on the agent, and agreement markers on the verb. Here OM stands for object marker, and AM stands for agent marker:

By-me the cat OM-see-AM	'I see the cat'
By-me the cat OM-will see-AM	'I will see the cat'
By-me the cat OM-saw-AM	'I saw the cat'

In the north-western languages of South Asia, we have a version of ergativity that is a bit more complicated: *split* ergativity. In these languages subjects turn into 'agents' only in the past-perfect tense. In all other tenses they remain subjects. SM stands for subject marker:

I	*the cat see-SM*	'I see the cat'
I	*the cat will see-SM*	'I will see the cat'
I	*the cat was seeing-SM*	'I was seeing the cat'
By-me	*the cat seen-OM*	'I saw the cat'

In the last example, in the past-perfect tense, the verb agrees *not* with what was the subject in the earlier examples, but with what was the object, and the 'subject' is now part of a phrase with 'by'. In these Hindi sentences the agent marker is the postposition *ne*:

mãĩ	*khānā*	*khātī hū̃*	'I eat food'	(agrees with 'I', fem)
mãĩ-ne	*khānā*	*khāya*	'I ate food'	(agrees with 'food', masc)

This sudden flip in the past-perfect tense is known as 'ergative realignment'. It is no problem for native speakers of these north-western languages: in fact, they don't even notice that they are doing it. If you draw their attention to it, they look confused. How this mutant version of ergativity emerged in the northwest is what we will explore in this chapter.

We first encountered ergativity in Chapter 2, where it was as a feature of Urdu that did *not* become a part of Dakkhini, and which was also missing in the Marathi spoken in the southern borderlands where Maharashtra meets Karnataka. Ergativity is found *only* in the languages of the Extended Indus Valley Periphery: a northwest that encompasses all of Pakistan as well as north India as far east as the Ganga-Yamuna confluence, and southwards into Maharashtra. It is conspicuously missing from the Dravidian languages of the south, and from the twilight zone that has Dakkhini and southern Marathi. The Māgadhan languages to the east of the Ganga-Yamuna confluence are also fiercely non-ergative.[2] This is a dragon native to the northwest, and it prefers to stay home.

According to Thomas Wier, a linguist at the Free University of Tbilisi in Georgia, the first person to coin the term 'ergativity' was Adolf Dirr (1860–1930), a German linguist who was a specialist in languages of the Caucasus.[3] In another *Quora* post, Wier says that the earliest written language, Sumerian, was actually an ergative language, and that languages over time have been known to lose ergativity (gain 'subjects'), or even acquire it (with their subjects becoming 'agents'), though 'in some language families ergativity is a deep, stable and persistent trait among all the daughter languages.'[4] What this means is that there is nothing out of the ordinary in ergativity showing up in South Asia too, though its presence and spread in the region have a feel of half-buried milestones along our old migration route.

Earliest Sanskrit did not have ergativity: you don't find ergatives in the Rig Veda. There were instead European-style past tenses:

Devadattaḥ pustakaṁ mitrāya adāt
Devadatta book to-friend gave

In this sentence Devadatta is the subject, and the verb agrees with him. Book is the direct object, the thing that he gave, not 'agreeing' with any verb. But by the Apabhraṁśa period this had changed:

Devadattẽ putthaya mittaho diṇṇa
by-Devadatta book to-friend given

The final *ẽ* on Devadatta contains the Sanskrit instrumental case ending *-ena*, which makes it 'by Devadatta', and the finite verb has been replaced by a past participle, 'given', which here agrees not with Devadatta, but with 'book'. In modern Hindi this evolved into:

Devdatt-ne pustak dost-ko dī
by-Devdutt book to-friend given

As in the Apabhraṁśa example, in modern Hindi Devdutt is no longer a 'subject' but an 'agent', taking an ending inspired by the old instrumental case ending *-ena.* And 'gave' has dwindled to become just a past participle, 'given', that agrees with *pustak*, book, which in Hindi is feminine (though in Sanskrit and the prakrits it was neuter).

This sort of ergativity first found its way into the prakrits and then Sanskrit as a past participle ending in *-ta*, and by the classical period it was all over the texts. It grew to be the preferred way of making past tenses in Sanskrit, and all the other old past tenses that had been there in the Rig Vedic period began to fall by the wayside. It is there in the works of Kālidāsa, in an example from *Abhijñānaśakuntalaṁ*, which translates as 'by Kuśa grass needle my foot-pierced', instead of her saying 'a Kuśa-grass needle pierced my foot'. What Shakuntala says is in prakrit, the first line below, but the Sanskrit translation is given as a sort of 'subtitle'. Both the prakrit and the Sanskrit translation have the same ergative structure:

aṇsūe. ahiṇavakusasūīe parikkhadaṁ me ćalaṇaṁ
anasūye. abhinavakuśasūćyā parikṣataṁ me ćaraṇaṁ

Oh Anasuya! My foot-pierced by a needle of young Kuśa grass.

Note this *ta* (with the ending *-ṁ*) in the ending of the participle *parkiṣataṁ*, and how it agrees in gender and case with *ćaraṇaṁ*, 'foot'.

And not just Kālidāsa: every single Ashokan pillar or rock inscription starts off with his byline, *this dhamma-inscription by-Devānāmpiya by-Piyadasi by-king caused to be written*, which means 'this dhamma-inscription caused to be written by King Devānāmpiya Piyadasi'.* The reference to Ashoka is in the instrumental case ending in *-ena*, which has the same function as *-ne* in languages like Hindi, and the verb 'was' is missing. The past participle *lekhita*, 'caused to be written', was already assuming the role of a verb, holding its place in the sentence

* Ashoka was referred to as 'Devanampiya Piyadasi' in many of his inscriptions.

without 'was', almost as if it were a finite verb. In Māgadhan Prakrit this was:

iyam dhammalipi devenampiyena piyadassina lajina lekhita.

And at about the same time, during the first millennium BCE, ergativity showed up in Iran too: exactly the same past participle ending in *-ta* became the standard way of making the past tense in Avestan and Old Persian.[5]

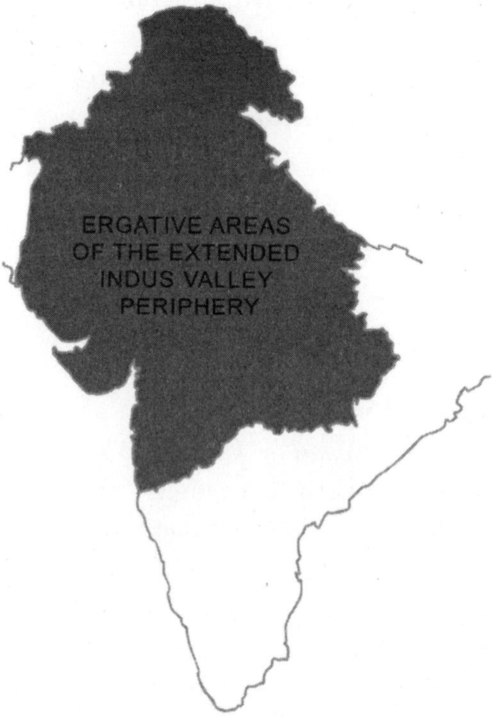

Map 3: The Extended Indus Valley Periphery, also the zone of ergativity

How did this ergativity, only in the past tense, appear in the prakrits using the Sanskrit instrumental case ending, *-ena*, which evolved into the modern ergative marker *ne*?

Early Sanskrit verbs had three 'voices', the active, the 'middle' and the passive. The middle voice[6] soon faded away, leaving only the active and the passive:

Active:	*rāmaḥ*	*phalāni*	*akhādat*
	Rāma	fruits	ate
Passive:	*rāmeṇa*	*phalāni*	*akhādyanta*
	by-Rāma	fruits	were eaten

In other words, there was already a way to turn sentences around to make them passive, converting the 'subject' into an 'agent', by-Rama, which was in the instrumental case. In the passive sentence, the object, *phalāni*, 'fruits', did actually become the subject: the passive verb *akhādyanta* was now in the plural to agree with a new subject, 'fruits'. It was still a finite verb, 'were eaten', and just as full of markers as any other finite verb. The passive in Sanskrit was not about simplification.

When the demand for simplification brought one-size-fits-all past participles, like *khādita*, 'eaten', into the game, there was already a precedent for how to 'realign' sentences in Sanskrit to make them passive, by turning objects into subjects and turning the earlier subjects into 'agents', with a marker meaning 'by'. Past participles, like 'eaten', 'broken', 'taken', are naturally passive in just about every language: they can be made active, but that always requires a special operation.[7]

At the time when signs of ergativity with *-ta* began to appear in the prakrits, the old IVC languages must still have been in use. People were using languages with ergativity in their daily lives and must have been frustrated by not being able to express ergativity when they spoke in prakrit. But there was a problem: prakrits had to conform to the rules of Sanskrit grammar. And there was a way to handle verbs that were passive: the subjects and objects had to be 'realigned'. The fruits were now eaten (by Rāma). The fruits were now the subject of the sentence. And so it would have to be if, instead of a finite verb, they used a past participle that had a passive flavour. The fruits eaten (by Rama). And since 'eaten' is a participle, and participles are basically adjectives ('the eaten fruit', 'the beaten path', 'the fallen tree'), they now had to agree in gender with their new subjects.

It was as simple as that.

~

Modern Punjabi, Sindhi, Pashto and some dialects of Balochi all have split ergativity, but when we look more deeply into the data, we see a varied spread.

In Punjabi the *-ne* marker is mostly missing. When the 'subject' is *I* or *you*, the *-ne* marker isn't used, though there is still gender agreement with the 'object'.[8] The marker *-ne* only surfaces when the 'subject' is third person, he/she or a noun.[9] But except for *-ne* not being there with *I* and *you*, it is business as usual: in the past tense, verbs agree in gender with what in other tenses would be their 'object'.

The first line below is in the present tense: the verb agrees with 'I' and 'Simran', which are female. The second line is in the past tense: 'I' and 'Simran' are still female, but there is an implicit *ne* after *mãĩ*, so the verb must agree with 'food', which is masculine. Simran is a girl's name:[10]

mãĩ	*khāṇā khāndī hã̃*	*Simran*	*khāṇā khāndī hai*
I	food eat (Pres-F)	Simran	food eat (Pres-F)
'I eat food'		'Simran eats food'	

mãĩ khāṇā khāddā		*Simran-**ne***	*khāṇā khāddā*
I food eat (Past-M)		Simran-by	food eat (Past-M)
'I ate food'		'Simran ate food'	

So, in Punjabi, the *-ne*, always there in spirit, only surfaces when the agent is he or she, or a noun (like Simran), not when it is *I* or *you*. But it still makes sure that the verb (the past participle 'eaten') is marked as masculine to agree with 'food', and not with 'I' or 'Simran'.

Marathi once upon a time used to have ergative marking on its first and second-person pronouns too, *miyā* and *tuvā*, but these old instrumental forms faded out, and modern Marathi joined languages like Punjabi that simply have *I* and *you*, with *-ne* only on he/she/it.

Some dialects in Haryana, Rajasthan and Gujarat also do not have *-ne* with *I* and *you*. And there are even some dialects that have taken it a step further, where *-ne* is now 'optional', even in the third person, though the gender agreement is still with what would have been the 'object' in any other tense.[11]

Sindhi too, like Punjabi, has ergativity and grammatical gender, with two genders, masculine and feminine, and does not take an ergative marker on first and second-person agents.[12] But in a strange twist that calls to mind an old 'double marking' feature that is still there in our northern Munda languages, Sindhi adds a suffix to the verb that agrees with the agent: (by me) food eaten-Masc-*Agent Agreement*. Suniti Kumar Chatterji, writing in 1926, gives the example: (*mũ*) *pōthī paṛh-ī-me*, '(by-me) book read-(fem)-by-me', where the 'by me' is repeated as a verb suffix, and he writes it in tiny letters.[13]

How did Pashto fit into this picture? It is supposed to be an 'Iranian language', but I was certain it would have its own tale to tell. It couldn't be a part of the Indus Valley, and it couldn't have retroflexion, without being . . . family. I made the journey to Jawaharlal Nehru University to meet a friend in the Persian department, and we sat sipping tea and waiting for Dr Anwar Khairi, a lecturer in Pashto from Afghanistan, to arrive. And then just as I began to have second thoughts about my strange quest, he burst into the room with a big smile and the energy of a strong breeze down from the Hindu Kush mountains and said: 'You want to hear about ergativity in Pashto? Retroflexion? I'll tell you!'

So I grabbed a pencil and the closest notebook and wrote down everything he said.

Pashto has two genders, masculine and feminine, and split ergativity, though there are no ergative markers at all. Intransitive verbs agree with their subject in person and gender, as do transitive verbs in the present and future tenses. In the past the only thing that changes is the verb, which now agrees with the 'object'. The present-tense forms are:

zı spāī winam (I see the cat)
halak spāī wini (the boy sees the cat)

Here *am* is a first-person marker, and *i* is a third-person (masculine) marker. In the past, however, the verb agrees with what was elsewhere the direct object in gender and number:

halak spāī wilid (the boy saw the cat: *id* is a masculine singular marker as cat is masc)

halak spyān wilidal (the boy saw the cats: *idal* is a masculine plural marker)
halak spıi wilidā (the boy saw the female cat: *idā* is a feminine singular marker)
halak spıi wilide (the boy saw the female cats: *ide* is a feminine plural marker)[14]

Balochi, like many other modern languages in the Iranian family, has no grammatical gender, but some dialects do have a semblance of ergativity in the past tense.[15] There is ergative *marking* in its eastern and southern dialects, which consists of sticking an ending, *ā*, on subjects, which then become agents, and only in the third person.[16] That is essentially it: the verb still agrees with the agent, as if it were the subject, though at times it follows the pattern of Pashto, and the verb may agree with the object instead. But in western Balochi, ergativity is totally missing. As we noted, our ergative dragon does not like to stray far from home.

~

And what about Burushaski, that well-known 'language isolate' spoken deep in the Karakorams, in the Hunza and Yasin valleys of Gilgit-Baltistan in Pakistan? It is an enigma to philologists, who are simply unable to match its words to any family they have ever seen, but something about its structure and sound system is surprisingly familiar. The vocabulary and some of the finer grammatical features of Burushaski are indeed unique. But it may well be that Burushaski shares a history with the modern languages of the Indus Valley Periphery: of local wives from early times, who married newcomers, and brought retroflexion into all our languages.

If there is one thing we have learnt in our time studying migrants and their languages, it is that migrants, the sort of people who get up and move to new lands, tend to be *men*. And those men, if they do not find wives locally, simply go extinct, along with the languages they brought. The survival of their languages comes at a high price: they have to turn themselves into grafted trees, as it were, with strong local rootstock, on top of which the pretty flowers and fruits, the words they remember from the old country, can have another life. But hidden below ground are the old features, from the languages of the women they married, invisible except to those with the eyes to see below the surface the sounds and grammar that did not die.

These structural resemblances to modern languages like Punjabi and Sindhi suggest that Burushaski too might be a mixed language, like the modern Indo-Aryan languages, and even Balochi and Pashto, both Iranian languages, where old grammatical features that go back to a time before the arrival of the migrant Vedic men might be preserved. Burushaski is not the final word on the IVC languages. It is just another language of the area, isolated from the others for a very long time. Does it line up with Punjabi, Sindhi, Pashto and Balochi in most of the ways that make them different from Sanskrit and the prakrits? And when it does not, could it point us towards things that might be logical precursors of the features we see in the other four languages of the Indus Valley Periphery today?

I did not for a moment think Burushaski would simply fall in line with the modern languages of the Indus Valley Periphery. But could it have a version of ergativity that was not too distant from the ergativity we saw on the plains? Something that could make us imagine the thing that spurred the prakrit speakers to invent split ergativity? A way of seeing that might go back to a time many millennia ago that lured the mixed descendants of the Vedic men and the women of the Indus Valley to dream of a different way of making verbs?

~

Peter Hook, my other dissertation adviser from half a century ago, suggested that I get in touch with Noburo Yoshioka, who had written his doctoral dissertation on Burushaski at Tokyo University, and gave me his email. I wrote to him and almost immediately got a reply, and soon he sent me a link to his dissertation. I went through it at lightning speed, and then I had to get up and take a long walk to wrap my brain around the fascinating things I had read.

Burushaski has ergativity. Not split ergativity: *full* ergativity. Its ergativity appears not only in the past tense, but in the present and the future tense too with transitive verbs: that is, verbs that can have objects. There are four genders. Yoshioka calls them HM, HF, X and Y: human male, human female, 'concrete objects including animals and fruit', and 'abstract object including liquids, trees and notions'.[17] As in Dravidian languages, gender agreement comes only with verbs, never with nouns and adjectives, and it comes only in the third person. Verbs agree with *I* and *you* using person markers, and in 'gender' with *he*, *she*, *X* and *Y* nouns and pronouns. But if the verb has an object, you will find ergativity in every tense, the verb taking markers to 'agree' with both the object as well as the 'agent'.[18] We are back to the old double marking we saw in Sindhi. Burushaski is a language that loves agreement.

~

What does all this mean for us trying here to trace our way back to the way we were? Well, ergativity in Burushaski, not split but full ergativity, is unique enough in modern South Asia that it doesn't seem to be a spin-off from the split ergativity we have now.[19] This kind of ergativity feels intuitively older and is eerily reminiscent of what we find in the languages of the Andamans. Anvita Abbi calls Present Great Andamanese a 'double-marking ergative language'.[20]

Other languages on the northern rim of South Asia also give importance not just to subjects but also to objects in their verb morphology. In the Munda languages of northern Jharkhand, for example, while there is no actual ergativity, verbs do carry object markers as well as subject markers.[21] And First Australian languages have ergativity: Grierson in the *Linguistic Survey of India (LSI)* states that 'Australian languages have a separate suffix to mark the agent', and that 'this is a characteristic feature of all the Australian languages'.[22] And, to complete the geographical arc between the Horn of Africa and Australia via South Asia and the Andamans, Amharic, the official working language of Ethiopia, our last port of call before our exit from Africa 70,000 years ago, has a feature where object markers often find their way on to the verb (though the rules governing these markers are not so simple). Could this be a relic from a time when there might have been something closer to ergativity in the Horn of Africa?[23]

All the Bantu languages of south of the Horn of Africa have object marking, languages such as Swahili in Tanzania on the East African coast, Lingala in the Democratic Republic of the Congo, Zulu and Xhosa in the Republic of South Africa along with a number of smaller Bantu languages and dialects, with the subject marker and object marker being prefixed to the verb stem.[24]

In Burushaski, what we get are verbs that are *stems* taking on markers of agreement. There is a present stem, and a past stem. When a sentence has a direct object—the boy sees *the cat's tail*—the one doing the action, the boy, gets an ergative marker, -*e*, often pronounced as *a,* and there is a marker *after* the verb that agrees, in gender, with boy, and a marker *before* the verb that agrees in 'gender' with cat:

The boy-ERG the-X cat-GEN <u>tail-X</u> (<u>X</u>)-**SEES-*Human Male*.**

There is an X gender marker *before* the verb 'sees' because 'tail', the object, belongs to gender-X, and a Human Male gender marker *after* the verb. That means there is gender agreement with both 'boy' and 'tail', while 'cat' has a genitive (or possessive) marker. The verb itself is a present stem, or a past stem.

And here is how 'he saw the cat's tail' looks in Burushaski:[25]

ín-e	*isé*	*búš-e*	*i-súmal*	*yeécimi*
he DIST-ERG	that-X	cat-GEN	3SG.X-tail-ABS	3SG.X-see-NPRS-3SG.HM[26]

'he saw the cat's tail'

If you couldn't recognize a single word, prefix or suffix in the Burushaski example above, you weren't supposed to. Burushaski is, after all, a language isolate: a language whose words have nothing to do with any other language on Earth. But if we look past the unfamiliar words to what is going on, its grammar makes a lot of sense. The ergativity we have in our modern north-western languages in just the past tense, Burushaski has in *all* its tenses. There is a verb stem with markers to agree not only with the 'object', but also with the ergative 'agent' too. The whiff of 'passiveness' that attaches to past participles like *seen* or *eaten*, however, is missing. The verbs behave more like stems with agreement markers, the sort of stems we get in Dravidian and Māgadhan languages. Ergativity in Burushaski feels less complicated than the split ergativity in our modern languages. There is no switching of roles, no realignment, verbs agreeing with 'subjects' in the present and the future, but then with 'objects' in the past. The alignments around the verb are the same regardless of tense:

> ***the-boy-e*** (the-cat-X) (X)-**SEES**-***Human Male***.
> ***the-boy-e*** (the-cat-X) (X)-**SAW**-***Human Male***.
> ***the-boy-e*** (the-cat-X) (X)-**WILL SEE**-***Human Male***.

In other words, this is the very same ergative pattern we outlined at the start of this chapter. If you had to design an ergative system from scratch, this is how you would do it.

Burushaski is not alone in this. Another language of the Karakorams, Gilgiti Shina, a Dardic language, 'is equally ergative in all tense and aspect categories'.[27] Shina is another example of *full* ergativity, ergativity not only in the past tense, but in all tenses. Like Burushaski, it uses an ergative marker, *se* (which makes immediate sense to us in north India as this is the very word that means 'from' or, actually, 'by'). As in Burushaski, the gender and singular/plural marker after the verb agrees with the 'subject' that carries the ending *se* but in Shina, unlike Burushaski, there is no object marker on the verb. The verb 'drinks' agrees only with 'boy', even though 'boy' is marked as ergative (MS is 'masculine singular'):[28]

*baál-**se*** *ča* *pí-an*
boy-**ERG** tea (F) drink-pres-MS
'The boy drinks tea'

~

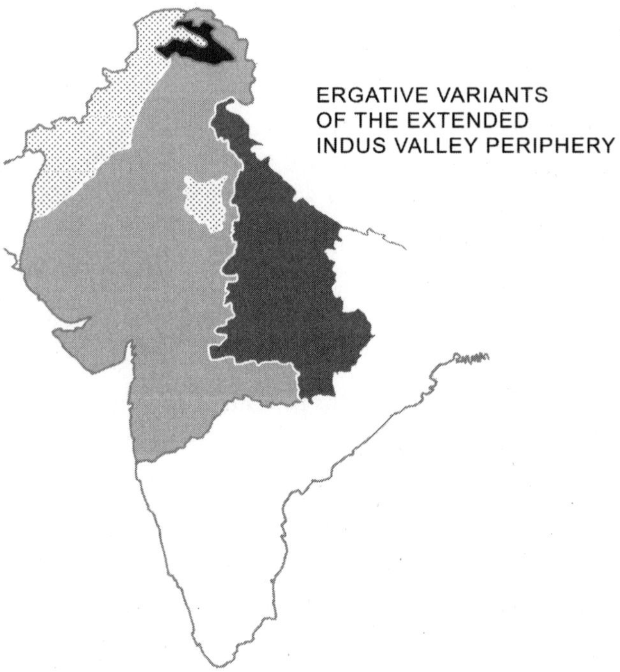

Map 4

Dark grey: split ergativity in past tense with ergative marking on agent for all persons

Light grey: split ergativity in past tense with ergative marking only in third person

Dots: split ergativity in past tense but without ergative marking on agent

Black: full ergativity in all tenses with ergative marking on agent

There is an amazing amount of variety in how ergativity is expressed:

> Full ergativity in Burushaski and agreement with agent and object
> Full ergativity in Gilgiti Shina with the marker *-se*, and agreement with the agent
> Split ergativity of Hindi with all agents marked with *-ne*
> Split ergativity in Punjabi, Marathi, Rajasthani, Hariyanvi with *-ne* only in third person
> Split ergativity in Pashto with no markers, but gender agreement with the 'object'[29]
> Full ergativity in Balochi dialects with the marker *-a*, but agreement with the agent
> No ergativity in some Balochi dialects

This sort of variety, especially in split ergativity, suggests the primordial variety of a centre of origin. And, indeed, this is the only part of South Asia where split ergativity emerged: the rest of South Asia doesn't have it at all.[30] Split ergativity may have come up separately in each dialect, with the maximum amount of marking (*-ne*) in the area around present-day Delhi. This does not suggest the spread of a feature from one area, but rather what one could call 'path dependency': a similar outcome reached from similar beginnings in response to the same need.

This is all strong support for a substratum. In other words, it is a signal that the IVC languages probably had ergativity.

If ergativity is so tightly bound up with agreement, and almost always has something to do with gender (or rather, noun classes), we need to understand gender before we go any further. Grammatical gender is something that has always been part of Sanskrit: it has three genders, masculine, feminine and neuter, but gender agreement in Sanskrit is with adjectives, not with verbs. Could the Indus Valley languages have had something like gender too before Sanskrit came on the scene? Burushaski has a sort of natural gender. Balochi has no gender at all. Pashto has two grammatical genders. Punjabi and Sindhi have grammatical gender, and gender agreement with both adjectives and verbs, and so do Hindi, Marathi and Gujarati and all the other western Indo-Aryan languages.

~

I paused. Then, on pure speculation, I searched on the Internet for articles on Australian aboriginal languages and Amharic to see what I would find. Australian languages have ergativity, and Amharic has an object marking on verbs that is a sort of 'ergativity-lite'. But did First Australian languages have gender? Did Amharic? I already knew that Present Great Andamanese had seven noun classes, which is another way of saying it had a strong 'gender' system, and that these noun classes played a major role in its verb marking.[31] Was gender also an important feature of the two language families at the opposite ends of the arc of migration? Was gender something *more* than just a feature that had forced its way into the Indus Valley via Sanskrit and the prakrits?

It was. Most Australian languages have four noun classes (while some have only two, and some have more than four), centring around a masculine-feminine dichotomy.[32] Amharic has gender too, a straight-up masculine-feminine dichotomy.[33] And, of course, all the Bantu languages of southern Africa have multiple noun classes as well as object marking. Amharic was no isolated example.

The evidence was mounting in favour of Language X having had full ergativity, as well as object marking and gender—if not grammatical gender, a strong semantically transparent form of natural gender, the sort we see in the modern Dravidian languages of south India.

~

I took a break to digest all of this, sat back to read everything I could lay my hands on about ergativity. And then when I was deep into a very good article about ergativity in the Indo-Aryan languages, I suddenly felt my antlers tingle. The writer had just spoken about Dakkhini, which, he said, 'unlike Hindi-Urdu, had *lost* its ergative case marking due to isolation from other IA [Indo-Aryan] languages, and long-lasting influence of Dravidian'.[34]

Lost! I felt like I had tumbled down a rabbit hole into a world of old grammarians. Dakkhini hadn't *lost* ergativity, because it had never had it to start with. Even poetry in Dakkhini written in the early 1500s does not have the ergative *-ne*.[35] Early texts that have it, and are included as 'Dakkhini literature', were actually written by migrants from the north who had only recently arrived in the Deccan, some Sufis who came spouting poetry which, despite their best intentions, did not feel local. The Dakkhini made by people who had been speakers of Telugu does not have ergativity, because Telugu does not have it. That is why we took that detour in Chapter 2 to test our model of language mixing on Dakkhini, before daring to speculate about other languages. That is the beauty of having a model that looks out on a larger world, instead of getting trapped in old texts. We chose to test our model on Dakkhini first because we already *knew* about its substratum, and that *that* would be the reason why the mixed language would not have ergativity.

As we can see with Dakkhini, it isn't as though split ergativity is the only option available to a community that wants simpler past tenses. If a language really does not want to do ergativity, even when it is there in its face as Urdu is with Dakkhini, it won't. Dakkhini treats these past participles as past tense stems, and gender agreement is with whatever the subject is in any other tense: *āp namāz paṛhe*? 'did you do your *namaz*'. No *-ne*. The verb agrees with *āp*, 'you'. Not the turned-around northern version, *āp-ne namāz paṛhī*, where the verb has to agree with *namāz*. They just leave out *-ne* altogether and treat it as though it is the past tense of *go*. A bit like they do in Dravidian languages. Or the Māgadhan languages. Or early Sanskrit. Except that it is a *gender* agreement. If people in the Extended Indus Valley Periphery ended up making split ergatives, they probably liked what they were getting into.

~

What sort of substratum do the western Indo-Aryan languages have, that they did not mind gender and ergativity? We can see that a language like Burushaski would not only allow ergativity, but maybe even push those grappling with Sanskrit to invent it afresh. Because every one of the Extended Indus Valley Periphery languages, from Hindi in the east, through Gujarati and Rajasthani to Punjabi, Sindhi, Balochi (partly) and Pashto in the west, and down south to Marathi and Konkani, has some sort of ergativity.

I needed to reach out to my Sanskrit professor, Madhav Deshpande, and brainstorm this with him. I sent him an email asking when and how ergativity had found its way into Sanskrit. He replied at once:

> While the past participle with *-ta* is already there in the Vedic language, it becomes more and more common in the post Vedic language, taking the place of the main verb, gradually becoming the dominant, but not the exclusive, usage. Ergativity-like phenomena begin to show up in late Sanskrit, when Sanskrit is clearly a second language, and under a strong influence of the local vernaculars. We also notice the gradual disappearance of the old finite verbs in Prakrit, but it takes quite a long time. Pali and Ardhamāgadhi do have past tense finite verbs. It takes the development of the Apabhraṁsas and later forms of the [Middle Indo-Aryan] and [Modern Indo-Aryan] for the old finite verbs to almost disappear.[36]

We were both on the same page. There was something about these writers' actual first languages that was causing a flood of ergativity into Sanskrit. It was not something basic to Sanskrit.

What were the local vernaculars these writers were speaking, when they were not penning literature in Sanskrit? Most probably prakrits, as they were elite writers, and not little people. But the prakrits were grammatically very close to Sanskrit. Something *else* was pushing the prakrits and Sanskrit towards ergativity, something older.

~

The first signs of ergativity leaking into Sanskrit texts were *after* the Rig Vedic era, when the epicentre of the Vedic presence had shifted from the Indus Valley to the Ganga-Yamuna Doab area. That would make the area around present-day Delhi the likeliest place where modern ergativity first emerged. This fits in with the Hindi zone being the place that most uses the ergative marker *-ne*, as it occurs with the first, second and third person:

māīne, *tūne*, *tumne*, *āpne*, *usne*, *unhōne*. Almost everywhere else it is only used with the third person: *I* and *you* do not take an ergative marker. It is as though the outward markers of modern ergativity fade the farther you get from the transmission tower.

We know that by the classical era, even the men who wrote in Sanskrit and spoke it on formal occasions lived the rest of their lives speaking prakrits and maybe other older vernaculars. Perhaps Brahman men had begun to secretly dislike all the verb conjugations in early Sanskrit. So while they abided by the rules of Sanskrit even when they were speaking prakrit, they tried to slip in simpler alternatives if these could be justified by the rules of Pāṇinian grammar. That is exactly what prakrits *do*: they bend the rules, but not so far that they end up breaking them. Indian English is a prakrit too, and it would like to avoid using the English verb *have*, which doesn't exist in Indian languages: *it is with me only*. That sentence isn't wrong, but when you notice that the English verb *have* is now gone for good, it becomes clear that we have stepped on to a different path. The inspiration for this technically correct but quaint sentence is not English, but Indian. We are speaking prakrit English.

And what about the First Indian languages, the totally imagined substratum of the Indus Valley languages, which were a mix of First Indian languages and the languages of the Iranian farmers from the Zagros mountains? Were they like the northern Munda languages, which, like Burushaski, have not only subject agreement, but object agreement too? If the Indus Valley languages had a substratum of First Indian languages, and if (like the northern Munda languages and, indeed, Great Andamanese) they had object marking on verbs similar to what we find in Burushaski, it would not be such a stretch for these objects to be ready for an enhanced role in sentences where finite verbs had been replaced by past participles. These past participles naturally go with objects, not subjects: *food-eaten* (*by-me*): the agent is almost an afterthought. Does the split ergativity we find in the modern languages go back to object marking in the Indus Valley languages? Were the Indus Valley languages more like Munda in this respect than like southern Dravidian languages? Was object marking the real driver behind split ergativity?

The simplification of the Sanskrit past tense had to take the form of a past participle with *ta*, which already existed in Sanskrit and Avestan, a solution that didn't violate the rules of Sanskrit: *khādita*, 'eaten', *likhita*, 'written' or the Persian *rekhta*, 'strewn'. Turning past-tense sentences into noun phrases with a past participle took the stickiness out of the spider web of Sanskrit verb conjugations, with all the person and tense markers in the past tense. In time the old aorist past that we saw in the Rig Veda essentially vanished. If we ever needed any evidence that Sanskrit was slipping away as a first language, this is it. Brahman men were *not* learning Sanskrit as a first language, or they would have had no problem with the most complex Sanskrit verb morphology. But by this time Sanskrit was something they slipped into briefly, before going back to their 'real' lives.

In the prakrits, constructions like *by-me food-eaten*, without even a finite verb there as a face saver, were now coming up, with the *by me* fading down to become just an optional add-on. The subject of the sentence got demoted, and nowadays may often even be deleted: you mostly say just *khānā khāyā* in Hindi-Urdu, 'food eaten'. Whoever ate it is implicit: you *know*, or you ask. All that is left is a noun phrase, *food eaten*, with a 'participle-adjective', *eaten*, that needs to agree with its noun, and the prakrits always had had gender, and case, to do this. And if Burushaski is anything to go by, the old ones really loved agreement.

One thing that continues to surprise me, as I speak Hindi, is how often I end up *not* inflecting verbs. Hindi has words like *ćāhiye*, analogous to *vēṇum* in Tamil and Malayalam, where the subject is more like an indirect object, and the form of the verb does not change: 'to me X is required', not '*I want* X'.[37] I remember, when I was a student learning Hindi, hearing people asking *kahā̃ jānā?* "where to go?' or *kyā karnā?* 'what to do?' And here I was, trying to inflect the verbs! 'Where *will we* go?' 'What *will we* do?' You could, but it wasn't necessary. In fact, the sentences with *will we* sounded strange. Like translations of English. Could this have something to do with the people who spoke earlier languages, and later the prakrits, and their search for ingenious ways to avoid inflecting verbs?

So for days on end, I went around noting my conversations in Hindi: *wāpas kab jānā? patā nahī̃. jānā hai. bād mẽ ānā . . .* When to go back? (When *do you want* to go back?). Idea-no. (*I don't know*). It is to go. (*I/you have* to go). To come later (*Why don't you* come back later?). We didn't avoid all finite verbs: we just didn't use them as often as we had thought.

~

Split ergativity did not come directly from the Indus Valley languages. It evolved under an intense spotlight of Sanskrit, when the Kuru kingdom was consolidating its hold on the Doab region, its Āryāvarta, the Ārya stronghold at that time, and had stopped at the confluence of the Ganga and Yamuna rivers, before the Māgadhan forests, unwilling to engage with the lands and people farther east.[38] Ergativity was a way of getting rid of the many verb conjugations and person endings of Sanskrit, with every verb form unique, a minefield where a non-native speaker was almost set up to make mistakes. Clearly the level of complexity in Sanskrit verbs did not appeal to the speakers of the old Indus Valley languages and, later, the prakrit-speaking Ārya men.

So they took it a step further in the modern languages, using verbal nouns to make other tenses too. In Hindi 'I do' is built from a prakrit version of *kartṛ*, 'doer', in essence a masculine noun with the nominative form *kartā*, which would become *mãĩ kartā hũ* ('I am a *kartā*'). This would have a feminine form, *kartī*, which would become *mãĩ kartī hũ* ('I am a lady-*kartā*'). *Doer* does not have the 'passive' flavour of *done*, so there is no realignment to get objects agreeing with verbs. Marathi dispenses with the verb 'to be' altogether and uses only the masculine and feminine verbal nouns: *khāto* and *khāte* for I/you/he eats and I/you/she eats. What began as simplification ended up being something that eerily recalls Burushaski and the languages of the Andamans, where verbs agree with their 'agents' and objects in gender. But in the modern western Indo-Aryan languages this does not only happen with *he-she-it*. These languages have gender agreement with *I* and *you* too.

It is almost with a sense of relief that I find that the old Indus Valley languages are not, after all, radically different from other language families of South Asia. They may have been predisposed to having ergativity, but that would have been an ergativity without the contortions we find now, where objects actually switch places with subjects in past tenses. Modern gender in the Extended Indus Valley Periphery resonates well with the *he-she-it* gender in the Dravidian languages, marked on verbs but not on adjectives. This may be where we get our love of gender marking, even though that would have started out as natural gender.

But from the time Sanskrit-style gender entered the picture, things really got going. There were prakrits busy at work on the sidelines, first copy-pasting gender from Sanskrit, and then finding an acceptable way to slip past the labyrinth of its verb morphology by turning all of its past tenses into one-size-fits-all past participles. And it worked so well that it even became a big hit in Sanskrit, where ergatives and past participles with -*ta* eventually became the favoured way of expressing the past tense. There was something of the old languages, it seems, in the way ergativity caught on in Sanskrit, instead of becoming just a passing fad. But most of all, it was a story of collaboration among all the stakeholders, reaching a solution that did not rattle Sanskrit's grammar while it made things a little bit easier for the Brahman men who now lived only a part of their lives in Sanskrit.

~

There is something about morning light that puts things together and brings a fresh perspective. We are still in olden times, looking at the Delhi area where ergativity first came to life, but now it is a wide-angle view, one eye trained on Maharashtra, to the south, which has Mahārāshtri Prakrit, and out of the corner of the other eye we can see Magadha, which has Māgadhan Prakrit. Both these prakrits have gender and ergativity: we need only look at Ashoka's inscriptions all over the land to see that the prakrits were a close family.

But only Mahārāshtri manages to pass on grammatical gender and ergativity to the modern languages and dialects coming up in the area. In Magadha this does not happen. What we see, instead, is a total disconnect between Māgadhan Prakrit, which has gender and ergativity, and the modern Māgadhan languages that emerged in the region. Bangla, Odia, Assamese, Maithili, Magahi and Bhojpuri do not have grammatical gender or ergativity. Why would these features survive and thrive in Maharashtra, but come to nothing among the Māgadhans?

Sumanta Banerjee, who writes on the history and culture of Bengal, says that 'Bengal had enjoyed a certain degree of independence from the political and cultural influence of the north-western part of India. In the epic age, Bengal used to be described as *Pāndava-varjita*, or rejected by the Pandavas, implying that it was unfit for settling down.'[39] He mentions that a *smṛti* warns people from the Āryāvarta lands west of the Ganga-Yamuna confluence not to travel to the peripheral lands of Anga, Bengal, Odisha, Saurashtra or Magadh except on pilgrimage, or they would have to do penance:

Aṅga-Vaṅga-Kaliṅgeṣu Saurāṣṭra-Magadheṣu ća
Tīrthayātraṁ vina yataḥ punaḥ saṁskāraṁ arhati.[40]

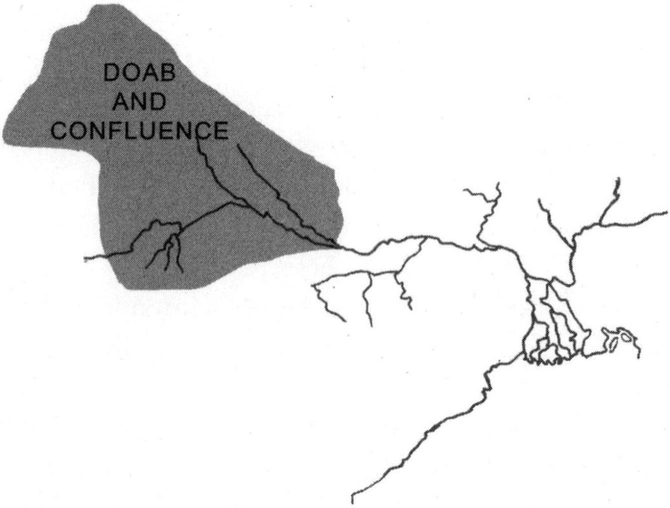

Map 5: The Ganga-Yamuna confluence: the eastern boundary demarcating the Extended Indus Valley Periphery from the Māgadhan zone east of the confluence

And in medieval times, in the south, Dakkhini came up, another new language, which, like Marathi, Gujarati and Rajasthani, took on grammatical gender. Against all expectations, it has exactly the same gender as Hindi-Urdu, which, in turn, is a lift from Sanskrit, pared down to two genders. What was it about languages like Marathi, Dakkhini and even the languages of 'Saurashtra' that made them so much more receptive to gender than the languages of the east?

What old Maharashtra had was a much stronger Brahman (and Sanskrit) presence than Magadha, and both Maharashtra and the Deccan have a substratum of Dravidian languages, all of which have natural gender, a bit like the natural gender we see in faraway Burushaski. The east has a substratum of Munda, a totally different family from Dravidian, which was tinged by an Austro-Asiatic migration 4000 years ago that turned the Munda languages into 'classifier languages', an identity that is at odds with having gender. Munda languages, probably ever since that migration, do not have gender, but instead have numeral classifiers like the iconic *ekṭā, dūṭā*, with the classifier *ṭā*, and *ekjon, dūjon,* which contrast with *ek, dū* for 'one, two' in languages like Bengali.[41] The old animate-inanimate 'gender' distinction that is supposed to be in Munda is almost like a faded memory of a feature that must once have been more robust.

It is hard to convince students who are native speakers of Dravidian languages that their languages 'do not have gender'. They insist that they *do*, just not in the first and second person. Tamil, Telugu and Kannada have a three-way contrast in the third person, *he*, *she* and *it,* linked to natural gender, and in Malayalam while the verb endings are gone, the pronouns are still there. It is only when they see how complex and arbitrary grammatical gender is in the north, where even nouns that *do not yet exist* are pre-assigned a gender (a hadron collider would have a gender, for example), that they sit back in wonder. Weapons we don't yet have. Scientific processes that are only now being developed. Made-up words. All of these have a gender in the Extended Indus Valley Periphery, and what is more, no one has any doubt about what it is going to be.

~

Banerjee suggested that I read *The Origin and Development of the Bengali Language*, by Suniti Kumar Chatterji, to see what he said about the modern Indo-Aryan languages and how they turned out as they did. I had actually read it when I was only twenty-five and busy writing my own dissertation, about Bhojpuri. But I was far too young to grasp what an amazing book it was. A full century ago Chatterji had seen what I am grappling with today. He spoke of . . .

> an almost wholesale disuse of OIA moods and tenses, reducing the verb system of Aryan to an indicative present form (and in some cases an indicative future), a past participle forming the past, a present participle, a conjunctive, and some verbal nouns . . . a similar decay has taken place in Iranian. But the whole principle of phrase building tended gradually to become nominal or adjectival from verbal in IA . . . and herein there is a possible influence of Dravidian, for in Dravidian the verb has an adjectival force, it being really a noun of agency with reference to the subject.[42]

Or, as Chatterji says, 'the most fundamental agreements are thus found between [the modern Indo-Aryan languages] and Dravidian, and all this began from early [Middle Indo-Aryan], as is seen from a comparison of Pali and the Prakrits with that of the modern vernaculars.'[43] After a strange interregnum with Sanskrit and the prakrits at the helm, the languages of the northwest and the south were re-manifesting their underlying . . . sameness. Below the 'flesh that does not last', astonishing family resemblances in bone structure were resurfacing. It was a story of people and languages who loved nouns, and would do almost anything, even adopt Sanskrit's grammatical gender, to escape from the Sanskrit verbs that had been plaguing them from the get-go.

But I would not put it down to mere 'influence' of Dravidian: languages do not share their basic DNA from casual proximity. In fact, languages themselves do nothing: they are only a reflection in a mirror. It is people who make the change. And there was a power shift, which brought a proper disconnect between the world of Sanskrit, Pali and the prakrits and the world that came up later. An age of Brahmans and kings was giving way to an age of traders and craftsmen and a new set of rulers from Central Asia. Lying quiescent for centuries, the maternal substratum was back in the game and had decided that the new languages, the languages of the one-time little people, would at last get to show their likeness.

This exploration of gender and ergativity has taken us on a long journey, where, at day's end, we have found tantalizing signs of these two features in Burushaski, and low-maintenance forms of ergativity in Balochi, Pashto and Shina, which tie in with a relationship that we were less certain of before. It always made sense that the route used by the early Dravidians into the subcontinent should run from the northwest to south India via the Indus Valley. But there were these two things in the western Indo-Aryan languages, gender and ergativity, that gave us pause and made us wonder if the Indus Valley people were not, perhaps, a separate branch of the Dravidian family. What we see now is a common ancestor that had natural gender, like the Dravidian languages and Burushaski do, showing up only in third-person pronouns but not in adjective agreement, and where verbs were stems with invariant agreement markers. But it would also have had full ergativity, in all its tenses (or, at the very least, object agreement on its verbs along with subject agreement).

And why not split ergativity? Because there is no reason for the split version to have existed in Indus Valley Civilization times. Split ergativity came up as a mutant strain when Sanskrit and its past participles had to be reconciled with a desire to do verbs like the old languages used to do them, using ready-made Sanskrit past participles with a passive flavour rejigged for the job. If there was ergativity in the old languages of the Indus Valley (and I believe that there was), it is hard to see why it would not have been full ergativity, using verb stems and not participles. And full ergativity, as we see in Burushaski, is mostly a matter of putting markers on 'agents' of transitive sentences and linking them to the verb stems with the right suffix. It is actually a more user-friendly system than the split ergativity we have now.

Map 6: Balochi (an Iranian language) and Brahui (a Dravidian language) in Pakistan

~

There is one language of the northwest that we have not yet discussed: Brahui, a Dravidian language spoken in Balochistan and in southern Iran by nomadic tribespeople who are rapidly moving on to the mainstream languages. Brahui has a core of Dravidian-origin vocabulary, and does not have grammatical gender or ergativity, features of other modern languages of the northwest.

The burning question about Brahui has always been: is this a relict early Indus Valley language, since it is Dravidian, and already present in the Indus Valley Periphery region? Or is it a Dravidian language of south or central India spoken by tribes that migrated into the area in more recent times? What does our discussion of ergativity mean for Brahui, which has neither gender nor ergativity? Brahui's vocabulary is full of recent loanwords from Persian and Urdu, but there seem to be no loanwords that go back to the time of the prakrits, or the time before Urdu when the modern Indo-Aryan languages of the region, like Sindhi and Punjabi and the other related languages, were taking shape. Consider these two Brahui sentences:[44]

> bādšāas *ass* – bādišā xudā *e*, xudānā rasūl *em* zamānanā*! – ki* awlād *a=matawaka-ta*
> 'Once there was a king – the King of the world is God, and his Prophet! – who had no son.'

> *ustaṭī tēnā* xīāl kare ki *dāsā rīš-ka piun mass*; āxir *kahoṭ, dā* bādšāī *pēntā dūṭī tammōe*
> 'Thought he to himself: "My beard has now turned white; at the last, and this kingdom will fall into the hands of others."'

Apart from the familiar-sounding xīāl kare (ki), which means 'thought-did (that)', the words from Urdu taken into Brahui are nouns linked to Islam and everyday words like *awlād*, 'son' and *āxir*, 'finally'. So in that sense it is reminiscent of Malayalam, a Dravidian language of south India with many Sanskrit nouns that go back to the twelfth century, added on to a Dravidian frame. Brahui does not even have the natural gender we find in the Dravidian languages of south India, and no ergativity.[45] Bray, writing in 1909, also says plainly that 'gender in Brahui is not expressed by grammatical forms'. Brahui has adjusted so much to its local environment that he feels the need to repeat Caldwell's (1856) question as to whether it should even be classed as a Dravidian language, or seen as 'derived from the same source as the Panjâbi and Sindhi, but it evidently contains a Dravidian element'. In the end he decides that '[t]he Brahui language is sprung from the same source as the Dravidian language group; it has freely absorbed the alien vocabulary of Persian, Baluchi, Sindhi and other neighboring languages, but in spite of their inroads its grammatical system has preserved a sturdy existence.'[46]

Brahui stands apart from the other languages of the northwest whose speakers would have been receptive to grammatical gender in Sanskrit and inclined to remake the Sanskrit verbs as stems with gender markers, giving a clear role for objects, at least in the past tense, and not just subjects. Brahui, in the absence of ergativity and gender, resembles only Balochi, its closest neighbour, which is also on the outer fringe of the region. Was ergativity there once upon a time in Balochi, but lost? Was the seed of ergativity ever there in Brahui? There is no way to tell. It is as if a huge swathe of history, the era of Sanskrit and the prakrits, simply passed it by.

We will discuss Brahui later. Suffice it to say, for now, that as Brahui does not have ergativity or gender, we can leave it out of the present discussion.

~

In this chapter we set out to tame a dragon. I don't know if our dragon is now tame, but it is possible that after this journey we understand it a little better and may even find some of its behaviour less unreasonable than before. In the process of traversing this terrain, a good deal of underbrush has been cleared, giving us a better view of the route into the remote past that it hid from our sight.

In the next chapter, in clearer daylight, we will use the model we tested in Chapter 2 as a map to lead us back a few thousand years in time to find out about Language X, the vanished language of old Harappa. We will carry forward the insights we have gleaned from this exploration of ergativity and hope to find out more about Language X by following the maternal line that underpins all our modern languages. What we end up with will only be a reconstruction, impossible to verify. We were not there to hear Language X while it lived. But, we hope, the exercise will take us closer to understanding how the old ones who lived before us spoke, and why we now speak the way we do.

4

In Search of 'Language X'

... the voice within the candle ...

The Silence of a Candle, Paul Winter

At the beginning of this book, I spoke of a song, a requiem for someone who had died, where the message was hidden in the chord structure, the substratum layer, while the tune, the first thing most people go to, to find meaning, floated in the air above it, ephemeral, forgettable, almost an afterthought. Flesh does not last, it seemed to say. But bones might. And so could the wonderful things we built when we were alive. You can still see us, if you know how to look, and imagine how we lived. But you will have to make do with an X-ray image.

The term 'Language X' goes back to a paper that Colin Masica from the University of Chicago presented at a meeting in Ann Arbor in 1978 about Aryan and non-Aryan elements in north Indian agriculture, where 'Unknown' was the heading of his longest list of words, because he either had no idea where they came from, or he was not convinced of the source he had listed.[1] 'Unknown', so call it X. The name caught on, and soon Michael Witzel at Harvard[2] and Franklin Southworth at the University of Pennsylvania were also speaking of 'Language X' when they mentioned the Indus Valley language. The hypothetical language that was the source of all Masica's enigmatic words now had a name.

There were probably many languages and dialects in the Indus Valley region, with one standard variety located at the centre of the civilization. But it would make sense for many of the little languages and dialects of the region to have belonged to a larger family, though there would probably have been some unrelated languages also looking on from the sidelines. In such great cities there would definitely have been local minority groups, as well as diplomats and traders from neighbouring lands who left behind communities to keep the relationship going.

Much of the early search for a lost Indus Valley language centred on the seals that were found when the old cities were excavated by archaeologists. These were small reliefs, many of which depict animals or people interacting with animals, besides more abstract markings that would appear to be 'writing' or some form of notation. What could these seals be? Could they be people's names? Perhaps the names of important merchants who needed to put a stamp on their transactions? Edicts? They were too short to be full sentences. And if they were words, what did they sound like? Were these markings meant to represent sounds? Or were they just symbols for concepts, like numbers?

Steve Farmer, Richard Sproat and Michael Witzel did not think they were words. In 2004 they went so far as to say that the seals were not writing at all, noting the 'extreme brevity' of the Indus Valley inscriptions, with the longest text having only seventeen symbols, something 'unparalleled in any literate civilization', which led them to declare the Indus Valley Civilization pre-literate.[3] They announced a prize of $10,000 for anyone finding 'just one inscription that contains at least 50 symbols distributed in the outwardly random-appearing ways typical of true scripts contemporary to the Indus system'.[4]

It isn't as though relics have never been decoded. The ancient Egyptian hieroglyphics all over the walls of their tombs, temples and monuments, and in old papyrus scrolls, were eventually deciphered, but it was because of one amazing piece of luck. In 1799 French soldiers retrieved a granite slab from a pile of rubble in the town of Rosetta, on the Nile delta. Carved into the stone surface were three texts, written in three different scripts. On top was a section in Egyptian hieroglyphics. Below it was text in Demotic script, an ancient Egyptian script used for more secular commerce. And at the bottom was a section in ancient Greek.[5] Was it possible that all three texts contained the same message? Could the Greek and the Demotic scripts be a key to deciphering the Egyptian hieroglyphics?

The Rosetta Stone

It took time. First the Demotic script had to be matched to the Greek. Then the names in the text had to be found and deciphered from the Demotic script. But it wasn't just a matter of finding one-to-one correspondences. The hieroglyphics were, after all, in a language, and that language had a grammar. The word order and grammatical markers in the three texts would not be the same. And the Demotic script, unlike Greek, turned out to be written from right to left, and was only partly phonetic, as it included symbols derived from hieroglyphs.[6]

It was only when French linguist Jean-Francois Champollion approached the problem through his knowledge of Coptic, an old language still used by the Coptic Christian Church in Egypt, that he was able to make out that the syllables written in the Demotic script were words he recognized from Coptic. The language of the hieroglyphics was a close cousin of the one used in the sacred texts of Coptic Christianity. Champollion had found not only the meanings of the words written in the hieroglyphics, but also how they had been pronounced.

It is lucky for Farmer, Sproat and Witzel that their challenge was so specific, finding a corpus of '50 symbols', as there probably aren't any. But tucked into their argument is the assumption that 'writing' must mean something like prose, or poetry, statements or narrative bound by rules of grammar. Documents like the Rig Veda were, after all, preserved orally for millennia through elaborate methods of memorization, so much so that we are now fairly certain of how the hymns sounded. We can treat the oral Rig Veda as a 'text'. It was quite feasible for a civilization, at that time, to do without written stories and 'literature'.

But was early writing really about that? Was 'literature' the first thing a society would wish to record in imperishable stone? And if a civilization did not choose to preserve its stories and hymns in writing, what sorts of things would it want to note down if it had a complex economy with multiple transactions involving exact measurements and currency? *Who* were the people who would want to set things like this in stone?

It took a radical approach to the issue to make headway on deciphering meaning in the seals. And in 2019, Bahata Ansumali Mukhopadhyay, a software developer in Bangalore, published an article in *Nature* describing the seals as 'formalized data carriers', but not in a phonetic script.[7] Mukhopadhyay's engagement with the Indus Valley seals began in 2014, and over the years her approach matured into an article in 2022, posted on the Elsevier SSRN preprint server, where she identifies a symbol for 'carat' based on the 'ratti' seed, known in English as the Rosary pea, which has traditionally been used in India as a standard measure for weighing gold and measuring its purity, and she also posits a symbol made from the image of a crucible with a goldsmith's blowpipe inside it as meaning 'gold'.[8]

I first saw her findings as a presentation from a video conference.[9] I myself come from a family of traditional Indian goldsmiths, and everything she said was instantly familiar. *Of course* it would have to be commercial people working with the substance linked to currency, and requiring exactness and certification, who would be the ones to first need to note down this kind of information. As Mukhopadhyay adds, the actual physical crucibles and blowpipes and gold testing stones depicted in the seals were found in Mohenjo Daro, *not* in some rich person's home, but along with unfinished jewellery pieces in a goldsmith's workshop, where the tools looked just like the ones I grew up with. I saw in my mind's eye the Paṇi, a mercantile community already living in the Indus Valley before the arrival of the Vedic men, and concerned with currency and the sorts of licence documents that allowed them to practise their trade. Early literacy would have been about *that*, not about stories.

Imagine, in a future age, archaeologists poring over our present-day barcodes and QR codes, or even the dhobi marks on our clothes, and wondering if they were 'meaningful', and whether they might be an ancient form of 'writing'!

The favoured approach to finding the Indus Valley *language* has been by linguists: philologists who bypassed the tempting Indus Valley seals and went straight to the words in the Rig Veda that did not seem to come from early Sanskrit, words for new things the Vedic men must have come upon when they reached the Indus Valley. Masica had his list of words and their possible sources.[10] The Finnish linguist Asko Parpola mentioned a number of words which, from their structure, seemed to him to be of Dravidian origin, and proposed Dravidian etymologies for these Sanskrit words.[11] Witzel, a professor of Sanskrit at Harvard (the same Witzel who declared the Indus Valley Civilization pre-literate) saw instead a 'Para-Munda' origin for the words he found that hadn't come from Sanskrit.[12] And Franklin Southworth and David McAlpin posited 'Elamo-Dravidian' as an origin, arguing that Elamite, an extinct language in southern Iran, might have been part of the Dravidian family. Munda languages trace back through their maternal line to the First People who came out of Africa, hunter-gatherers who reached the subcontinent 65,000 years ago,[13] and Dravidian words go as far back as the first farmers who came to the Mehrgarh area of Balochistan in the northwest of the subcontinent about 9000 years ago from the Zagros mountains in southern Iran and mixed with First Indians.[14] These two families would have to have been the first ports of call in any search for Language X.

But philologists who pore over texts in classical languages tend to have a strong fixation on *words*, so much so that they think of the substrata of the Indus Valley languages only in terms of words that appeared in Sanskrit from other old languages that must have been circulating in that area at the height of the Indus Valley Civilization. They are focused on the last traces of the 'flesh' that does not last. But to me, the substratum is mainly about structure, the 'bones' that do not go away so easily. The 'operating system' that underpins the language. And, as we have seen in mixed languages like creoles that go on to become native languages, the old languages that precede them are always erased, not so much their grammars, which tend to linger on as features of the creoles, but their vocabulary. If I had to look for substrata that had any chance of surviving after their languages had been lost for millennia, I would expect to find them only in the sound system and the grammar.

Let us now recap an old story, but this time with a slightly different spin.

Once upon a time there was a language, early Sanskrit, with a structure that looked a lot like Avestan, Greek and Latin. In its earliest days it did not yet have the almost ubiquitous South Asian retroflex sounds—*ṭ, ḍ, ṇ, ḷ* and *ṣ*.[15] It was a language where nouns took eight different case endings, depending on which class they belonged to, and could be singular, dual or plural. Verbs too had different conjugations, or paradigms, the same tenses as verbs in Avestan, Greek and Latin, and the subject was the same in all tenses. *I* eat, *I* will eat, *I* ate. Verbs agreed with their subjects using person markers, not gender markers, even though Sanskrit had three genders, masculine, feminine and neuter: *khādati* meant 'he/she/it eats'.

As the Vedic migrant men took local wives and had children, spoken Sanskrit would have taken on a few local features, mainly in its accent. The children would have brought in a local pronunciation, adding *ṭ ḍ ṇ*, *ṣ* and maybe *ḷ*, since their mother tongues had these sounds. It is usual in mixed families of this type for children to learn their mothers' languages first, and boys are generally taught their fathers' language only when they are about five years old.

Sanskrit was oral: for centuries it had no writing system, and when it did get one, it was not much used, as there were elaborate procedures in place for memorizing texts. Maybe it was a good decision to keep it oral, as this restricted access to all but a small and inbred group of Vedic men who had full control of the valuable *śrauta* rituals. As a result, the sound of the language was the first thing anyone would notice, and this made it clear who was 'us' and who was not. Small differences in accent, or in *saṁdhi* (sound assimilation) rules, would make a huge difference to Brahman listeners: like the word *loka*, the world, being pronounced as *loga* with a Dravidian *saṁdhi* rule. This would lead to these non-standard varieties being dismissed as 'prakrits'. Not the way 'people like us' speak.

Prakrits were not spoken by the little people: they were the elite 'almost' varieties of Sanskrit spoken by the first local men to meet the new Vedic migrant men, and by the local wives of the Vedic men. The first prakrits would have been just Sanskrit with a local accent, but in time each began to pick up a character of its own and become an important language of religions like Buddhism and Jainism, and of kingship, as with the Ashokan pillars and rock inscriptions. Still, even after the prakrits went their separate ways, they all held on tight to the grammar of Sanskrit. The prakrit nouns all had cases like Sanskrit did. And their verbs stayed close to the Sanskrit of their time, adding only the local features that were acceptable in Sanskrit too.[16] Sanskrit and the prakrits, to a modern linguist, were close cousins. The prakrits did not represent any sort of 'midpoint' between Sanskrit and modern Indo-Aryan languages. Change, real change, had not yet begun.

It is only after the tenth century, and definitely by the twelfth century, that we begin to see languages that are radically different from the prakrits used by the elites in each area. These modern languages, like creoles, have all their words and affixes drawn from the local prakrits, but there are many features in their grammars that are strikingly different, not based on Sanskrit and the prakrits. While the prakrits formed a close family, with a grammatical sameness to them wherever they were found in the subcontinent, all of a sudden the north of the subcontinent was divided into two distinct families, with two linguistic 'tectonic plates' colliding at the confluence of the Yamuna and the Ganga rivers. To the east were languages of the Māgadhan region: modern Bengali, Odia, Assamese and the Bihari dialects of Maithili, Magahi and Bhojpuri. And to the west were the modern languages of an Extended Indus Valley Periphery: the 'Hindi family' in the east of the region, and as one moves westward, the Hariyanvi and Rajasthani dialects, Gujarati, Punjabi and Sindhi,[17] and then south to Marathi and Konkani. All the Extended Indus Valley Periphery languages had grammatical gender, besides several features not found in Sanskrit and the prakrits.[18] The Māgadhan languages had no grammatical gender, but they had other unique features, besides many of the 'new' features in the Extended Indus Valley Periphery languages. A fault line older than Sanskrit and the prakrits had reasserted itself in the structure of the modern Indo-Aryan languages.[19]

When did these modern languages first appear? We don't know, beyond noting that it was in the tenth or twelfth centuries that they began to make their presence felt in the written record, which is usually all we have to go by in discussing the past. And like what Bahata Mukhopadhyay suggests about the information in the Indus Valley seals, the subject matter of this early writing tended to be secular, and about mercantile and legal matters, a far cry from the topics of the earlier Sanskrit and prakrit texts: epics, religious treatises, edicts. While the twelfth century was a yeasty time, full of mysticism and free-spirited exploration, with Bhakti poets and Islamic Sufis fanning out all over the land and spreading the new languages that were coming up, there were also new writers in the towns producing written material, as craftsmen and traders were emerging into the sunlight.

Did all the new languages appear exactly when these new players started writing? Was writing the thing that brought these languages, with prakrit-derived vocabulary, to life and stabilized them? Or were they already there in the airwaves as spoken languages for a good while before, in songs, in poetry remembered over the ages? If they were, how long would they have been there? In the spoken language the transition probably happened gradually, as a slow process of vocabulary adoption, the old and the new existing side by side as they traded vocabulary. And what were the little people speaking before? What made the little people shift to new languages? Did they shift gradually, or all at once?

It is unlikely that all these new languages sprang up looking like the standardized written languages we have today, though some of the evidence we have from those early days, like samples of Amir Khusro's verse composed in the Dehlavi dialect, is strikingly like our modern standard languages. This mention of Amir Khusro points to what 'happened' to bring these local dialects to prominence as full-fledged languages: the Delhi Sultanate, which arrived from the Uzbekistan region of Central Asia, and sidelined the old crumbling order, ruled by prakrit-speaking kings, for good.[20] These dialects would have emerged locally, with a degree of variation similar to what we find even today within our regions. Certainly, many dialects of the 'Hindi family', like Awadhi and Braj, were not yet seen as subsets of the Delhi dialect that eventually spread and monopolized the literate activity in the region. The expression *kos-kos par badle pānī, chār kos par bānī*, that the water and 'voice' change every few kilometres, the same distance as the horizon of a village, must have been as true back then as it is now.

Our most important takeaway from this story is that just as we have, in archaeological terms, an Indus Valley Periphery region, we also have, in linguistic terms, something I like to think of as an Extended Indus Valley Periphery region. This is a linguistic terrain where the languages fall into one mega-family connected by their common features that do *not* link back to Sanskrit and the prakrits.

The image we are after is how our hypothetical Language X would have looked in the late Harappan period, just before the Vedic people and Sanskrit arrived. There may have been many twists and turns in its history before that, with all sorts of groups adding to the vocabulary in the area, and lots of variation within the larger Indus Valley zone. This is not an attempt to recapture that entire history. All we want is an X-ray snapshot of Language X as it was spoken before it began to fade from sight, and with its early history far behind it.

~

At the heart of my approach to finding the skeletal structure of the Indus Valley languages is my belief that the features of the modern Extended Indus Valley Periphery languages that do not come from Sanskrit and the prakrits are likely to be *calques*, literal translations of structures that existed in languages that lived in the region before Sanskrit and the prakrits appeared. This is why, in Chapter 2, we looked in such detail at Dakkhini, to get a model of the fusion process when older languages of an area come into contact with a new language of power.

While the languages that found their way into these modern calques were probably not the actual standard varieties of the cities of Harappa or Mohenjo Daro, which would have been abandoned by then, the *sameness* of the features we see in this region strongly suggests that they correspond to a family of languages that was there just before Sanskrit arrived. 'Family' is an interesting word: why would the little people's languages have formed a continuum? Wouldn't it have been more likely that they would have been distinct languages, separated by drift over time, the way the central New Guinea highlands separated into at least 800 distinct languages, despite there having been no outside influence on them?[21] The idea that the Indus Valley Civilization must have had a continuum of related dialects reflects our belief that, in the process of building a civilization, the group in power would have absorbed other local communities and their languages, some of them probably isolates, languages unrelated to any of their neighbours.

In a way, we are lucky we do not have to deal with words, the superficial differences between the early languages and the dialects of the area, and with the knotty issue of some languages being isolates. At the skeletal level they seem, at first glance, to fall into a single substratum. And since the civilization that immediately preceded the Vedic influx into the region was the Indus Valley Civilization, it is a short but reasonable step from there to thinking that the substratum of the modern languages of the Extended Indus Valley Periphery must be that of the vanished IVC languages and dialects themselves.

So in the early period of Vedic influx into the subcontinent, most of the local people would have spoken languages and dialects linked to the languages of powerful Indus Valley groups, along with some unrelated minority languages too. Some of the local women would have been pulled into the Vedic community as wives, and some elite men would have made the effort to learn the vernacular language of the Vedic men as a second language. But if the daily lives of the little people were not too disrupted, they would probably have continued speaking their earlier languages for as long as their world remained stable.

How long could this have continued? That would depend on how much the little people were able to ignore the presence of the newcomers. Was the Vedic migration enough of a shock to bring change all the way down to the little people? Or were the elites the only ones really affected, the men whose activity brought them into contact with the Vedic men? The text of the Rig Veda is the only 'document' we have of those times, composed from the Vedic men's point of view, and it may be giving us a distorted picture of their numbers and their initial importance in the land they had entered. After all, we know that for centuries until the emergence of the Kuru Empire there were skirmishes, between the Vedic men and locals, between the different Vedic tribes fighting each other, and even battles where some of the Vedic men allied with locals.

Would it have been possible for the little people to look away from all that activity and continue with their earlier lives? The Vedic men were not inclusive, the way the Deccani elites were, happy to welcome ordinary locals into their community. They had a strong sense of who was 'us' and who was 'other'. They would probably have been fine with the little people keeping to themselves if they didn't get in the way. Did something happen to remove that stability and catapult the little people into a more urban, networked existence, the way the Deccan Sultanate was able to transform the lives of little people who had earlier been Hindu and speakers of Telugu? At what point, between the influx of the Vedic men in 1700

BCE and the twelfth century CE, did the last little people let go of the Indus Valley languages and move on?

Was it like Latvia, which I mentioned in *Wanderers, Kings, Merchants*, where an earlier language, Livonian, a Finno-Ugric language related to Estonian, Finnish and Sami spoken in Lapland, lived on beside its Indo-European replacement, Latvian, with the last native speaker dying as late as 2003?[22] Latvian as a language emerged relatively late, with the first texts appearing in the 1500s, in a process that began in the thirteenth century with the Livonian Crusade that imposed Christianity in the region. This is very late for the evolution of an Indo-European language, and it gives a precious glimpse of the process of language replacement while it was still a work in progress.[23] Was the Latvian and Livonian story a model with implications for us? Were there people who still spoke the old languages in the Indus Valley Periphery region until maybe as late as a millennium ago?

These are questions to ponder. We are also not interested in tracking the in-between elite varieties of the Middle Indo-Aryan languages in the written record. What we are concerned with are the insights we can glean from the modern languages, in which we can clearly see an old substratum that was not there in Sanskrit, or in the prakrits.

We will also take the term Indus Valley Periphery literally, and consider all the modern languages of the area, regardless of whether they are classed as Indo-Aryan or Iranian or anything else. There is no reason to exclude them. On the contrary, they are very important because most seem, at first glance, to have exactly the substratum features we are interested in.

~

There is already one language in the region recognized as Dravidian: Brahui, spoken in Balochistan and in southern Iran by nomadic tribespeople who are rapidly moving on to the mainstream languages. It has a core of Dravidian-origin vocabulary, but it stands apart from the other languages of the region in having no gender or ergativity. It has loanwords from Persian, Balochi and Urdu, but its grammar and basic vocabulary are mostly Dravidian.

The big question about Brahui has always been: is it an example of an old language from the IVC family, as it is a Dravidian language, and already present in the Indus Valley Periphery region? Or is it a Dravidian language from peninsular India, spoken by people who migrated into the northwest in more recent times?[24]

In a genetics paper on this issue, Luca Pagani and Vicenza Colonna say that the Brahui people 'currently reside in south-western Pakistan, surrounded by Indo-European [language] speakers with whom they share a common genetic origin' as 'overall in Pakistan genetic relationships are more accurately predicted by geographic proximity than linguistic origin'.[25] When they compare the Brahui with other population groups in Pakistan, they find that the Brahui have exactly the same amount of Dravidian heritage (genetics similar to what is found in south India) as neighbouring groups in Pakistan who speak Indo-European languages.[26]

This is not surprising. It is totally expected that the people who lived in the Indus Valley Periphery did not vanish. Most must have stayed in place after the IVC de-urbanized, and moved on to become speakers of newer languages, which took their vocabulary from local prakrits, retaining a large number of features in their sound systems and grammars that trace back to IVC times. We are mostly still there. But there are questions that remain.

The geneticists do not rule out the possibility of a small number of Dravidian language speakers arriving from peninsular India in Balochistan, drawing locals into their group and spreading their language more than their genes. Their measurement was about the *amount* of Dravidian heritage in the different Pakistani groups, not whether these specific Dravidian genes go back to south India or whether they are unique to the IVC region. It looks like these groups are not easy to tell apart on a genetic test.[27] Grierson, in the *Linguistic Survey of India*, kept comparing Brahui not with the major mainstream Dravidian languages of south India, but with tribal Dravidian languages on its northern fringe, specifically Kurux/Kurukh and Malto.[28] So if we are looking to find a Dravidian tribe that migrated in the last millennia or so, maybe we should be looking past the big southern languages. However, it is just as possible that something of the IVC language family and its original speakers *did* stay back in the IVC lands, preserving their old language.

I sometimes amuse myself by speculating about a time after I am gone. Who, in my generation, will still be around to talk about me? I have no doubt that it will be the ones who knew me the least, never sat and talked to me, never read my books, the ones who survived well into old age because they had distanced themselves from this present-day world. But by virtue of being my family, they will have the last word. How will they portray me?

If Brahui is part of the original IVC family, now deceased, could it, likewise, be a distant cousin who stayed apart from family politics? An area as large as the IVC would not have had a single language, but at least as much variety as the region has today. There would have been standard urban varieties, and a large number of little dialects spoken in the hinterland, differing in their proximity to the standard urban varieties. The most urban people would probably have been the first to adapt to unstoppable change, while the poor, looking away from evidence of decline, would have lingered in their old worlds, preserving the old languages and culture.[29] Would Brahui have been on the edge of the group then, the way it is now, in the lands closest to the original Mehrgarh settlement? Would it have been, even then, reasonably different from the mainstream languages of the IVC? And how much has it changed since those times, bringing it more in line with neighbours like Balochi?

Could Brahui be another mixed language? A language which, like Burushaski, incorporates some structure from neighbouring languages, brought in by wives from outside the community, but with vocabulary and iconic bits of grammar preserved from its earliest days?

Brahui, for example, does not have ergativity, while almost all the other modern languages of the region have some form of ergativity. That in itself is not a problem. The Dravidian languages of south India do not have ergativity either, but neither do most dialects of Balochi, its neighbour in Balochistan. Brahui also does not have gender, not even the natural gender in third-person pronouns found in south India, and in this it lines up with its neighbour, Balochi, and not with the Dravidian languages of south India.[30] But its verbs have the typically Dravidian feature of negative conjugation (a single verb form that means 'it isn't'), which none of the Indo-Aryan languages of the region has. This is interesting, as a negative verb is precisely the sort of feature one would expect to be preserved in the modern Indo-Aryan languages of the region if a language like Brahui were the substratum.[31] From a distance Brahui looks like a pared-down version of the Dravidian languages of peninsular India, with loanwords from Persian, Urdu and Balochi.

Brahui has a role to play in helping us find Language X, but with these caveats borne in mind. Whether it is an original IVC language, or a recent migrant from south India, it will have vocabulary that links to the lost vocabulary of the IVC languages, though vocabulary is the most variable thing in a language family.

~

As we go feature by feature, constructing a model of the Indus Valley substratum out of the modern languages of the area, we will need to look at data from one more language of Pakistan that has not drawn its vocabulary from the Indo-Aryan prakrits, whose vocabulary is from a completely different source: Burushaski.

Burushaski is a language isolate spoken deep in the Karakorams in the Hunza and Yasin valleys of Gilgit-Baltistan in Pakistan. Pagani and Colonna report that the speakers of Burushaski, like the Brahui, are not genetically different from their neighbours.[32] This again is not a surprise. While philologists have had no success in matching its vocabulary to any other language family they have ever seen, there is still something about the structure and sound system of Burushaski that is surprisingly familiar.

The vocabulary and some of the finer grammatical features of Burushaski are unique. What is interesting about Burushaski, enough for us to include it in our comparison, is its structural similarities with Punjabi, Sindhi, Balochi and Pashto, all modern languages of the Indus Valley Periphery. It is quite possible that these five languages share a history: a shared 'female substratum' provided by women, the wives of early Burusho men, who probably spoke languages related to those of the IVC. As we see again and again, migrants into South Asia have generally been men, who would have gone extinct with their languages if they had not found local women to marry, going on to have half-local children whose first languages would have coloured the 'father tongues' they preserved.

In other words, Burushaski too might be a mixed language, exactly like the modern Indo-Aryan languages are, where old grammatical features that go back to IVC times might be preserved. Burushaski is no Rosetta Stone that will take us straight to Language X. It is just another language of the area, out of touch with the outside world for a very long time, adding a distant corner to the base of our pyramid and giving us a bit more confidence as we triangulate our way back to IVC times. If it lines up in structure with the other modern languages of the region, that is important to note. But just as important is when it does not, as it may give us an idea of earlier structural options that the others have moved on from, and a possible glimpse into features of Language X.

~

Who were the *people* of the Indus Valley? We often jump and call them Dravidians, since there is genetic evidence of a migration of farmers from the Zagros mountains just before farming began in Balochistan and the Indus Valley. But, as we have seen again and again, migrants into South Asia have always tended to be men. Even with the best of intentions of including women, it is always hard to get even a 30 per cent share of women in a migrating group anywhere.[33] That means that *most* of the early Iranian farmers would have had to find

First Indian wives, which means that there is another strand to the Indus Valley people and languages, something we could call Proto-Munda, the language of First Indians at that time. Proto-Munda would take us back to the First Indian languages spoken by hunter-gatherer populations in the northwest, varieties without the tinge of 'Austro-Asiatic' that now attaches to the Munda languages spoken in the Māgadhan lands beyond the Ganga-Yamuna confluence. But we must not take it for granted that the old Indus Valley languages would match up exactly with the present-day Dravidian languages of south India.

Punjabi and Sindhi are the modern languages that have come up in the Harappa and Mohenjo Daro regions. This is both positive and negative: on the plus side, they might be closest to the standard forms of the old Indus Valley languages, but at the same time they are the ones most exposed to 'modern' influences from Sanskrit and the prakrits, as well as Urdu, the official language of Pakistan, which, having started out in Delhi, is actually an Extended Indus Valley Periphery language.

We will go through each feature, one by one, where the modern languages of the IVC region differ from Sanskrit and the prakrits. These features are retroflexion; aspiration; word order; light verbs; ergativity and gender; compound verbs; reduplication; honorifics.

Retroflexion

Retroflexion in South Asia is the existence of dental consonants, like *t* and *d*, along with a parallel series of retroflex consonants, like *ṭ* and *ḍ*, which are pronounced with the tongue curled backward and touching the area in front of the hard palate in the mouth. This is a *phonemic* contrast, which means that using *t* in place of *ṭ*, or *d* in place of *ḍ*, can change the meaning completely. In Hindi, for example, *dā̃nt* means 'tooth', while *ḍā̃ṇṭ*, with the retroflex phonemes *ṭ* and *ḍ*, means 'a scolding': *dā̃nt* and *ḍā̃ṇṭ* are two different words.

Retroflexion is a feature of every language in the subcontinent, except for Assamese and the languages of the Indian North-east. Even the Munda languages Sora, spoken in Odisha and Andhra, and Korku, spoken in Madhya Pradesh and Maharashtra, which do not *now* have retroflexion, seem to have had it as recently as a century ago. When in 1906 George Grierson published the *Linguistic Survey of India, Volume IV: Mundā and Dravidian languages*, he did not single out 'Kūrkū' and 'Savara' as not having any retroflex consonants, though he noted that in 'Savara', there was a tendency to 'free variation' between *d* and *ḍ*,[34] like pronouncing *deś*, 'country', as *ḍeś*.

Retroflexion seems to go back to earliest times, as it is found almost everywhere in South Asia. D.N.S. Bhat, in his study of the incidence of retroflexion worldwide, discusses the presence of retroflex sounds in First Australian languages, and in the languages of the central New Guinea highlands, both of which groups were the fellow travellers of First Indians on the first successful migration out of Africa, which began 70,000 years ago.[35] It is easy to search the Internet and find videos of First Australians explaining how to pronounce the retroflex sounds *ṭ*, *ḍ*, *ṇ* and *ḷ*, with ultrasound images of the tongue curling back as they make these sounds. Many Indians sitting in restaurants in Australia and hearing First Australians speaking their languages say that they turn around to look, thinking they are hearing some sort of Tamil!

Retroflex consonants like *ṭ*, *ḍ*, *ṇ* and *ḷ* now occur more frequently in Dravidian languages than in other languages of the subcontinent, even if languages like Punjabi, Garhwaḷi, Gujarati and the Rajasthani dialects have all these same sounds. But there is a dental-retroflex contrast even in the tribal languages of the

Andaman Islands, which have not been in contact with mainland South Asia for thousands of years, so it owes nothing to Dravidian influence.[36] That would make retroflexion something very old, and almost like a South Asian genetic tag.

Every single language of modern Pakistan, the immediate Indus Valley Periphery, has retroflex consonants. Urdu, the official language of Pakistan, also has retroflex consonants, but we will not include it in our list here as it is not from the Indus Valley Periphery. It began as a twelfth-century Delhi dialect,[37] and thus belongs to the Extended Indus Valley Periphery. Here is the line-up for Punjabi, Sindhi, Balochi, Pashto, Burushaski and Brahui:

Punjabi:	*ṭ*	*ḍ*	*ṛ*	*ṇ*	*ḷ*		
Sindhi:	*ṭ*	*ḍ*	*ṛ*	*ṇ*	*ṣ*		
Balochi:	*ṭ*	*ḍ*	*(ṛ)*				
Pashto:	*ṭ*	*ḍ*	*ṛ*	*ṇ*	*ṣ*	*ṭṣ*	*ḍẓ*
Burushaski:	*ṭ*	*ḍ*	*ṣ*	*ṭṣ*	*ḍẓ*		
Brahui:	*ṭ*	*ḍ*	*ṛ*	*ṇ*			

Retroflexes are the sounds that trickled into Sanskrit, in early times, when the first locally-born Vedic children began to speak. If you look at the text of the Rig Veda, you will see very few of these sounds, as they would not have developed in most of the words originally brought by the Vedic men. Sounds like *ṇ* and *ṣ* in Sanskrit mainly occur when there is an *r* or *r̥* earlier in the word triggering retroflexion, as in *ramaṇa* ('pleasing'), or *r̥ṣi* ('rishi'), and *n* becomes *ṇ* before *ṭ*, *ṭh*, *ḍ* or *ḍh*. They are not meant to be phonemes in their own right, even if they sometimes turn up in words like *maṇi*, 'jewel' and names like *uṣā*, 'Usha', the goddess of the dawn, and *kavaṣa*, a *dāsiputra* whose mother was a local slave woman. And the sounds *ṛ* and *ḷ* are not a part of Sanskrit at all.[38]

Burushaski, like the other four languages, definitely has retroflexion. If any proof were ever needed that Burushaski has picked up features from the languages of the plains, this is it. It is impossible to imagine Burusho men trekking into the subcontinent already speaking with lots of retroflexion, because retroflexion is quintessentially a South Asian thing. Burushaski has *ṭ* and *ḍ*, but not *ṇ*, which I expected to see, and it does not have *ṛ*, which, in Pakistan, is probably a recent addition from Urdu, which is not a local language. Burushaski does, however, have *ṣ*, and also a few retroflex affricate sounds, *ṭṣ* and *ḍẓ*, which are also found in Pashto. Retroflexion is so well established in Burushaski that it speaks of a relationship that goes back to the time when the first Burusho men arrived and took local wives, after which the families lived far away and almost in isolation. Burushaski is just the language we need to keep us on track as we try to see our way back into the past.

The most likely retroflex sounds in the old Indus Valley language/s out of this line-up would therefore seem to be *ṭ*, *ḍ*, *ṇ*, *ṣ*, coincidentally the same ones as in Sanskrit. Could *ḷ* have been there too? In modern days *ḷ* only seems to turn up in Punjabi, where it has begun to fade away, but it seems to have been all over the literary prakrits. Local people were clearly using it a lot in early times. And it is still a part of Garhwali, deep in the Indian Himalayas.

Why am I so convinced about *ḷ* being part of the line-up? Because this sound still keeps coming up in more rural forms of Punjabi on both sides of the India-Pakistan border. We have words like *nāḷ*, meaning 'with', and a number of other words like *goḷī*, meaning 'bullet', where *l* becomes *ḷ* because it occurs in between vowels, a well-known Dravidian *saṁdhi* rule. It is also easier to think of *ḷ* fading out from Punjabi than being a recent addition. The list, then, at least for Harappa, is *ṭ*, *ḍ*, *ṇ*, *ṣ* and *ḷ*.

Aspiration

Aspiration is the h-like hiss that follows some consonants in languages of the subcontinent. *ph*, *th* and *kh* are *voiceless* aspirates, pronounced with no vocal cord vibration, and *bh*, *dh* and *gh* are *voiced* aspirates, where the *b*, *d* and *g* involve vocal cord vibration.

Among the Dravidian languages of south India, the only one that resolutely lists no aspirated consonants is Tamil. The other main Dravidian languages, Malayalam, Kannada and Telugu, do list alphabet symbols for the aspirated Sanskrit consonants, *kh gh ćh jh ṭh ḍh th dh ph bh*, but make sure to mention that these occur only in loanwords, and that they are almost always pronounced without aspiration, and that very few speakers can pronounce the voiced aspirates *gh jh ḍh dh bh*.[39] There is clearly something about aspirates, especially voiced aspirates, that does not sit well with most native speakers of Dravidian languages.

Voiced aspirates are technically a challenge to pronounce, because while *g j ḍ d b* have vocal cord vibration, the following *h* does not. That means that immediately after pronouncing the *g j ḍ d b*, the tension on the vocal cords has to be relaxed for a split second and the vocal cords thrown wide apart to make the voiceless *h*, before coming back into alignment to pronounce a following vowel or *r*. Even children who speak languages with voiced aspirates, like Hindi, or Marathi, or Bengali, do not get these sounds right until they are past infancy (though their parents do not notice it). I actually remember the moment when I was six years old in our backyard one evening when I pronounced the word *bhājī*, our word for *chaulāī*, or Amaranth leaves, with a proper *bh*. I realized that up until then I had been saying **phājī* but no one had noticed and corrected me.[40] I could feel the gymnastic achievement of getting the timing of the vocal cord action right as adults did. Experimenting further,

I found that it was impossible to whisper a voiced aspirate, or I was back to saying **phājī*. It could only be said out loud.

The languages of the Indus Valley Periphery in Pakistan are all uncomfortable with the sounds *gh jh ḍh dh bh*. In Punjabi *gh jh ḍh dh bh* exist as phonemes, but are pronounced *not* as voiced aspirates, but as *k ć ṭ t p* with a falling-rising tone. The Hindi/Urdu word for house, *ghar*, is pronounced in Punjabi as a sing-song *kàár*, or *kàr*, with a falling tone. In Sindhi, too, voiced aspirates are there as phonemes, but on the ground what they have are *implosive* versions of *g ḍ d b*, which are pronounced with the airstream going *inwards*, not outwards.[41] So Punjabi and Sindhi do make a distinction between sounds like *b* and *bh*, but it is not pronounced as *aspiration* (hence the use of ? in the table below). This tells us that these sounds were not a natural fit in Punjabi and Sindhi. Balochi and Pashto have no aspirates at all.

Punjabi:	*k kh g ?*	*ć ćh j ?*	*ṭ ṭh ḍ ?*	*t th d ?*	*p ph b ?*
Sindhi:	*k kh g ?*	*ć ćh j ?*	*ṭ ṭh ḍ ?*	*t th d ?*	*p ph b ?*
Balochi:	*k g*	*ć j*	*ṭ ḍ*	*t d*	*p b*
Pashto:	*k g*	*ć j*	*ṭ ḍ*	*t d*	*p b*
Burushaski:	*k kh g*	*ć ćh j*	*ṭ ṭh ḍ*	*t th d*	*p ph b*
Brahui:	*k kh g*	*ć j*	*ṭ ṭh ḍ*	*t th d*	*p ph b*

It is impossible to imagine that there could have been voiced aspirates in Language X. But could the voiceless aspirates *kh ćh ṭh th ph* have been in the old Indus Valley languages before Sanskrit? Tellingly, Brahui and Burushaski have them. Balochi and Pashto, both Iranian languages, have retroflexes, but no aspirates. The Munda tribal language family of central India has voiceless aspirates.[42] Anvita Abbi also finds voiceless aspirates in the languages of the Andamans, which never had any contact with Sanskrit.[43] Brahui has the voiceless aspirates *kh ṭh th ph*.[44] So the likeliest group in Language X would have been:

k kh g *ć ćh j* *ṭ ṭh ḍ* *t th d* *p ph b*

All the western Indo-Aryan languages in present-day India besides Punjabi—that is Hindi/Urdu, Gujarati, Rajasthani, Marathi and the Māgadhan languages farther east—have voiced aspirates, *gh jh ḍh dh bh*, just like Sanskrit. So much so that the official name of India is now *Bharat*, with *bh*, originally the name of one of the Rig Vedic tribes. It is unthinkable that the earlier local languages they sprang from had these sounds. How did these sounds, more prominent in Sanskrit than even in the prakrits, which often reduced them to just *h*,[45] get to be so well established in modern north Indian languages?

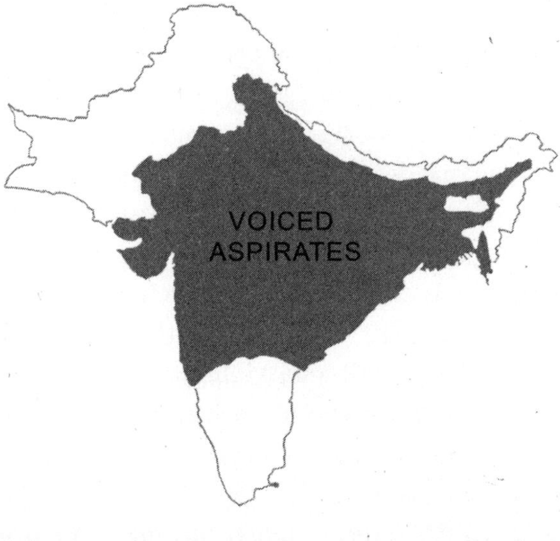

Map 7: The areas where voiced aspirates occur in South Asia: note that the indigenous languages of the Indus Valley area (modern Pakistan), the Dravidian languages of South India and the tribal languages of the North-east do not have voiced aspirates.

Could it be that this is like Dakkhini having grammatical gender even though Telugu, its substratum language, does not have it? Could it be another example of *porosity*, which makes mixed languages sometimes adopt grammatical features from their *lexifier* languages, which are otherwise donors of vocabulary, not grammar. There is, after all, a history of voiceless aspirates even in the Indus Valley Periphery, the first camel's foot inside the tent, as it were. Could it be that there was more early contact, in towns, between Sanskrit, the prakrits and the newly formed Indo-Aryan languages in what is now India? Or are these crisp, clear voiced aspirates relatively new? This, too, is something to ponder.

Word order

Almost all languages of South Asia (except Kashmiri and Khasi) are 'SOV' languages: the normal order of words in a sentence is typically subject-object-verb.[46]

Punjabi, Sindhi, Balochi, Pashto, Burushaski[47] and Brahui[48] are all SOV languages. This is not surprising. Even Sanskrit is essentially an SOV language, though its word order is not as strictly fixed as in most languages, as it also has case markers to clarify what word is a subject and what is an object.[49]

More revealing are *postpositions*, the words like *mẽ* in Hindi and *il/yil* in Tamil and Malayalam that mean 'in' and come after nouns. Even the tribal languages of central India have postpositions.[50] Postpositions do the work of the case endings in Sanskrit and are found in all South Asian languages that have an SOV order. English has an SVO word order, with the verb coming in the middle of the sentence before the object: <u>the man</u> <u>saw</u> <u>the dog</u>, where 'the dog', the object, comes last after 'saw'. SVO languages have *pre*positions (*in* the house), while all the SOV languages in South Asia, including Burushaski[51] and Brahui,[52] have *post*positions (house-*in*). Balochi, however, an Iranian language, has a mix of *pre*positions and *post*positions.[53]

The languages of the Indus Valley Periphery, Punjabi, Sindhi, Pashto, Brahui and Burushaski, line up with almost all the other South Asian languages in being SOV languages, and in having postpositions, with Balochi being something of an Iranian outlier.

Light verbs

One thing I was hoping to get to the bottom of in Indian languages was what I call a 'love of nouns': putting into nouns the sort of things languages outside of South Asia would express as verbs. To *do* marriage, instead of 'to marry'. To *do* love. To *do* memory, instead of 'to remember'. Or memory *came*, instead of 'I remembered'. And 'it is *pasand*', for 'I like it', where *pasand* is a noun and *I* comes as 'to me', something known as a dative subject. I talked about this in Chapter 1, calling it a feature of Indian English that makes it a prakrit, rather than a clone of British English. I was sure this love of nouns and diffidence about verbs came from Indian languages and went all the way back to a time before Sanskrit, which likes verbs, but I had no idea how to take this idea forward.

Then I happened upon an article by Piar Karim, a linguist and native speaker of Burushaski, in *Pakistanaat: A Journal of Pakistan Studies*, where he discussed 'light verbs' in Hunza Burushaski.[54] Karim says that 'Burushaski like Persian has probably the smallest lexicon of single word verbs or simple verbs. A limited set of more than 15-20 Light Verbs (LV) form an infinite number of verbal constructions in Burushaski.'[55]

Balochi and Pashto too use a small number of Persian-style light verbs to keep their verb inventory low, depending on nouns to carry the semantic load. As Mousa Mahmoud Zehi says in his book on 'simple verbs' in Balochi: 'The number of simple verbs in Balochi is more in comparison with that of Persian and the ability of word-formation through derivation is easier in Balochi than in Persian.'[56] And Talat Masood, writing about Pashto, quotes linguist Miriam Butt as saying that light verbs 'seem to be more of a verbal licenser for nouns [though] the verbs are clearly not entirely devoid of semantic predicative power either: there is a clear difference between take a bath and give a bath'.[57] Pakistan, with Pashto, Balochi and Persian present in the air around, seems to be a more fruitful place for linguists to see and understand light verbs. Linguists in India seem to take them for granted, and do not even mention them. Wikipedia, however, does discuss light verbs in Hindi-Urdu (Hindustani), describing this feature as 'highly productive'.[58]

In Pakistan light verbs are a 'thing' in languages like Punjabi too. In her MPhil thesis on the subject Tabasum Saba discusses them in detail: 'Punjabi manifests a productive formation of light verb constructions which are integral to the structure of the language . . . Punjabi light verbs tend to combine with N, Adj, V, Adv, and prep [nouns, adjectives, verbs, adverbs and prepositions] to form light verb constructions in Punjabi.'[59] And Brahui is just as full of light verbs, like *barām kanning* (to 'do' marriage), *aḍ kanning* (to 'do' wait) and *nishān tining* (to 'give' show), where nouns carry the semantic load.[60]

That would seem to answer my original question, about the languages of the Indus Valley Periphery having a 'love of nouns', and a much less productive relationship with verbs. This is not the case with earliest Sanskrit, which, like Greek and Latin, was very happy using verbs to express feelings and actions.

So we can add light verbs to the list of features that must have been in Language X.

Ergativity and gender

The distinctive grammatical features that set the modern Indus Valley Periphery region apart from the rest of the subcontinent are ergativity and gender: full ergativity as well as split ergativity, where ergativity appears only in the past perfect tenses. Ergativity is such a big boulder in our way, and such a daunting topic in itself, that it made sense to extract it from this discussion and give it full space to run and tire itself out in Chapter 3.

Full ergativity, or ergativity in all tenses, is something we find only in a few remote languages deep in the Karakorams, like the isolate Burushaski and the various dialects of Shina, which feel almost like versions of Burushaski with prakrit-derived vocabulary. These languages are important to our discussion, as they just might preserve features that date back to a time before Sanskrit and the prakrits played a role in the evolution of the languages of the IVC region. Features like retroflexion in Burushaski strongly indicate that the migrant men who came into the area, even with a language isolate like Burushaski, would have had to take local wives simply in order not to go extinct with their old language in mint condition. If survival meant a degree of local influence in the structure of Burushaski, while the next generation of half-local children spent its early years exposed to IVC-type languages, it would have seemed like a reasonable trade-off, especially if the earlier vocabulary was kept. This makes Burushaski and the Shina languages likely repositories of precisely those old features, like early ergativity, that we want to know more about.

In the lowland areas, more exposed to the direct glare of Sanskrit and the prakrits, we get split ergativity: ergative *realignment* in the past perfect tense, where all of a sudden the verb agrees not with its earlier subject, but with what was its object. The *by-me food-eaten* structures that are such a problem for South Asians from outside this region. As we saw in Chapter 3, these were the result of a growing dislike, among Brahman men, for the Sanskrit verb conjugations, with different person forms as well as singular-dual-plural distinctions, and gender in adjective agreement (but, mystifyingly, never between nouns and verbs).

This brought a compromise, which took the form of a simplification of the prakrit past tenses, replacing the finite verbs with participles (*eaten*, *broken*, *gone*), which now behaved like adjectives, and agreed (in case, number and gender) with nouns. And then, over time, this simplification found its way into Sanskrit. 'I/you/he/we (dual)/we (plural) *ate* the food' of earlier Sanskrit would be simplified to 'food-eaten', with *eaten* taking a gender-number-case marker to agree with food. In languages like Hindi, where case no longer existed, this would become *khānā khāyā*, where *khāyā*, 'eaten', would agree with the masculine singular *khānā*, 'food', no matter who ate it. The price to be paid was that the verb, now just a past participle, would have to agree in gender with its noun, the thing that was *eaten*. But as we saw in languages like Burushaski, gender was in any case seen as something that had to do with verbs, never with adjectives, so this sort of arrangement would have satisfied both the demands of Sanskrit/prakrit grammar and an older sense that verbs with gender markers, at least in the third person, were a very normal thing.

There is also the point that a language like Burushaski has verb agreement with both subjects and objects, as do the northern Munda languages, and even a distant relative like Great Andamanese. Maybe once upon a time First Indian languages were double marking, verbs agreeing with both subjects and objects, and fully ergative too. If they were, and these traits were retained in the vanished IVC languages, it would be strong support for the case that the IVC languages played a role in transforming and simplifying the Sanskrit/prakrit verbs into one-size-fits-all participles, where objects were ready to take a starring role. Gender, it seems, did not bother the old ones as much as the alien Sanskrit need to conjugate verbs (not to mention having many different paradigms where verbs behaved differently).

Grammatical gender, as it now exists in the IVC Periphery region, is not something retained from earlier IVC languages. It is too identical to grammatical gender in Sanskrit, whittled down from three genders to two, masculine and feminine in the north, for it to be anything but a straight lift from Sanskrit, via the prakrits. But grammatical gender is not the only kind of gender. As we see from Burushaski and the Dravidian languages of the south, there is also natural gender, showing up in the third-person forms of the verb. There is the *he/she/it* distinction in Tamil and Kannada verbs, the masculine vs non-masculine distinction in Telugu, Gondi and many other Dravidian languages, and the four-way gender split in Burushaski, and even the vestigial animate-inanimate noun distinction in the Munda languages. Could this sort of natural gender have been a part of Language X, a gender distinction only in third-person verb endings? Could this have sweetened the deal, a natural gender that was only linked to verbs, later accepting adjectives into its ambit?

Brahui has no gender or ergativity at all.

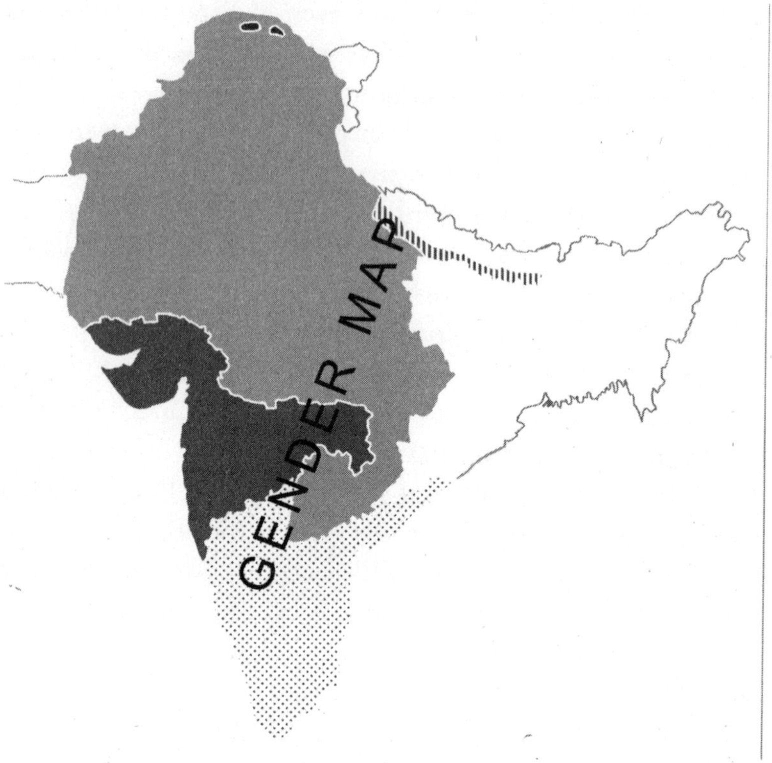

Map 8: Gender map of South Asia

- Small black areas at top: 4 grammatical genders with verb agreement
- Dark grey: 3 grammatical genders with verb and adjective agreement
- Light grey: 2 grammatical genders with verb and adjective agreement
- Dots: 3 natural genders, he/she/it, with verb agreement
- Stripes: 2 natural genders, with verb and adjective agreement
- White: no gender, natural or grammatical

What does this imply for Language X? Well, what we can imagine is a hypothetical language that had natural gender, like the Dravidian languages and Burushaski do, showing up only in third-person pronouns but not in adjective agreement. In other words, a language like Burushaski and the southern Dravidian languages where verbs are stems with invariant agreement markers. And Language X would almost certainly have had full ergativity, with ergative marking in all its tenses (or, at the very least, it would have had object agreement on its verbs as well as subject agreement).

And why not split ergativity? Because there is no reason at all for the split version to have existed in IVC times. Split ergativity came up as a mutant strain when Sanskrit and its past participles had to be reconciled with a desire to do verbs like the old languages used to do them, using ready-made Sanskrit past participles with a passive flavour, by realigning sentences as if they were Sanskrit passive sentences—not *I ate food*, but *food was eaten by me*, leaving out the finite verb *was*. Language X would have been under no pressure to model its ergatives on Sanskrit passives, because Sanskrit had not yet arrived on the scene. It would have had full ergativity, using verb stems, as in Burushaski, and not participles, which had a passive 'feel' to them. Full ergativity, as we see in Burushaski, is mostly a matter of putting ergative endings on the 'agents' of transitive sentences and linking them with an ending to verb stems. It is a less labour-intensive system than the one we are saddled with now.

If you think about it, Punjabi and Sindhi, both modern Indus Valley Periphery languages, have handled the Sanskrit and prakrit demand for ergative realignment in the past tense exactly as they handled the Sanskrit voiced aspirates *gh jh ḍh dh bh*. They did not ignore them. They left slots for voiced aspirates (but did not pronounce them as aspirates), and realigned their past tense sentences to look like Sanskrit passive sentences (but used past participles instead of finite verbs). And it worked: they avoided having to pronounce voiced aspirates, and they got away from the verb conjugations in Sanskrit and the prakrits by using one-size-fits-all participles.

Compound verbs

If you speak a South Asian language, you have undoubtedly come across expressions like *huā* and *ho gayā* in Hindi, both of which mean 'it happened'. The two aren't exactly the same. The second one, *ho gayā*, has *gayā*, from 'go', at the end and has a sense of completiveness that *huā* lacks. Here *gayā* no longer means 'go'; it has become a *vector*, a grammatical element that adds force to the main verb, which is *ho*. *Ho gayā* means that whatever happened didn't partially happen: it is over and done with. It can even mean 'no, no more for me', after a meal. All the same general idea. With *huā*, however, you are almost waiting to hear 'but actually . . . there's a bit more left to do'. You can say *huā* and you can say *nahī̃ huā* (it didn't happen). But you mostly can't say something like **nahī̃ ho gayā*,[61] unless you are expressing a contradiction. To say that something 'conclusively happened' and at the same time 'did *not* happen' is otherwise strange.

There are other verbs besides 'go' that turn into vectors. 'Give' and 'take' also do the job, keeping just a tinge of 'giving' and 'taking': *bhagā diyā*, with 'gave', means 'chased away' (which was good for others), and *haṭā liyā*, with 'take', means 'took away' (which was good for whoever took it). That is just for starters. A good way to translate these compound verbs into English is with prepositions or adverbs: eat it *up*, take it *away*, write it *down*.

Compound verbs seem to be in all the major languages of South Asia. In Punjabi, right in the Harappan zone, the pair would be *hoyā* and *ho gayā*. In Malayalam down south we have *āyi* and *āyippoyi*, where *āyippoyi* means that something didn't just happen, it got completely botched up. Not a good outcome. In Marathi it would be *jhāla* and *hoūn gela*. In the Māgadhan zone we have Bhojpuri with *bhail* and *hoi gail*. Bengali has *hoyeche* and *hoye gaeche*. And Nagamese, the newest Māgadhan language, has compound verbs too.[62] When I needed iconic features that would help me see whether someone was a native speaker of Trinidad Bhojpuri or not, compound verbs were the first thing I thought of.[63] It was exactly the sort of exotic structure that a non-native speaker would leave out.

Does Brahui have compound verbs? I reached out to Peter Hook, who has written about compound verbs in a number of South Asian languages, and he gave me the email of Masato Kobayashi, a Japanese linguist doing research on Brahui. He responded immediately. Yes, Brahui has compound verbs. He pointed me towards a book by Sanford Steever on serial verbs in Dravidian languages and told me exactly which page I would find examples on, and agreed that there was a mistake where Steever thought he saw a gender marker. Brahui, too, has 'at least one' compound verb, with *hin*, 'go', as the vector:[64]

kask	*hinā*
die-*PST-3*	go-*PST-3*

'He died (outright)'

There is something strange about this compound verb. In compound verbs what you expect is a stem plus a 'vector verb', with only the vector a finite verb. In Hindi, *mar gayā*, the translation of the example above, *mar*, 'die', remains a verb stem, while *gayā*, from the verb 'go', has tense and gender agreement markers.

But in Brahui, both *kask* and *hinā* seem to be inflected as finite verbs, something like 'he-died + he-went'. This is when Dravidian languages usually do not like more than one finite verb in a sentence. Here, now, are two, one after the other. This struck Steever as strange, something unique to northern Dravidian languages like Brahui and Kurukh: 'since inflection of both main and auxiliary verb does not occur . . . in general Dravidian . . . it is very probable that we have here a North Dravidian innovation'.[65]

We are back to an uncomfortable question, just when we were warming up to having a cousin who never left the IVC: is Brahui just a north Dravidian language like Kurukh?

What about Burushaski? I asked Noburo Yoshioka, my go-to person on Burushaski. He wrote back to say that he didn't think that there were compound verbs in Burushaski. The language has 'complicated verb morphology', he continued, but it 'does not have syntactic combination of verbs'. In other words, Burushaski, like Sanskrit, likes to keep it all within one word, and not go around making strings of verbs. He thought that most Indo-Aryan languages in northern Pakistan did not have compound verb systems either, 'while compound verbs are regularly found in Tibeto-Burman languages'.[66] True: Peter Hook mentioned that when he was doing fieldwork on Shina in Gilgit and Skardu, despite a lot of 'badgering', he was not able to get any examples of compound verbs, but that Balti, a Tibetan language spoken in the same area, had them.[67] Was a section of the Karakoram mountains 'out of signal range'?

But something inspired by compound verbs did find its way into Sanskrit. Not Vedic Sanskrit, or even classical

Sanskrit. What Deshpande told me was that in late Sanskrit and Pali, what you begin to see are 'constructions like *gantum dadāti*, in the sense of someone allowing someone to go. The infinitives combined with verbs like *dadāti*, *śaknoti*, *anujānāti*, *ājñāpayati*, etc. become common. This is already allowed by Pāṇini.'[68] He 'gives' someone to go. He 'is able' to go. And variants of these. 'Give someone to go' is not exactly the same as a compound verb, but it is a breakthrough. A little local weed sticking its head up into a lawn of Sanskrit grass. And as with the ergativity story, the prakrits and late Sanskrit had to use the grammatical resources they had, and Sanskrit didn't do verb stems and vectors.

What is significant for us in this example is that it gives us an approximate time when something resembling compound verbs pushed its way into Sanskrit, where, as Deshpande says, 'the perfective sense was already built into the past participle *-ta/tavat*.' There was no need to bring in compound verbs, as the Sanskrit verb by itself could express perfectiveness anyway.

But ah! It was not about *need*. They must have *wanted* to get that buzz like in the old languages when they spoke Sanskrit. The way English speakers miss their present continuous tense when they speak French, which doesn't have it, and we find ourselves saying 'I am in the process of' a bit too often. All this happened before the time of Pāṇini, who lived some time between the fourth and sixth century BCE,[69] so whatever inspired this would have been around in the local languages for a while before that. The only question is: *which* local languages? The Indus Valley area, this time, was a borderland.

Did Language X have compound verbs? The safest answer based on what we know now is a tentative 'maybe'. If there were compound verbs in South Asia as far back as IVC times, it would have. It is possible that many or most IVC languages back then had something like compound verbs: it looks like they were okay with what Yoshioka would call syntactic combination of verbs. Maybe an early form with two finite verbs strung together, like we find in Brahui now. The languages of the Extended Indus Valley Periphery all have a way of saying *having done this*, *having done that*, *they left*. These nested structures are known as conjunctive participles, which end with a punch and a finite verb. Think of the Hindi sentence *khā-ke ćalā gayā* (having eaten, he went away). 'He ate and left'. Brahui also has conjunctive participles, where the *kar ke* form in Hindi has *sa* instead of *ke*: *dari-sa* (having taken), *huri-sa* (having seen), *hini-sa* (having gone).[70]

Burushaski has conjunctive participles too: you can say 'having hidden, sit', in the sense of 'lie in wait',[71] as you can in all the modern Indo-Aryan languages. The mechanism for saying it is not exactly the same, but it is close enough to be familiar. What do we make of this? One kind of verb string is allowed, while another, the compound verb, is missing. It reminds me of the way, in Trinidad, we have *chokhā*, a Bhojpuri roasted vegetable puree, but not the *liṭṭī* that goes with it in India now. Because we left India before wholewheat flour, and *liṭṭī*, had reached our part of India. *Chokhā* is actually older than *liṭṭī*.

The only hiccup here is that conjunctive participles also exist in Sanskrit, where they are not new. Not only do they go back to earliest times, they even exist in Latin, where they are called the 'ablative absolute'. When I studied Latin in school, I remember our teacher telling us that, now that we were done with mugging up case declensions for nouns and verb conjugations, this was where Latin was going to get 'interesting'.

Take a look at this Sanskrit sentence:[72]

gṛhaṁ gatvā rāmo jalaṁ pibati,
'having gone home, Rāma drinks water'

This structure using a gerund ending in *-tvā* is a transformation of a longer sentence that uses a clause beginning with 'when':

yadā rāmo gṛhaṁ gaććhati, tadā sa jalaṁ pibati
'when Rāma goes home, then he drinks water'

Did Sanskrit, like the Dravidian languages, dislike having more than one finite verb in a sentence? Find it . . . not elegant? What an amazing coincidence! Because if Burushaski also has this feature, it cannot be a Sanskritism that found its way into essentially all the languages of South Asia. This is an exciting moment where, despite expressly looking for grammatical features that 'feel' pre-Sanskrit, we have happened upon one that was, independently, part of Sanskrit too. And for essentially the same reasons why it existed in Dravidian languages: to avoid repeating the same finite verb endings.

In fact, conjunctive participles exist in the Munda languages too, and even in the Andaman languages, so they would definitely have been part of Language X. But compound verbs are more . . . iffy. It is hard to imagine them *not* being older than Sanskrit, but sprouting together all over South Asia (*except* in the high Karakorams) on one rainy monsoon night not too long ago. They *feel* like part of a substratum, but we just cannot prove it. So we list conjunctive participles as a feature of Language X, but leave compound verbs as 'maybe'.

Reduplication

Some time back a friend wrote to me from Trinidad to ask how one would express something like 'it kept raining' in

Trinidad Bhojpuri. He wanted a verb tense, but somehow the past continuous did not really capture the feel of 'kept raining'. It felt the same as 'used to rain'. I asked others in Delhi who knew Bhojpuri and pondered over it for a week. But it was only when I got out of tense-mode and started thinking laterally that I got a flashback of an old woman saying into my tape recorder *ćalat-ćalat ćalat-ćalat*. Walking-walking walking-walking. Reduplication. How could I have forgotten?

Reduplication is basically repeating a word (or part of it), altering the meaning. For example, the word *ek* in Hindi means 'one'. Make it *ek-ek* and it means 'one each'. When *ghar*, 'house', becomes *ghar-ghar* it means 'from house to house'. If you add the verb 'play' it becomes 'playing house', as children do, or homebound adults did during the lockdown. This is a feature that occurs with all sorts of things. Nouns. Verbs. Numerals. Pronouns. Adjectives. Adverbs. Even onomatopoeic sounds like *kaṭ-kaṭ*. Twisting the basic meaning in the same sort of way.

I was surprised to find this feature even in Burushaski, where *hin*, 'one-Masc', reduplicates as *hi-hin*, and *han*, 'one-Fem', reduplicates as *ha-han*, with the same meaning of 'one each'.[73] There were even pairs like *bésan-bésan*, from the word for 'what?' meaning 'what all?' and *men-men*, from the word for 'who?' meaning 'who all?'. Yoshioka in his dissertation also gives examples of other types of words being reduplicated: *thaláa-thaláa*, meaning 'slow-slow' (gradually), and *béurman-béurman*, 'how much how much' (quite a lot of)[74] though he said in an email that he didn't think they occurred very often.

It didn't seem likely that a language isolate like Burushaski could have arrived in the subcontinent with such a local-looking feature. Yoshioka wondered if expressions like these were not calques from other languages of Pakistan. I wondered too, but I was thinking about calques from a different era altogether. I wasn't worried about it not being an original feature of Burushaski. What I wondered was if it went back to the time when the Burusho men first arrived in the subcontinent and took local wives. Reduplication, after all, seemed to be everywhere you looked. Was it that old? Had it been in the Indus Valley region long enough to have been a part of the language of the first Burusho wives who, even as late as Sanskrit times, might still have been speaking the old languages? Could reduplication be a glimpse of Language X?

Reduplication is something you find all over South Asia, even in tribal languages far off the beaten path. Anvita Abbi thinks it originally came from Munda into Indo-Aryan and Dravidian languages, and Munda traces back to First Indians.[75] But Munda also traces back on its paternal line to Southeast Asian languages, which are full of reduplication. Did reduplication come from Munda's Southeast Asian side? Or is it First Indian?

And there is more: echo words. I grew up in Trinidad hearing echo word pairs like *gahanā-ohanā*, 'jewellery and that sort of thing', *ćiṛāi-oṛāi*, 'birds and things like that', *khīsā-oisā*, 'stories and things like that'. Not exactly a plural, but widening the circle. Abbi gives examples from Tamil like *uppu-gippu*, 'salty things', from *uppu* (salt), Marathi *gela-bila*, from *gela* (went) meaning 'went (perhaps)', Hindi *agal-bagal*, from *bagal* (side), meaning 'all around', and *gāy-vāy*, from *gāy*, 'cow', meaning 'all sorts of cattle', and examples from tribal languages.[76]

Burushaski has them too, and they work exactly the same as they do in the rest of the subcontinent. Yoshioka says they add the meaning 'and/or the like' to the original meaning of the base noun. Some of his examples are *yamú-mamú*, from *yamú*, 'ice', *urk-murk*, from *urk*, 'wolf', and *makái-šakái*, from *makái*, 'corn'. Is it the handiwork of the first Burusho wives?

Brahui also has reduplication, as in *sit-asit* which means 'one by one'. And it has echo words, which add 'and things like that': *iragh-miragh*, from *iragh*, 'bread', *ćuna-muna*, from *ćuna*, 'child', and *ura-mura* from *ura*, 'home', all using *m-* as an associative prefix.[77]

It would be unlikely, given the spread of reduplicatives and echo words in South and Southeast Asia, that they would have been missing from Language X, as there is every indication that they have been around a very long time. We can safely add reduplicatives and echo words to our feature list.

Honorifics

Some time back I got a WhatsApp from Devdutt Pattanaik, who writes about Indian mythology, asking me where the honorific *-jī* that you find in languages like Hindi, after names and titles, came from. Like *Devdutt-jī*, for example. Or *swami-jī*. I passed the question on to everyone I could think of. I even asked all my students to think about it. I got a few interesting suggestions, but, in the end, there was no proper answer. Nobody knew.

Of course, I did not expect it to be a single answer. I had already split it in my mind into two questions. The first was: what brought the *need* to express something like this? And the second was: where was the *form* of *-jī* derived from? Or it could even be three questions: about the need for honorifics at all, the need to attach them as endings on names and titles, and about the final form a suffix like *-jī* took.

The form *-jī* we can leave aside for the moment, but about the need for honorifics, a need not felt in early Sanskrit, there is room for us to explore.

All the mainstream languages in South Asia have a distinction in second-person pronouns and finite verbs linked to an honorific hierarchy, with two or three ways of saying *you*, going from familiar and intimate to formal and respectful. Tamil and Malayalam have *ni* as the familiar *you*, and *niŋgaḷ* for the polite formal *you*, and they both have a third even more honorific form, *tāŋgaḷ* in Tamil, *tāŋŋaḷ* in Malayalam, which you only hear in very formal speech. Telugu has *nūwu*, *mīru* and *tamru*; Bengali has *tui, tumi* and *apni*; Hindi has *tū*, *tum* and *āp*; and Marathi has *tū*, *tumhī* and *āpaṇ*. These threesomes do not match up well across languages. Marathi *āpaṇ*, Tamil-Malayalam *tāŋgaḷ/tāŋŋaḷ*, Telugu *tamru* and Bengali *āpnī* are very formal and much less used than Hindi *āp*, which is now almost a default for many people, especially in Urdu. Bhojpuri, when my family left India in the 1870s, had only two ways of saying *you*: *tū* and *tō̃*. Now it seems to have a third, *rauwā̃*, which corresponds to Hindi *āp*. Honorifics seem to be blooming all across the land!

I sent a WhatsApp to a Tamilian friend, to find out if Tamil had a word like *tāŋŋaḷ*, as Malayalam did. He phoned back at once, full of apologies that maybe his Tamil wasn't good enough, but he just had no memory of any word like that. He hadn't grown up in Tamil Nadu or gone to school there. For him it was only *ni* and *niŋgaḷ*. I calmed him down and put the same question to another friend, who knew *tāŋgaḷ* well.

According to Chinmay Dharurkar,[78] the words *āp*, *āpnī* in Bengali and *āpan* in Marathi hark back to the Sanskrit word *atman*, which means 'self'. The Tamil word *tāŋgaḷ*, Malayalam *tāŋŋaḷ* and Telugu *tamru* are also related. What this suggests to him is that these highest-level honorifics did not emerge independent of each other: their evolution is connected. This means that high honorifics may be a recent innovation, going back only to a time when the modern languages of the subcontinent had begun to compare themselves with each other.

You see where this is going, don't you? That while the two-way division into familiar and polite might be old, there is something about the three-way division of *you*, with an extra top layer, that feels . . . newer. A bit forced. There is a very top-down elitist feel to the topmost honorific *you* that does not sync with the idea of an old substratum leak. Needing to be specially acquainted with the schooling system and modern officialese to have a sense of some of these most honorific *you*-forms is something of a giveaway. Honorifics are also unstable: in languages like Hindi you almost feel the old *tū* dropping out of circulation, like the square five-paise coins made mostly of aluminium that some of us older folk grew up with. I can't remember the last time I used *tū* in Hindi! Can honorifics also fall prey to inflation?

If you did not grow up with more than one way of saying *you*, it is hard to get an instinctive feel for who needs to be at which level in the hierarchy, especially when families and larger communities decide this differently. For some traditional people caste plays a role, with those perceived as lower in caste being addressed with the most familiar form of *you*. Other families use the most respectful *you* even with children, as a way of teaching them to be polite. Some hedge their bets: using the Hindi word *āp* together with the verb form that goes with *tum*: *āp jāo!* A friendly but deferential 'please go!' Honorifics are not simply about words and grammar. They are about one's place in a social pecking order, and that hierarchy first has to exist.

Burushaski is one of those rare languages of South Asia that does *not* have different ways of saying *you*. There is just the one way. And that is not strange: why should a small community far away from the rough and tumble of the modern South Asian plains want to divide its members up in this way? They live very well without it. And Brahui, for its part, has no honorific forms with *you* and no 'plural of respect' in the third person at all.[79]

This absence of a *you*-honorific in Burushaski and Brahui should give us a moment of pause. Given how easy it seems to be for at least a two-way division of *you* to emerge in South Asia (Tamil and Malayalam only had to pluralize the basic *ni* to get *niŋgaḷ*), one would expect that this was exactly the sort of thing that deferential local wives could slip into the language of their menfolk without too much fuss. They could easily have extended the ambit of a plural form of *you* to use as a singular honorific. But they didn't.

Was it there at one time, but lost? Isolated groups do lose these things: we in Trinidad only kept *tū* in our Bhojpuri, with the oldest speakers using *tõ* (like Hindi *tum*) in the first few minutes after meeting you for the first time 'until they got to know you better'. The ones who persisted with *tõ* were Brahman women.[80] Not exactly a substratum layer. Could it be that in Burushaski and Brahui, making this distinction had no support from old IVC languages?

Vedic Sanskrit did not have these honorific distinctions either, and for a good while after the Vedic era there was no such thing. But I had a winking memory of an honorific used in later Sanskrit, *bhavat*. This word was not very old, and it felt to me like a bit of a patch. An item slipped into what felt like an empty slot. Definitely not based on a dual or plural form of *tvaṁ*, like *yuvām* or *yuṣmān*. It seemed to go only as far back as a time when even Brahman men were speaking prakrit most of the time, and maybe older vernaculars too. A time when Sanskrit would have been, for them, more like a scholarly second language.

Deshpande confirmed this: Vedic Sanskrit did not have 'the use of *-bhavat*. By the time of the Upaniṣads, we start seeing *bhagavat* used as an honorific. The epics have the full-blown use of *-bhavat* and *bhagavat*. Kātyāyana and Patañjali refer to Pāṇini as *bhagavān ācārya*, but there is no use of the honorific plural. We don't see the honorific plural even in the epics.'[81] So *bhavat* came up in the last few centuries BCE, just before the time of Pāṇini, in the same era when the past participles ending with *-ta* were starting to replace the old past tense forms in the prakrits, and showing up in Sanskrit itself.

Was it just the perfect weather for a local weed to sprout? Or was this not an old weed at all, but something new emerging into daylight for the first time? Was this the sort of social hierarchy the Indus Valley people would have had, a civilization with no temples or palaces? Was it Manu's caste system finally finding expression in the language? These were, after all, used only for eminent individuals. Not for loved family members as they are now.

The honorific plural is when *he*, *she* and *it* forms are made into 'they' to mark respect. You do not, for example, refer to your father in the singular (unless you want to insult him). In Hindi you say *veh mere pitā-jī hãĩ*, with the words for *he*, *my* and *is* in the plural (*is* is now actually *are*, 'they are my fathers'), as you would in most languages of South Asia. But in the Rig Veda the gods are referred to in the singular: *sa devām eha vakṣati*. The first hymn of the Rig Veda, the *agnisuktaṁ*, speaking of Agni, says that *he* (singular) brings the other gods to the fire sacrifice. And no insult is intended.

As Deshpande clarifies:

> It is in much later Sanskrit that we begin to see the use of the honorific plural, and adding the respect-indicating use of words like *-caraṇa* or *pāda* to a word like *ācārya*. The full-blown expression becomes something like *ācāryapādāḥ* or

> *bhagavat-pādāh*. This includes all possible ways of showing respect to a person. But this is a relatively late development. The influence of Dravidian is very likely, as a significant number of Vedanta Ācāryas, like the great Śankarācārya, came from the south.[82]

Our question here is whether this sort of distinction goes back 4000 years to the languages of the IVC. And from what we see here I am not convinced. Honorifics in South Asia have a more modern feel to them, as poor people do tend to use the basic form of *you* most of the time among themselves. These honorifics smack, to me, of the sort of division that comes up in societies with a strong sense of hierarchy, which it is just possible that the old Indus Valley civilization did not have.

Is this kind of social hierarchy older than Manu's caste system, which did not bring honorifics into Sanskrit? Older than the Vedic era? It could be, but it takes a huge leap of imagination to think that. It makes sense to err on the side of caution and not add honorific forms of *you* and third-person plurals as honorifics to our list of features of Language X.

~

And what about *jī*? To answer the first part of the question, there certainly seems to have been a way of tagging eminent people with a suffix similar to *jī* in later Sanskrit, as we see from *bhavat*, *ćaraṇa*, *bhagavat-pādāḥ* and *āćāryapādāḥ* slipping into Sanskrit when the stars were right, and change was in the air.

About *jī* itself, Deshpande thinks the sense and the form of *jī* might go back to *jit*, which occurs in the epics, in words like *āśvajit*, *indrajit* and *viśvajit*, with *jit* having the sense of 'conqueror'. In Pali *āśvajit* becomes *assaiji*, he says, with *ji* over time evolving into a general honorific. You also get it in pre-modern Marathi in names like Śivāji, Śahaji, Maloji, Udhoji, Dhanaji, Santaji, Dattaji and Tānāji. As he concludes: 'This is my theory. This is similar to how the ending *-vatī* in Sanskrit gets reduced to *-vaī* in Prakrit/ Apabhraṁśa [*līlāvatī* > *līlāvaī*], and eventually getting generalized into modern *-bāī* in languages like Marathi. In Marathi, this develops into a full-fledged new word *bāī*, "woman".'[83]

But Jawaharlal Nehru, India's first prime minister, writing on *jī*, had another theory: that *jī* had come from the word *ārya*, meaning 'honourable' in Sanskrit, and in the prakrits pronounced as *ajja*. The same word from which, in languages like Bhojpuri, Marathi, Konkani and Kannada, we get the term *ājī* or *ajjī* for grandmother (in Bhojpuri *ājī* is only a paternal grandmother). The word 'honourable' itself, it seems, may have evolved into an honorific tag.[84] I remember as a child being struck by the resemblance between *ājī* and *jī*, as though there were an honorific *jī* attached to *ājī* that wasn't there on its Hindi equivalent, *dādī*, where *jī* had to be added to do the job: *dādī-jī*. If it did come from *ārya*, why did it become *jī*, which sounds like the feminine version? Still, it is something to think about.

It might also be significant that around the time that we began to hear *jī* after the names of famous Marathas, there were newcomers in the Delhi region and spreading south, from Uzbekistan, who used the tag *jān* after the names of family members and friends, and after the word for their relationship: like *bhāī-jān*, 'elder brother'. We also get *bībī* (or just *bī*) after women's names, and a more honorific tag, *sāhab*, after some men's names. Could the Central Asians have played a role in popularizing the use of a tag after people's names, not for exceptional people but for respected family and friends? Could they have amped up the feeling in the air that tags like *jān*, as well as the more local *jī*, after names and titles were the civilized thing to do?

~

Language X

What we see of Language X after this long journey together is an X-ray image. It has no flesh, in the sense of words, which, in any case, would have changed over time and varied a lot from place to place. It is also a *probabilistic* image: it is a backward projection, using a model of language change and all the data at hand to try to see the past. In exactly the way that words in Proto Indo-European are projections, this reconstructed image, never seen by any of us from today's world, would have to have something like an asterisk in front of it as a warning. This does not mean that the reconstructed image is wrong: it just means that we are squinting at something whose real form none of us was ever there to see, and that this is as close as we can get. Here is a snapshot of how Language X lines up with Tamil, Burushaski and Brahui:

	Language X	Tamil	Burushaski	Brahui
Retroflexion	**yes**	**yes**	**yes**	**yes**
Voiced aspirates	**no**	**no**	**no**	**no**
Voiceless aspirates	**yes**	**no**	**yes**	**yes**
SOV word order	**yes**	**yes**	**yes**	**yes**
Postpositions	**yes**	**yes**	**yes**	**yes**
Light verbs	**yes**	**yes**	**yes**	**yes**
Gender	**natural**	**natural**	**natural**	**no**
Ergativity	**full**	**no**	**full**	**no**
Compound verbs	**maybe?**	**yes**	**no**	**yes**
Conjunctive participles	**yes**	**yes**	**yes**	**yes**
Reduplication	**yes**	**yes**	**yes**	**yes**
Echo words	**yes**	**yes**	**yes**	**yes**
Honorifics	**no**	**yes**	**no**	**no**

A big surprise is how similar Burushaski, Brahui and Tamil look in terms of these features, how much of a resemblance you find when you are not looking at the words themselves or the fine morphological details that make Burushaski such an enigma. Language X comes across as a Dravidian-type language that has Burushaski-style ergativity, an early form of ergativity that simply had markers in all tenses on the subject-as-agent, in sentences with direct objects, and without the flips in alignment that you get in the modern languages of the area that tell of Sanskrit and prakrit influence. This is not to say that the ergativity in Language X came *from* Burushaski. It is just that this *type* of ergativity is generally the older version, and the most logical sort of ergativity to expect if it had to evolve from scratch. Connecting the dots, we could also imagine that Language X would have done its verbs as stems with agreement markers, the way that Tamil, Burushaski and Munda languages do, with person markers for *I* and *you*, but gender markers for *he*, *she* and *it*.

Here now is the same list of features showing Punjabi, from modern Harappa, Bhojpuri, a Māgadhan language and Rig Vedic Sanskrit:

	Language X	Punjabi	Bhojpuri	RV-Sanskrit
Retroflexion	**yes**	**yes**	**yes**	**yes**
Voiced aspirates	**no**	**no**	**yes**	**yes**
Voiceless aspirates	**yes**	**yes**	**yes**	**yes**
SOV word order	**yes**	**yes**	**yes**	**yes**
Postpositions	**yes**	**yes**	**yes**	**no**
Light verbs	**yes**	**yes**	**yes**	**no**
Gender	**natural**	**grammatical**	**no**	**grammatical**
Ergativity	**full**	**split**	**no**	**no**
Compound verbs	**maybe?**	**yes**	**yes**	**no**
Conjunctive participles	**yes**	**yes**	**yes**	**yes**
Reduplication	**yes**	**yes**	**yes**	**no**
Echo words	**yes**	**yes**	**yes**	**no**
Honorifics	**no**	**yes**	**yes**	**no**

And here is the breakdown of how much each language differs from Language X:

1 feature: Burushaski
2 features: Brahui
3 features: Tamil, Punjabi
4 features: Bhojpuri
8 features: Rig Vedic Sanskrit

There is nothing strange in how different Language X looks from Sanskrit: we did, after all, choose features in the modern languages of the Indus Valley Periphery and the Extended Indus Valley Periphery that were *not* from Sanskrit. But it is still interesting that a glance at the text of the Rig Veda shows the total *quantum* of retroflex sounds to be far fewer than we expected. Rig Vedic Sanskrit, after all, does have *ṭ ṭh ḍ ḍh ṇ* and *ṣ*. The only retroflex consonant Sanskrit did not take in was *ḷ*.[85] Retroflexion, however, is not only a matter of individual sounds, but also about the *frequency* of their occurrence, which keeps increasing as we go south. Punjabi, Rajasthani, Gujarati and Garhwali all have *ḷ*, but Marathi has much more of it, and Malayalam and Tamil even more. And the immediate Indus Valley Periphery starts out with much more retroflexion than the 'Hindi family' and the Māgadhan lands to the east of the doab.

Retroflexion is one feature we always expected Language X to have, simply because retroflexion is as old as the First Indians and practically ubiquitous in the subcontinent: even the Andamanese languages, separated from the mainland for thousands of years, have it. And so do Iranian languages like Balochi and Pashto, at the edge of the northwest.

But the real surprise is Burushaski, which has five retroflex phonemes, three of them shared with Pashto. This is a revelation, as it says louder than any other data could that our original hunch was right. There is simply no way that the Burusho men could have arrived in the subcontinent with retroflexion already in their language, because retroflexion is such a South Asian feature.[86] This is our clinching proof, besides the genetic evidence, that the Burusho *did* have strong initial contact with the Indus Valley region in olden times, because as migrants, who would have been mostly male, they would have married local women who spoke languages with retroflexion. And if retroflexion could slip into the language, there would have been other features in Burushaski that could take us back to the early days when the Burusho men had just arrived. Burushaski differs from our hypothetical Language X only in one feature (and that feature, compound verbs, was only a *possibility* in Language X).

It is disorienting to think that it is Burushaski, and not an Indo-Aryan or Dravidian language, that has turned out to be so very, very close to Language X! But then, Burushaski, in seclusion in the high Karakorams, was always likely to be the one most unchanged from the days when some of the IVC languages were still being spoken.

The other big surprise is Brahui. Except for having no ergativity or gender, it lines up perfectly with our reconstructed Language X, down to not having any honorifics. I will admit that I started out sceptical about Brahui being an Indus Valley language hiding from us in plain sight. And I don't think we have yet proved conclusively that it is, or that it is not. But the findings peeking out at us from these charts are like a jolt of electricity, making this chapter feel like a family reunion.

We are way past the point where we can decide the status of Brahui by guesswork or wishful thinking. It is time to put Brahui under the scanner in a more rigorous way, with more data and better models, and actual historical evidence to support the claim of a more recent migration from south or central India, to determine whether it is the 'last of the Harappans', or just a lucky Dravidian language from peninsular India that found its way back home.

Both Punjabi and Bhojpuri look much more like Language X than Sanskrit does, but Punjabi is much closer. Unlike Bhojpuri it has ergativity and gender, and the familiar Dravidian dislike of *gh jh ḍh dh bh*.

Ergativity and gender appear to be the most *probative* features in our list. *Probative* is a legal term used to signify 'the extent to which relevant evidence will tend to prove the proposition for which it is proffered'. Or, as Peter Hook explains it: 'The more unusual a trait the stronger its weight in showing the relation between a superstrate and a substrate, or between a putative earlier language and the one which later overlies or replaces it, but is influenced by it.'[87] Could this concept be turned around when we are working backwards, doing a reconstruction of an old vanished language? Ergativity and gender stand out as the most defining features of Language X, while all the others, found in many modern languages of South Asia besides Sanskrit, do not have that make-or-break quality to them. Language X may or may not have had compound verbs, depending on whether this almost universal feature goes that far back in time. We just don't know, but we imagine, based on the appearance of verb strings in later Sanskrit, that there could have been *something* like compound verbs in Language X. Or Language X may have had honorifics, or it may have been too early to expect them in the subcontinent. Ergativity is unusual, though, and unique to the Extended Indus Valley Periphery, and on this hangs a long and interesting tale.

So what would Language X have looked like, if it had some flesh? Burushaski?! Maybe not in vocabulary and fine details, but in broad strokes? Brahui, maybe if it were not so stripped down and rustic? A Punjabi-Tamil chimera with natural rather than grammatical gender and full ergativity? It would have had the sort of gender we find in today's Dravidian languages, gender agreement with verbs (and not adjectives), and the sort of ergativity we find in Burushaski. And that is what we should expect: a language of people from the northwest, with some of them continuing south, and a hint of the language spoken in present-day Harappa.

Punjabi, Tamil, Burushaski, Bhojpuri and Brahui, together with Language X, look like one big extended family, and Sanskrit the foreign guest who came to stay.

But is chimera the right word for the resemblance between Punjabi and Tamil? Wouldn't it be more accurate to say that the two are cousins dressed in different clothing? There are other telling things in Punjabi that have a strong Dravidian flavour. Like the large number of retroflexes, *ṭ ḍ ṇ* and *ḷ*, the same ones we now find in south India. As well as *saṁdhi* rules that turn *n* into *ṇ* in between vowels, and *l* into *ḷ*, exactly as they do in Tamil and Malayalam. For example, we have *pāṇī* for 'water' (which is *pānī* in Hindi), and *jāṇā* as the verb 'to go' (*jānā* in Hindi), *vaṇiyā* (*baniyā* in Hindi), and *huṇa* for 'now'. We also do get *kāḷā* for 'black' (*kālā* in Hindi), *wāḷā* for 'belonging to' (*wālā* in Hindi), *goḷī* for 'bullet' (*golī* in Hindi), *hauḷe* for 'slowly' as well as *nāḷ*, 'with'. There is a lot of discussion of this *ḷ* sound in Punjabi on both sides of the Indo-Pak border on Internet forums: the general feeling is that it is not something new, but an old feature that is fading out, so much so that many young people don't know it any more.[88]

Punjabi also has a number of Dravidian-style geminate consonants (geminate coming from the Latin word for 'twin'), double consonants like *bb*, *jj* and *ḍḍ* that make you think of south Indian languages. Like *kabbo* and *sajjo*, 'left' and 'right', *vaḍḍā*, 'big' (*baṛā* in Hindi), *gaḍḍī*, 'car' (*gāṛī* in Hindi). *Jaṭṭ Sikh* (*Jāṭ Sikh* in Hindi). And how about *Pañȳabbī* ?

Hindi has geminates too, but less than Punjabi, and it also has less retroflex sounds than Punjabi: *ṇ* in Hindi generally only comes before *ṭ ṭh ḍ ḍh* (think of *ḍāṇṭ*, 'scolding'), except for speakers who are conscious of Sanskrit pronunciation, and *ḷ* does not exist at all. Is Hindi different from Tamil because it is more northern? Or is it less Dravidian because it is on the eastern fringe of the Extended Indus Valley Periphery, with Māgadhan breezes taking away some of the Dravidian heat? Hindi is just a bit off the great Dravidian highway from the northwest to the south, on a turn-off to the east. Punjabi, on the other hand, even though its original Dravidian vocabulary has been lost, is right on track.

So while our image has no flesh, we are almost in a position to imagine what the old Harappan language looked like. Language X would have had full ergativity, simpler than the split ergativity in modern Punjabi, in all tenses, and with no past-tense realignment. And Language X would have had the natural gender you get in Tamil, verbs as stems and not participles, gender agreement only with the third-person forms of verbs, and basic words and verb endings looking a lot like Tamil.

And why specifically Tamil? Why not Malayalam? Or Telugu? Or Kannada? Or Brahui? Well, this exercise is imaginary, but I am guessing that Tamil would score over all the other Dravidian languages in being the most distant from Sanskrit and prakrit influence. That would mean that vocabulary, the main thing to be restored in Language X, might be more like Tamil than any other south Indian language. In any case, pronouns and numbers in the different south Indian languages do resemble each other to this day, and that is an interesting start to any project to reimagine the 'flesh'. Could we speak Punjabi with Tamil numbers, pronouns and nouns, the way we speak Hinglish? I have heard of Indian techies speaking Japanese with Tamil nouns (and Japanese thinking this must be just technical jargon). And even if words are the first thing to change when languages drift apart, a few old words do linger on for thousands of years.

~

One big question remains, a question I do not have the information to answer, but I will ask it anyway. What about relative clauses? If Language X is as Dravidian as it looks, wouldn't it have had the kind of relative clauses we get in the Dravidian languages of the south and in Dakkhini? Like *kaun bolā-ki us-ku ich* pūchho, meaning 'ask the person who said it', based on the Telugu *ewaru annāru-o wāḍni aḍugu?*

Did Language X have this sort of relative clause, the reverse of what you get in north Indian languages like Hindi-Urdu, with *us-ko pūchho jisne yeh kahā*, where the clause 'who said it' comes last?

Even Brahui has changed in how it does its relative clauses: it now takes after Balochi not only in the form of its relative clauses, but even in using the marker *ki*, which comes from Balochi. Did Brahui, too, once have Dravidian-style relative clauses? I can imagine, with no evidence, Language X having Dravidian-style relative clauses. The kind of relative clauses we get now in the north typically came up later: '*who* is sitting there, ***she*** is my sister', with the question word *who* being repurposed and used as a relative pronoun. All this means is that if we ever wrote a hypothetical Punjabi song with Tamil words to see what Language X might have sounded like, one more feature we should think about is Dakkhini-style relative clauses. It just might be the final touch Language X needs for its little heart to start beating.

~

There are few surprises in the way this story ends: many in the south were inclined to think this anyway, mainly on the strength of genetic evidence of 'Iranian farmers', essentially seen as the male ancestors of the Dravidian people, migrating from the Zagros mountains into the Indus Valley, the presence of Brahui in the region, as well as reports of Tamil-like words found in early Sanskrit. But modern things like gender and ergativity were an enigma. And for those of us in the north who looked past what we were told in school about our languages and were sceptical about all the Sanskrit things we were taught as 'our' grammar (like cases and noun compounds), the broader resemblance between the northwest and the south was always plain to see.

The only thing missing was: *how*. What brought this resemblance? Without a model that gave importance to the substratum, and a sense of languages as two-stranded with a maternal as well as a paternal side, linguists and historians spoke instead of 'influence', and when they could not find features like gender in the Māgadhan languages and ergativity in Dakkhini, which they had seen in earlier prakrits and early literature written by elite men, they said that they had been 'lost' without ever saying why. Concepts like 'influence' and 'loss' were magic wands: there was no need to explain how they worked.

What our explanation says is that it was not 'influence'. There was a continuity in the population of the region. *We ourselves in the Extended Indus Valley Periphery today are still the Dravidians.* Just as many of us speak English now, without being British, our ancestors listened to local prakrits and added the prakrit words into their existing languages. Languages are not that hard to learn and adopt, if they make life a little easier. Even if a few in our male line might have been steppe migrants, our female ancestors were local, and they would have passed on their languages to their children first, keeping the old tongues alive even as they engaged with Sanskrit and helped make the prakrits. But most of the little people would not have been related to the steppe migrants in any genetic sense. They would, over time, have picked up whiffs of the prakrits spun off from Sanskrit simply because they were languages of empire, the way English spread in India when the British arrived, and even more so after Independence when the British themselves were gone. But in those times, as now, a whole ecosystem of older languages had survived, sitting quiet and biding its time, waiting for a new age when it could shine again.

And between the tenth and twelfth centuries there was a Great Disconnect. Prakrit languages, the languages of royalty, which had united the elites of the larger land mass, were *replaced*, and our modern languages began to appear in documents written by a new set of players. Merchants. Craftsmen. Townspeople. In smaller more organically compact regions. These new languages took their words from the prakrits, but their grammars retained many of the features of the old languages that went back to the time of the Indus Valley Civilization, because the old languages themselves probably were alive and being spoken for longer than we thought, not only by the 'little people', but even by elites who would have known them too. Paradoxically, when the prakrits spoken by the rich and powerful faded out of sight, an even older kinship across the land between the little people resurfaced, in structure but not in words, new languages that drew their words from the very prakrits they displaced.

Somewhere in the thousands of years of separation between the northwest and the south, an IVC feature, ergativity, failed to emerge in the south. This was the feature that, in the northwest, had added to a push for simplifying Sanskrit verbs, bringing in Sanskrit past participles that had a passive flavour. *Done. Eaten. Broken.* This started a whole train of events in the prakrits, which found their way into Sanskrit too, and which survived into the modern languages as Sanskrit-aligned grammatical gender and split ergativity. This set the whole Extended Indus Valley Periphery apart from the Māgadhan east and the Dravidian south. When we untangled how all this happened, we saw that this was not about two separate groups of Dravidians, but about one language family that had got divided as the Dravidians who went south encountered new First Indians whose languages did not have ergativity, and became a further iteration of Tiramisu bear Dravidian creoles. Meanwhile, in the Extended IVC Periphery, ergativity mutated under the spotlight of Sanskrit and the prakrits to give us modern languages full of grammatical gender and agreement with adjectives as well as verbs, and a split ergativity, only in the past tense, where objects swapped place with subjects, following the logic of the new evolutionary path it had set its feet on.

Our next chapter takes us across the confluence at the end of the Ganga-Yamuna doab to see another migration story, even more hidden in the mists of time. Here migrations over the millennia combined to make a family of modern languages separate from the languages of the Extended Indus Valley Periphery and the Dravidians of the south. In what used to be elephant forests, and fanned by more Asian winds, the Māgadhan language family was born.

5

Across the Sangam

. . . drawing me near to a path that is clear . . .

The Silence of a Candle, Paul Winter

In South Asian folklore there are many stories that tell of a different world that awaits us on the other side of a river. My favourite, from just beyond the Ganga-Yamuna sangam, or confluence, at the modern city of Allahabad, or Prayagraj, in Uttar Pradesh, is the story of Rani Saranga who began life as a monkey in the forest and jumped off a branch into the river below when the stars were right, and was instantly transformed into a woman.[1] A river, or better yet the meeting point of two great rivers, is after all a watershed. Things are not supposed to be the same on the other side.

In olden times the eastern side of this confluence was the start of the Kālaka forest,[2] where landscape, people and fauna changed. Before the time of Manu the law-giver, this was the eastern limit of Āryāvarta, the territory of the Vedic people,[3] and Vedic Brahmans were strongly dissuaded from crossing to the other side except for short visits.[4] For linguists, the confluence is in another sense a major watershed, because it marks the eastern edge of the Extended Indus Valley Periphery, after which we enter a new language zone. The languages on the other side belong to the Māgadhan family.

Map 9: The terrain of the Māgadhan languages

I came to this meeting point full of questions about the past. The biggest question on my mind was one that one of my students had asked, when we were studying the Emperor Ashoka's pillars and rock inscriptions. How is it that Ashoka was a Māgadhan, but his prakrit was so much like the western prakrits? It had gender and ergativity, just like western Indo-Aryan languages do, but Māgadhan languages are not supposed to have that.[5]

I had no immediate answer. We had already discussed the great disconnect between the prakrits, which all had grammars like Sanskrit, and the languages that came up after the tenth century, based on local languages that were older than Sanskrit and the prakrits. We knew that the modern languages would be radically different from the prakrits everywhere. But even then, Māgadhan Prakrit, Pali and Ardhamāgadhi, the sacred languages of Buddhism and Jainism, felt alien in the Western region. Ashoka, Buddha and Mahavira were supposed to stand apart from the brahmanical world of the doab. Were these three leaders, all of them Kshatriyas, not truly Māgadhan after all?[6] How was it that the languages of the educated and the powerful in ancient Magadha all bore the stamp of the Āryāvarta lands?

Walking around the Harish-Chandra Research Institute in Allahabad where I had come to give a talk on Language X, it was obvious that all the professors and students, and all my local friends, spoke standard Hindi, the language of the old Āryāvarta lands.[7] And English too, of course. But the little people who worked at the guest house doing the cooking, waiting on us and arranging our transport looked different, and spoke with a cheerful lilting accent that I recognized from another life in faraway Trinidad. The little people were speaking Bhojpuri, not just among themselves, but telltale phrases would sometimes slip out even when they were talking to us. It took me a while to grasp that when they spoke to me without gender agreement, it was not the usual dumbed-down baby-talk Hindi I get in Delhi from people who mistake me for a foreigner. There *is* no gender in Bhojpuri! So one day I couldn't stop myself: I replied to one of the bearers in Bhojpuri, and saw his look of bemused surprise. A professor . . .?

For a brief moment, I had time-travelled back across the Kala Pani.

2500 years had passed since the time of Ashoka, the Buddha and Mahavira, but the gulf between the elite and the little people of the Māgadhan zone was still as deep as ever. While Bhojpuri was there marking the fault line between the Indus Valley Periphery and the lands to the east, Hindi was there too for the elite, just as the prakrits had been in olden times, to cover over the cracks and give an outward appearance of one continuous seamless north.

And yet the mere existence of Buddhism and Jainism, and of an emperor like Ashoka, told another story. An emperor who unabashedly had his edicts carved in stone—*lekhita*—all over South Asia not in Sanskrit, but in local prakrits to record history his way. A ruler who did not surround himself with Vedic Brahmans to 'validate' his royal status with their *śrauta* rituals. It was a different land, with an older culture that already leaned towards *ahiṁsā*, *tapasyā* and a belief in karma and rebirth, which were not yet a part of Vedic Hinduism. Non-violence. Performing austerities to erase past transgressions. Living as an ascetic. Believing that our actions have consequences in terms of how we will be reborn. Remaining wilfully inactive so as not to add more negative karma. Wanting the lightest possible ecological footprint. This old Māgadhan world view segued smoothly into Buddhism and Jainism and the cult of the Ajīvikas, whom we only know from what others wrote about them, religions that stood for centuries as bulwarks against brahmanism and Manu's caste system that ruled in the west.[8]

It was a contradiction: being resolutely different from the world of Vedic Brahmans outside of Magadha, while maintaining 'social distance' within Magadha by using languages based on the prakrits spoken by Kshatriyas in the western lands.

The elite always speak like outsiders. We have lived with this in South Asia for as far back as our history goes.

~

There is something else that was special about the Māgadhan region which set it apart from the northwest, where we have to resort to reconstruction to get a feel of the languages spoken there in Harappan times. Exactly as the Māgadhans preserved their forests, instead of cutting them down for farmland, and the elephants that fought alongside them as battle tanks, they preserved the old languages too. There is no mystery today about what the old Munda languages of the area were like. They are alive, and still spoken natively by tribal people who retreated into the Chota Nagpur forests instead of adjusting to the unstoppable influx from the west that ultimately brought Sanskrit and brahmanism to Magadha.

The term 'Munda' used in this sense means not just one of the tribes in the Jharkhand region of India, but the entire group of tribes. The Munda people share DNA with almost all modern South Asians, an M haplogroup that is like a genetic tag of South Asia that dates back to that first successful migration of Homo sapiens out of Africa. 'Successful' in the sense that the group went on to leave descendants among the present population of the planet, instead of going extinct without progeny after a bricf spcll outside of Africa. This migration took the southern route, crossing from the Horn of Africa into what is now Yemen during an Ice Age when oceans were shallower and the gap between Africa and Arabia not more than 10 kilometres at the closest meeting point. They could have *seen* the other shore. At that time the northern Sinai route that took modern humans to Europe and onward from there would not have been viable: it was an Ice Age, so that route would have been desert, without the flora and fauna that would have attracted early Africans to keep wandering north.[9]

An Australian blog *X23andMe* written in 2009 talks about a genetic study that explored links between 'relic' populations of early tribes in India and First Australians,[10] both of which have been thought to trace back to this first successful migration out of Africa:

> The team, led by Satish Kumar [of the Centre for Cellular and Molecular Biology, Hyderabad], reasoned that if the hypothesis of an ancient migration along the Indian Ocean towards Australia was accurate, there would be evidence in the DNA of modern people living along that path. So they compared the DNA of modern Australian Aborigines to that of tribes from India, such as the Baiga of central India and the Birhor of eastern India . . . After comparing the two groups, they came to a startling conclusion: two specific genetic mutations on the mtDNA of the Indian and aboriginal samples matched perfectly. Not only that, but these particular mutations do not exist elsewhere in the world; they are shared exclusively between a few isolated tribes in India and native Australians.[11]
>
> Kumar and his colleagues concluded the two groups must share a common ancestry. To lend further credence to their theory, they calculated the date when the ancestors of the Indian tribes and Aborigines must have split. Their calculations produced a date of 55,000 years ago.[12]

In my earlier book on Indian languages I wrote that the languages in South Asia with retroflexion are essentially the same ones whose speakers have the macrohaplogroup M tag, and that that is something 'scarily close to being more than just a metaphor'.[13] Almost every South Asian has this M tag on the maternal line, except the ones whose languages do not have retroflexion.[14] Aboriginal Australians share haplogroup M mutations with First Indians, and their languages too have retroflex consonants: *ṭ ḍ ṇ* and *ḷ*, the same as ours.[15] In other words, we are fellow travellers on that first great trek, related in language and in DNA. So whatever the twists and turns Munda genealogy has taken in the last few thousand years, it is fair to say that Mundas trace back all the way to the first modern humans in the subcontinent.

But this digression about First Australians has another purpose: to show, with genetic evidence, that the Baiga and Birhor tribes are ultimately part of the same ancestral group, and that both go back to First Indians. Because over the years, linguists have categorized them as 'Dravidian' and 'Austro-Asiatic' tribes, as though they have fundamentally different origins and nothing to do with each other or with First Indians. The Baiga are officially listed as a 'Dravidian' tribe,[16] while the Birhor are 'Munda', and thus 'Austro-Asiatic'.[17] We will look at the Dravidian tribes separately, in the next chapter.

The Munda tribes live in a large tribal belt that covers five states of India: Jharkhand, Odisha, Chhattisgarh, Madhya Pradesh and West Bengal. They fall into two linguistic groups, North Munda and South Munda. The Santali speakers are the largest group, followed by Mundari, and the other groups are speakers of Asur, Bhumij, Birhor, Bonda, Gorum, Gta?, Ho, Juang, Kharia, Kodaku, Korku, Korwa, Sabar and Sora. There are other tribal groups from the first migration out of Africa that are now identified as Dravidian tribes: First Indians, in their 65,000 years in South Asia, met and mixed with different groups of newcomers. There are also undoubtedly other Munda languages that once existed, and which have disappeared over the ages as their speaker populations moved on to new languages of power. And since almost everyone in South Asia, barring some tribal groups in the North-east, has a trace of the First Indian M haplogroup on the maternal side, we need to remember that the Mundas are not just the people in the tribal belt who continue to speak the old languages.

It is telling that Grierson opens Volume IV of his *Linguistic Survey of India*, on Munda and Dravidian languages, with this question, and he shows himself to be conflicted about separating the tribes in this way. He admits up front that the early discussion of the tribes of India was originally driven by race, a popular theme in colonial times. He defers to 'the eminent German philologist Friedrich [Max] Müller' who claimed that 'man can only have developed real language after having split up into races, and the various languages in actual use must therefore be derived from different racial bases',[18] a bold and unsupported assumption. Grierson is careful to step back from this position, and point instead to significant differences in vocabulary, grammar and number systems between the Munda and the Dravidian languages, with Munda languages counting to Base-20* but Dravidian to Base-10.[19] He concludes that 'for our purposes it is sufficient to state that the languages of the Muṇḍās and the Draviḍas are not connected, but form two quite independent families'.[20]

Max Müller's final comment, however, is that the Munda languages 'have traces of a language spoken in India before

* In Hindi, for example, like in most South Asian languages, the numbers 10, 20, 30, 40 follow the decimal system, Base-10: *das*, *bīs*, *tīs*, *chālis*. In Bhojpuri, which maintains the old Munda vigesimal, or Base-20, system, we get *das*, *bīs* (or *koṛi*), *koṛi ā das*, *dūi koṛi*, or ten, twenty, twenty-and-ten, two-twenties. 85 would be *ćār koṛi ā pā̃ć*, four twenties and five.

the Tamulic conquest . . . [which] may have merged into the Tamulic in places where they have been living together for some time.'[21] In other words, even tribal languages now classed as Dravidian are probably the result of populations mixing or new languages of power being adopted over the ages. These 'Dravidian' tribes trace back to First Indians too.

I do not like the exclusive label 'Austro-Asiatic' to define a language group that includes not just a large portion of the First Indian people, but also the very first humans to migrate out of Africa. The idea of linking the Mundas to Southeast Asia emerged when archaeologists decided that the stone tools excavated in the Munda lands in India were so similar to those found in the Malayan Peninsula that 'they appear to be the work of one and the same race'.[22] Grierson adds that 'comparative philologists agree that the Muṇḍā languages, Khasi, Mon-Khmer, Nancowry, and the speech of aboriginal races of the Malay peninsula contain a common substratum, which cannot be anything else than the language of an old race which was once settled in all those countries'.[23]

By 'aboriginal people' Grierson meant the people now called the 'orang asli' in modern Malaysia.[24] These are indeed the first people of Southeast Asia, genetically linked to Indian Mundas and Andaman Islanders, and part of the first human migration out of Africa. These people have mostly been replaced by Austro-Asiatic migrants who settled there later, coming in from south China. A 2019 genetics article by Kai Tätte et al. expresses surprise that 'Malayan Peninsular tribes rather than the geographically closer Austro-Asiatic language speakers like Vietnamese and Cambodians show the highest sharing of IBD segments with the Munda'.[25] So in that sense Grierson is right: the people who made those stone tools *are* the same group as the Munda people of India. They are also the same people who went on to Australia and New Guinea. But the 'orang asli' were not Austro-Asiatic. In early times they would have made up the entire population of Malaya and the archipelago between Malaya and Australia, and any Austro-Asiatic populations there now would have come maybe 50,000 years later. But there is no way Grierson and the early philologists could have known that.

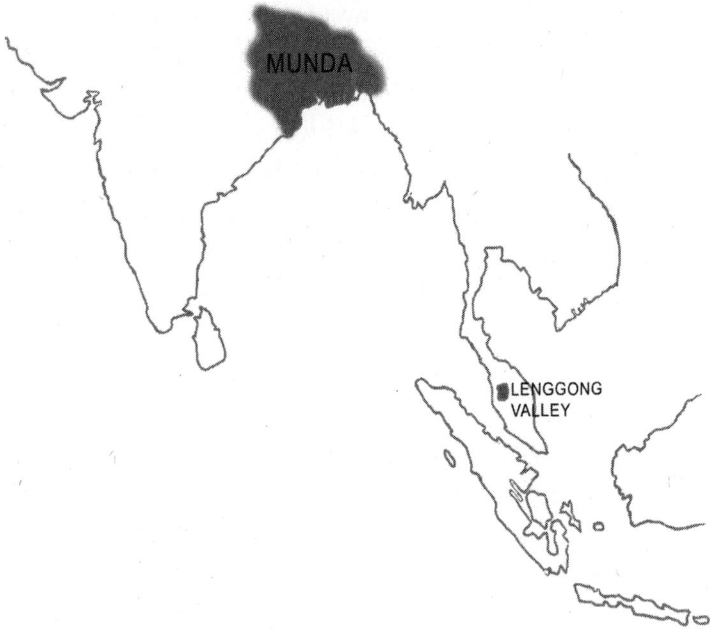

Map 10: The Munda lands in South Asia and the Lenggong Valley, Malaya, with archaeological excavations of First Peoples migrating onward from South Asia

Still, it is amazing that these early linguists were able to detect a link between Austro-Asiatic languages and the Munda languages in India, because there was indeed a migration from Southeast Asia into India about 4000 years ago, the same sort of male-driven migration that we have seen in the subcontinent time and time again. This migration is not in any historical record, or folk memory, but was something uncovered by geneticists. What they noticed was Southeast Asian japonica genes going back 4000 years in rice, which had been hybridized with rice that Munda farmers had been cultivating in the Lahuradewa area in the Gangetic basin for 3000 years already. These men settled down in India and had children with Munda women. In time even the remote tribes in the forest showed mostly Austro-Asiatic Y-DNA—Southeast Asian lineage on the paternal side—but essentially only Munda mtDNA on the maternal side.[26] It was the same old story, of men coming into the subcontinent and creating mixed people with mixed languages. The old philologists had found a connection that it would take more than a hundred years for geneticists to confirm.

Clearly the philologists had a theory in mind. With no idea of any westward migration of Southeast Asians into the subcontinent 4000 years ago, or any theory of language mixing, what some of them decided was that there had to have been a single 'racial' group that extended from 'Nearer' to 'Further' India, with a 'common substratum, over which there have settled layers of later immigrants, but which, nevertheless, has retained such strength that its traces are still clearly seen over the whole area'.[27] They thought that the Austro-Asiatic people in Southeast Asia *now* and the Mundas must have started out as a single group.

What our model helps us see is a fusion of an older Munda strand on the maternal side with a much *later* Austro-Asiatic strand contributed by migrating men. Before the idea that languages could be born of two parental streams, linguists thought only in terms of *one* descent line, the one defined by vocabulary. While they had always known that words could be borrowed, they thought that there was a certain core of vocabulary that had to be original, that languages would never borrow words for hand, foot, sun, moon, or basic numbers.

Creoles changed this: Caribbean creoles had emerged recently, almost in living memory, with grammars drawn from their African side, and vocabulary (and some bits of structure) from men in power who had come from Britain and Europe. To this day, creoles are not what philologists think of when they see a new language, nor do they think that most languages in the world must at some point have emerged from this sort of fusion. But creolists knew it, and now geneticists are adding their support to a notion of 'father tongues'. In short: even the 'relic' tribal populations and languages in India today are mixed.

When I was a child growing up in the Caribbean in the 1950s, we hadn't yet heard about creole languages. All we were told, since English-based creoles had essentially only English vocabulary, was that we were speaking 'bad English'. What decided that it was English was its vocabulary, and English class in school was intended to stamp out this flawed local usage. It is only when I went to the University of the West Indies in 1970 that I learnt that the creole we spoke, and our native-speaker intuitions, were valuable in studying the substratum, which went back to West African languages. Soon people began to see the way we spoke not as 'bad English', but as an important link to our history.

The case of the Munda languages in India is so much déjà vu, except that in Munda there was no continuing Southeast Asian colonial presence, with pressure to phase out the agglutinative structure of the languages in favour of short words, no endings and tones, where, like in Chinese, *ma* would have different meanings depending on whether it was *má* or *mà* or *mǎ* or *mā* (that is, a rising tone, a falling tone, a falling-rising tone or a level tone). It was great detective work for the early European philologists to find resemblances to modern Vietnamese and Burmese dialects in Munda vocabulary: it was nowhere near as obvious as the link to English, or French, or Portuguese or Dutch was in the Caribbean.

But once they found it, academic obedience, and an ability to see only the paternal lineage of any language, kicked in. Linguists, not only in India but everywhere, began to piously assert their membership in the community of linguists by calling Munda languages 'Austro-Asiatic' (even as they studied their agglutinative structure). To raise the issue that they were actually *mixed*, and that the Austro-Asiatic presence was long gone, was just being 'difficult', not conforming to the rules of the group. It is amazing how long this 'good behaviour' has lasted.

There is one useful takeaway for us from the separation of the First Indian tribes. What this tells us is that the strongest influence in the east was not Dravidian, as it had been in the Indus Valley. Could the tribes with Dravidian mixture be separate from the Mundas, at least in not having been exposed to the influx of Austro-Asiatic men?[28] Was the confluence of the Ganga and Yamuna rivers, at the end of the doab, even in pre-Vedic times, already a watershed? Not a hermetically sealed border, but a barrier to significant Dravidian culture and language in the east. Visitors, maybe. But not rulers. Rulers would come later, after the time of Manu, when the Brahmans, the mixed children of the Vedic men and Dravidian women, the local kings brought on board by their *śrauta* rituals, and all the little people in their retinue, finally brought the Dravidian substratum to Magadha.

~

Munda languages do have a fair amount of basic vocabulary from Southeast Asian languages, something expected in a creole language, even if the 'operating system' of the earlier maternal languages is still essentially intact. In fact, it often takes so much excavation to unearth these vocabulary resemblances that they almost feel unreal. Creole languages are impossible to understand from words like these.[29] The Southeast Asian words in Munda go back to the migration 4000 years ago that gave us hybrid rice. Philologists, delving into words in 'Nearer and Further India', came upon their own likely matches, and Grierson has listed some of these words in Volume IV of the *Linguistic Survey of India*. Below is a part of his list, exactly as it is in the *LSI*. On the left of the semicolon are the Munda languages, and on the right are the Southeast Asian languages. Bahnar, Stieng and Hue are spoken in Vietnam, and Mon is from Thailand and Burma:

I.—Parts of the body

Back.—Santālī *dea,* Khaṛiā *kuṇḍaōn,* Savara *kiṇḍoŋ* ; Bahnar *kedu*

Blood.—Santālī *māyām* ; Stieng *maham*

Eye.—Santālī *māt'* ; Bahnar, etc. *mat*

Foot.—Santalī *jaŋga,* Juang *ijiŋ* ; Bahnar *jön* ; Stieng *joŋ*

Hand.—Santālī *ti* ; Bahnar *ti*

Nose.—Santālī *mũ* ; Bahnar, etc. *muh*

II.—Animals

Bird.—Santālī *sim* ; Bahnar *śēm*, Mōn *chē̃*

Crab.—Santālī *kaṭkâm* ; Bahnar *kötam*

Dog.—Savara *kinsor* ; Huey, Sue, etc. *śor*

Fish.—Kūrkū *kākū* ; Bahnar, etc. *ka*

Peacock,—Santālī *marak'* ; Mōn *mrāk*

Snake.—Santālī *biñ* ; Bahnar *bih,* Steing *bēh*

Tiger.—Santālī *kul,* Muṇḍārī *kulā* ; Mōn, Bahnar *kla,* Kuy *khola*[30]

Vocabulary, however, is not the only thing that can swim through cell walls into a creole language: sometimes grammatical features can too. We saw with Dakkhini that grammatical gender could be incorporated from Urdu, and the existence of natural gender in Telugu, the substratum language, must have helped. We were prepared to find the old gender system of Sanskrit making its way into all the western Indo-Aryan languages, and even fading down in the north from the three-way contrast in Sanskrit and the prakrits to a two-way contrast between masculine and feminine. There too we guessed that the Indus Valley substratum languages, if they were Dravidian, would not have been hostile to grammatical gender, as, being Dravidian, they would probably have had natural gender.

Munda languages do not have this sort of gender. What they have is a distinction between animate and non-animate nouns. The animate class includes humans, animals and 'heavenly bodies' like the sun, moon and stars, and it is linked to a 'system of concord between subject, object and verb'.[31] This is something linguists would call a gender system, if we take 'gender' to mean a class of nouns, and not something only to do with being male or female. In any case, most masculine and feminine nouns in north Indian and European languages are not male or female. Chairs? Cars? Books?[32] No way.

But I was thinking of another sort of gender system, one that didn't mark adjectives or verbs, but instead marked numbers. I was thinking of the numeral classifiers I had heard in Bhojpuri all my life, where *ek* and *dūi* for 'one' and 'two' were different from *ego* and *dū-go*, or, as some people said, *ek-ṭho* and *dū-ṭho: go* or *ṭho* meant that these were countable items. One shoe. Two separate glasses of water. Without the marker it would be the total quantity of water in two glasses, or the number as an abstraction. I had spent a lifetime thinking that this sort of distinction was special in Bhojpuri, as Hindi didn't have it. And I knew it was also in all the other Māgadhan languages, like Bengali, Odia, Assamese, and Magahi and Maithili in Bihar. Bengali and Odia also had a marker, *jon*, for a human 'gender', exactly like the word *hitori* in Japanese, that means 'one person', as distinct from *ichi*, which simply means 'one'. Assamese had many more. Since this was a Māgadhan trait, I thought it had to go back to the Munda languages in our substratum. The Munda languages were supposedly Austro-Asiatic, and so were numeral classifiers: all the other Austro-Asiatic languages in Southeast Asia—in fact, all the languages of Asia, like Chinese, Japanese and Korean—had numeral classifiers.[33] This had to be an old Munda feature that got a new life in the 'Indo-Aryan' Māgadhan languages. It never crossed my mind that it could be anything else.

But when I opened Grierson's *Linguistic Survey of India*, Volume IV, on Munda and Dravidian languages, it wasn't mentioned. After all the loud insistence on the Munda tribes being from an Austro-Asiatic 'race', as if the people in the Munda lands in India could be mistaken for people from the Mekong Delta, what was starkly missing was the most iconic feature in all the Māgadhan and Southeast Asian languages: numeral classifiers. All that had struck Grierson about numbers in Munda was that the Munda languages had a three-way number contrast: singular, dual and plural, and that they counted to Base-20. Even I knew this Base-20 counting from Bhojpuri in Trinidad, down to *dūi-kamtī bīs*, two-less-than-twenty for eighteen, and *tīni koṛī ā pāñć*, three twenties and five, for sixty-five, using the tribal word, *koṛī*, for twenty. That was the sum total of what Grierson had to say in his hugely influential *Linguistic Survey of India* about Munda numbers, and once the *LSI* was published it became linguistic truth. To be fair: he had never said that Munda *didn't* have numeral classifiers. He just didn't mention them in the *LSI*.

I sat for a long while as the world spun crazily around me. Had I dreamt it all up? That the Māgadhan languages and the Munda languages were related? All of a sudden, the Munda languages looked like strangers. But that was impossible! I had to rewind and start my search again to get to the bottom of this situation.

My first port of call was Suniti Kumar Chatterji's magnum opus, *The Origin and Development of the Bengali Language*, written a century ago. From page 777 to 781 he had listed all the possible forms these markers could take in Bengali, not just the familiar *ṭā*/*ṭi* and *jon*, but more obscure ones like *khān*, for flat rectangular objects, *gāćh*, for long stick-like objects, *goṭā*, for round objects, and *thān* for flat objects. He even said that 'the employment of these enclitic words or fragments of words lacks the range and variety of the numerative or qualifying words of many other languages, *e.g.*, Chinese . . . and Japanese . . . although there is some resemblance in the general principle.'[34] But he made no definitive comment on how they might have come into Bengali. They were simply . . . there.

Emeneau, thirty years later in 1956, revisited the issue, citing Chatterji: 'Finally, I would present in detail a matter which has not been noticed before. The phenomenon is of limited areal range, but appears in all three families, having spread from Indo-Aryan, though it is not an Indo-European phenomenon. This is the use of "classifiers" or "quantifiers".'[35] Emeneau saw the contradiction in their coming from Indo-Aryan, but not being an Indo-European thing, and went on to say that 'conspicuous as having such systems are Chinese, Japanese, Korean, Vietnamese, Khmer, Thai, Burmese, and Malay'.[36] He concluded that since all the Māgadhan languages 'use practically the same morphemes, the modern descendants are all descendants of a system that originated in the Māgadhan Apabhraṃśa at the end of the Middle Indo-Aryan period'. But he can't have been satisfied with that, as he kept looking, in Marathi and tribal Munda and Dravidian languages, for the source, though in the end he gave up: 'Until a more searching study has been made of the various stages of Middle Indo-Aryan, the history of the systems will remain a subject of speculation.'[37]

In other words, numeral classifiers are *not* Indo-European, but they *are* Indo-Aryan. They erupted spontaneously out of the blue some time in the medieval era, almost only in the Māgadhan region where the tribal substratum languages are 'Austro-Asiatic'. An identical feature exists in all the languages of Southeast Asia, but it somehow missed Munda, so numeral classifiers in Māgadhan languages did not come from Munda, but out of thin air. Only Emeneau could see a problem in this reasoning. But for almost everyone else, it made an eerie sort of sense.

Numeral classifiers are not from Sanskrit. They also do not exist in Māgadhan Prakrit. Ashoka's first rock edict has a paragraph where three numbers occur without any classifiers in a situation that in the modern languages would require them: *duve majula eke mige . . . etāni pi ća tini pānāni no alabhiyisanti*, 'two peacocks (and) one deer . . . and even these three creatures are not slaughtered regularly'. Not a single numeral classifier for countable items and animals.

My first break in the clouds was an article by two Australian linguists, Richard Barz and Anthony Diller, about noun classifiers in South and Southeast Asia, which goes into the question of why the path leading to numeral classifiers is so muddy.[38] As they find:

> In archaic Sanskritized varieties of Bengali classifiers are not used even though they may well have been common in ordinary speech. Vivid confirmation of this occurs in Kṛṣṇadās Gosvāmī's *Caitanya Caritāmṛta*, a 16th century work at the apogee of the Sanskritized style of Bengali. A careful perusal of the verses of this biography of the Hindu saint Caitanya has failed to turn up even one classifier either in the poet's descriptive verses or in the conversations of Caitanya with his followers. On the other hand, classifiers appear in the quoted speech of people expected to use a non-Sanskritic purely colloquial type of language. For example, a Muslim Pathan soldier says to Caitanya (Bhaktivedanta 1975, vol. 7: 220-221):
>
> 'ei ṭhak cāri-jana'
> *these rogues four-CLF*
> *'(Here are) these four rogues'*
> Caitanya's reply has no classifier:
> 'ei cāri dayā kari karena pālana'
> *these four mercy having done do maintenance*
> *'These four (men) by their mercy maintain (me)'*[39]

We are right back to the start of this chapter, at the confluence, where the rich and the educated simply do not speak like the little people, even now. And here we are, trying to find numeral classifiers in the written record from medieval times, which is *only* about elite usage! Numeral classifiers are just the sort of stigmatized speech that would make the Māgadhan gentry cringe! They would simply delete them and hope no one saw that they had ever been there. Just try to imagine the educated people you know in Allahabad saying *dū-go bhāī rahal*, 'there were two brothers', with the classifier *go* on the word for two. I cannot even recall my own grandmother saying something like that. She would understand, of course. I would often hear her in conversation with voluble village women who used classifiers freely. But my *ājī* maintained a dignified reserve in her own usage. Like the Emperor Ashoka, she would have put all she had to say into a more western Hindi dialect, something closer to Braj, which her father knew, while still signalling that she was a part of the community. Māgadhan features, even in my family, were strictly for the little people.

Let us take a step back. What exactly are numeral classifiers, and when are they used?

To my surprise, Barz and Diller found their answer in a 1978 publication by P. Mohan. It was *my* doctoral dissertation. I had been trying to make sense of the numeral classifiers in my recordings, sitting in our old family home in rural Trinidad, far from any libraries that might give me ready-made answers.[40] I had to work it all out for myself. My data was as old as the data Grierson had used for the *Linguistic Survey of India*. *LSI* was published in 1919, the same year that Bhojpuri-speaking migrants stopped coming to Trinidad. And some of the old people I had recorded had actually been on the migrant ships. They were *jahājīs*.

In fact, on this topic my data was better than Grierson's: I had just let people speak, tell me long stories, without getting them to repeat the same biblical parable as Grierson did (where the only number that ever occurred more than once was 'one': and the other one was 'two', which came up only once). Many of the stories and narratives I recorded had lots of numbers in them, so I ended up with a good sprinkling of classifiers. I instinctively avoided the sort of speakers who knew Hindi and might try to tune their speech away from Māgadhan usage: not pundits, but definitely their wives. I got my *ājī* to help me with my transcriptions, but I never recorded her. I already knew that speakers like her would only confuse me.

After I looked at all the numeral classifiers in my recordings, I concluded that the numbers with the classifier *go* (or *ṭho*) were things that were countable: *dū-go ghuṛkī pānī*, two (separate) glasses of water, while *dūi* by itself meant the total quantity of water in the two glasses. I also found in a story one instance of *jana* as a classifier for humans, but it was not a productive feature: you couldn't make more numbers with *jana*. The distinction boiled down to whether the items were separate or a single mass, like a quantity of water, or money, or distance, or an abstract concept.

Barz and Diller listed my findings as twelve 'guidelines governing the use of the Bhojpuri classifier', which 'while intended for the Bhojpuri of Trinidad are equally applicable to all forms of Bhojpuri . . . from India as well as Mauritius and Trinidad':[41]

1. If the number is used as an adjective with a noun: <u>two</u> glasses of water: *dū-go ghuṛki pānī*
2. If the noun is understood but not expressed: take <u>six</u> (of them): *ćhau-go le lo*
3. No classifiers in compounds like <u>three</u> hundred, and no classifiers beyond 100: *tīn sau*
4. No classifier for mathematical symbols: <u>ten</u> plus <u>five</u> equals <u>fifteen</u>: *das ā pā̃ć bane panrāh*
5. No classifiers for days, weeks, hours or other measurements: <u>one</u> day: *ek din*
6. No classifiers for money (except bills or coins): *$10: das ḍālā;* two penny-coins: *du-go kāpā*
7. No classifiers with units of weight: ten loads of sugar cane: *das lāḍ ketārī*
8. No classifiers with reduplicated numbers: <u>one</u>-<u>one</u> house: *ek-ek ghar*, each individual house
9. No classifiers if two numbers represent a span: <u>eight</u>-<u>ten</u> sticks: *āṭh-das lakaṛī*
10. No classifiers with fractions except <u>half</u>, <u>one and a half</u>, <u>two and a half</u>: *ḍeṛh-go ghuṛkī*, 1½ cups
11. No classifiers with ordinal or aggregative numbers: <u>second</u> or <u>all four</u>: *dūsar*, *ćāro*
12. The classifier is after the number, but before other adjectives: <u>one</u> more thing: *ego aur bāt*

And they refer to this list as 'Mohan's rules'.

Why, then, is Grierson's data on numeral classifiers in languages like Bhojpuri, Magahi and Maithili so patchy? I suspected that it had to do with how he had got his data. Not every narrative is about numbers, and the parable of the prodigal son, a biblical story that Grierson depended on for data easy to compare across a spread of dialects, only mentions the number 'one' a few times, and 'two' once. I would have been sceptical about telling someone a story they didn't know, and then asking them to repeat it in another dialect.[42] That was practically the same as feeding them what you wanted to hear. Translation had not worked as an elicitation technique with my speakers in Trinidad. The kind of speakers who understood what translation was were educated, and conscious of not wanting to sound like villagers, and inclined to suppress what they saw as rustic features, while those who did not understand what I was after got confused and gave me long paraphrases, thinking I didn't understand a particular word. I had opted to go with the speakers who had not been to school, and to just let them speak and see what the language itself turned up. That way I found many features I was not expecting: like numeral classifiers.

But according to Barz and Diller, there was more going on: in many of Grierson's data samples the classifiers were deliberately suppressed:

> Contrary to modern usage, old texts like the poems of Vidyāpati do not contain the classifier and, even as late as the last decades of the 19th century, many learned Maithilī writers preferred to suppress its use. For example, between 1883 and 1887 George Grierson produced a set of grammatical sketches of Maithilī, Magahī—which he termed 'Magadhī'—and Bhojpurī. In order to obtain illustrative and comparative material he asked an educated speaker of one or more dialects of each language to translate the same set of fables into his particular form of speech. The results are informative. Not a single classifier is employed by

> the translators of the northern Maithilī (Grierson 1887: 30-38), mixed southern Maithilī-Bengali (Grierson 1887: 82-89), mixed southern Maithilī-Magadhī (Grierson 1886: 88-94), southern Maithilī (Grierson 1887: 94-101), and mixed Maithilī-Bhojpurī (Grierson 1884: 92-98) translations. Since it is unlikely that classifiers were not used at that time in speech uniformly all over the Maithilī area, the explanation seems to be that some translators were writing in a traditional literary style in which classifiers were omitted.[43]

That is a kind way of putting it. What these translators were doing was *suppressing* a feature that they thought made them look 'uneducated', something they—like my *ājī*—never used themselves. My *ājī* had dismissed *go* as 'just a password', and left me to figure out for myself what its function was. While some markers did sneak through into Grierson's data, he was not told that they were the same as the numeral classifiers he had seen in 'Indo-Aryan' Māgadhan languages. As far as Grierson knew, numeral classifiers existed *only* in Bhojpuri and Magahi, not even in Maithili: and he assumed that they had nothing to do with Munda. To this day almost no one in the field has questioned this intuitively wrong assumption: I see again and again in the literature that numeral classifiers, if they did at all come into Munda, had to be there because of 'influence' from Indo-Aryan languages like Bhojpuri and Magahi.

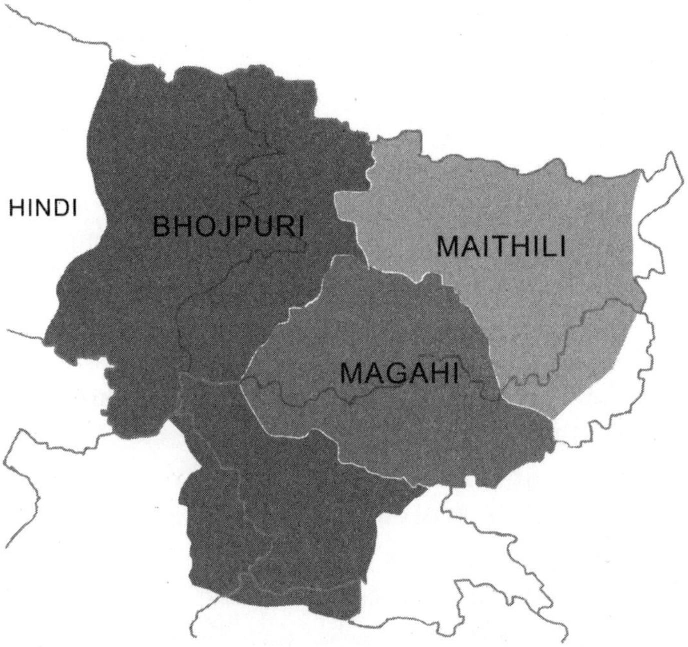

Map 11: Bhojpuri, Magahi, Maithili—the three westernmost Māgadhan languages. The terrain of these languages does not correspond to state boundaries.

We are back to *diglossia*, the kind of bilingualism that occurs in unequal societies where the elite are conscious of how the less educated speak and go to great lengths to keep it out of the record, as if it cast a shadow on the whole community. In a way, this is an early stage of what we otherwise welcome as standardization, where before one prestigious urban dialect is selected for an upgrade, many others have to be eliminated. But the little people in the Māgadhan region are still hanging in there, over long millennia, holding on to precious features in their languages. In exactly the way they had preserved their forests, their tribes, their old languages and their elephants. Numeral classifiers were a familiar episode in an old Māgadhan story.

~

As one travels east into the Māgadhan lands, two things change. First, the sense of embarrassment about numeral classifiers as something very downmarket vanishes: Odia, Bengali and Assamese actually regard numeral classifiers positively, as a part of their basic identity. Second, going eastwards towards Assam, the number of classifiers keeps increasing. In Bhojpuri, the westernmost Māgadhan language, the distinction is only between numerals marked with *go/ṭho* and those without this marker. In Maithili, a human vs non-human distinction emerges with the appearance of *jon*, used only with persons, giving it two classifiers. Odia has three: *goṭe*, *jaṇe* and *khaṇḍe*, with *khaṇḍe* coming for the word for 'piece'. Bengali has six: *ṭā* (with a diminutive *ṭī*), *jon*, *goṭā*, *gāchā*, *thān* and *khon*.[44] And Assamese lists twenty-one: *jon*, *joni*, *jona*, *to*, *ta*, *ti*, *khon*, *khoni*, *sola*, *soli*, *dal*, *dali*, *zopa*, *zupi*, *gos*, *gosi*, *goraki*, *pat*, *khila*, *sita* and *sota*.[45]

This led some, like Emeneau, to speculate that classifiers might have entered Indo-Aryan from the east, and that their use spread westward,[46] citing Bloch and Grierson who actually put it down to 'substratum influence' from Tai, which entered Assam with the Tai-Ahom migration in the mid-thirteenth century.[47] In Tai-Ahom the number and the classifiers come *after* the noun, not before: *khai song tu*, where *khai* is buffalo, *song* is two and *tu* a numeral classifier with animals, meaning 'two buffaloes'.[48] In Assamese there are two possible placements. The number can come first, followed by the classifier, and then the noun: *dui-ta moh*, 'two-CL buffaloes', as in the other Māgadhan languages. Or the number and the classifier can follow the noun, as they do in Tai-Ahom: *moh du-ta/dui-ta*.[49]

Numeral classifiers exist in Tai-Ahom, but they probably did not come into Assamese from Tai-Ahom, though having them also in Tai-Ahom would have reinforced the classifiers and given Assamese an extra stylistic option for their use. But the *forms* of the Assamese classifiers are derived from prakrit words. That would link them back to the time when the Māgadhan languages themselves were coming into existence with a fresh coat of 'prakrit paint' on top of their earlier vocabulary. Also, Odia, Bengali and Assamese do not use all these classifiers in normal speech: they tend to go mostly with the equivalent of *go/ṭho/ṭā* and the equivalent of *jon*. If there are many more classifier *forms* in Assamese now than in the other Māgadhan languages, it is more likely that in Assamese, like in modern Thai, their number has been growing because they are seen as a very good thing.[50]

Our entire wild goose chase, looking for the origins of numeral classifiers in early Indo-Aryan languages, and then in Tai-Ahom, is only because researchers helping Grierson with the *LSI* managed to make these forms invisible to him in the Munda languages, while, paradoxically, agreeing with him that the Munda languages, the languages of the First Indian tribes, were 'Austro-Asiatic'.

~

So, did numeral classifiers come from the tribal Munda languages? My first written confirmation of this was from Toshiki Osada, a Japanese linguist who is married to a native speaker of Mundari and has written a lot on Munda. He mentions (in passing) that they do:

'As Emeneau has pointed out, numeral classifiers are an Indian areal feature. Mundari uses *hoṛo* "person", *oṛaʔ* "house", *booʔ* "head [of cattle]" as classifiers.[51] Thus,

api	*hoṛo*	*hon-ko*	"three children"
three	person	child-PL	

The word *jan/jon* (from Indo-Aryan) is also currently used in Mundari. However, *jan/jon* always co-occurs with Indo-Aryan numerals. For example,

tin	*jan/jon*	*hon-ko*
three	Num Cl	child-PL'[52]

It is interesting to see this use of *jan/jon*, and a glimpse of how prakrit vocabulary has been slipping into Munda languages from the time that they began to refit themselves as 'Indo-Aryan' Māgadhan languages. The word *jan/jon* is taken from a prakrit word that means 'people', the same as *hoṛo* in Mundari. This is exactly the process we have been talking about in the Extended Indus Valley Periphery, the great vocabulary replacement, except that there we had to imagine the Indus Valley languages, because they are gone. But Munda languages are still here with us. And we are getting to see the fusion process happening before our eyes: a prakrit *form* that stands for what is originally an Austro-Asiatic *concept*, being adopted and used, but only with Indo-Aryan numbers. It was never the *idea* of numeral classifiers that had come from Indo-Aryan. It was only the forms, which stood for something in Munda that was much, much older. Emeneau had been led astray by the *forms* being from the prakrits.

All I needed now was to know that this was not a one-off, that this was true of other Munda languages too. So I wrote to Probal Dasgupta, a retired professor of linguistics living in Kolkata. He and I had had long conversations about Bengali having emerged from a Munda substratum, and about whether languages could have gender or numeral classifiers, but not both. He wrote back to me saying: 'Write to Arun Ghosh. He is a specialist in Munda languages and very proficient in Santali. He can give you data.'

Ghosh responded, sending me information from two of his publications.[53] He listed for Santali the classifier *ṭɛn* (also found as *ṭɛc'*), which is used with the numeral for 'one', with 'non-living human beings, non-human living beings, non-human non-living objects and the inanimate [along with] human beings when specified'.[54] In other words, the word for 'man' at the start of a story would not have a classifier, as it would be 'a' man, rather than 'the' man. Elsewhere a classifier would be used: *mit'-ṭɛn gɔc' hoṛ*, 'one dead man', *mit'-ṭɛc' uric*, 'one bullock', *mit'-ṭɛn rakkhos*, 'one man-eater', *mit'-ṭɛn hətiər*, 'one weapon', *mit'-ṭɛn hoṛ*, 'one man' (someone who had previously been mentioned in the narrative).

The next classifier he gave was *ea*, which is used for 'two' to 'four' and for 'twenty': *barea bogga*, 'two ghosts', *pɛa sim*, 'three cocks', *ponea jinis*, 'four things' and *ponea gatɛ*, 'four friends'.

The last classifier he gave was *gɔṭɛn* (with a variant *gɔtɛc'*), which occurs with the numbers 'five' to 'ten': *mɔṛɛ-gɔṭɛn kaḍa*, 'five buffaloes', *turui-gɔṭɛn bogga*, 'six ghosts', *ɛae-gɔṭɛn putul*, 'seven dolls'.

Ghosh's numeral classifiers in Santali looked familiar. I was sure I had seen them in Grierson's raw data. I went back to the *LSI* Volume IV, *Munda and Dravidian Languages*, to check out this hunch.

They were easy to find: I had already marked them all with highlighter in the text, thinking that they had to be classifiers. All Grierson's data corpora that told the parable of the prodigal son in Santali began with *mit'*, 'one', *mit' hâr*, 'one man', without any classifier after 'one', as classifiers do not occur with indefinite humans (one sample starts with *mit'-hoṛ haṛmā*, 'one man', using *hoṛ* as a classifier with humans, as in Osada's Mundari example).[55] But there were also examples with *mit'-ṭäch'*, *mit'-ṭhän* and *mit'-ṭāŋ*, which, despite the differences in spelling, are the same classifiers with 'one' as Ghosh had listed.

Going beyond 'one', the *LSI* also has many instances of *bar-ea* for 'two', in *bar-ea koṛa*, 'two boys' in the parable of the prodigal son, and in another story *bar-ia haṛam-buṛia-kiŋg*, 'two-CL old-man-old-woman-DUAL SUFFIX',[56] meaning a couple.

Grierson had actually had numeral classifiers in his samples all along, though no one had ever pointed them out to him! The rules governing their use were not exactly the same as in Māgadhan languages like Bhojpuri, but they were doing the same thing. In some samples the 'translators' had indeed left them out, but in most of his data the classifiers were there. And, except for *gɔṭɛn* (which does not turn up in any of Grierson's samples), the forms of the classifiers did not show any influence from the 'Indo-Aryan' languages (like Bhojpuri *go*, which with *ṭɛn* or *ṭɛc'* make *gɔṭɛn* and *gɔṭɛc'*). All Grierson's primary data was in the *LSI* for everyone to see: the classifiers were hiding there in plain sight. Could I be the only one who had checked Grierson's raw data to see what all was there? Or were classifiers something that only Māgadhans and Mundas with our finely tuned antennae could detect?

That removes one huge roadblock. Māgadhan languages got numeral classifiers from Munda when the languages were born from a Munda substratum and prakrit words. And while numeral classifiers would not have been there in proto-Munda, the mixed Munda got them from Southeast Asian languages at the time of the migration of Austro-Asiatic men who brought new words and japonica rice. Which is exactly what I had always thought. And whenever a modern Māgadhan language has more classifiers, as Assamese does, they are new, as the feature is alive and growing.[57] Now, at last, it is all making sense.

As Dasgupta remarked when he heard the result of my long odyssey: 'Home at last—after scouring the shire . . . We are all hobbits!'

~

Now we can get on with the story of the Munda people that began 65,000 years ago, when the first modern humans reached the subcontinent and settled. Over the millennia there must have been other migrations that added small numbers of people to their population, but the genetic record does not show them. In any case, it is really only groups with political power that leave a linguistic mark. Small bands and individuals who try to blend in tend to leave their old languages behind. The Munda people were mostly on their own. 65,000 years is a very long time. We cannot assume that Munda remained the same pristine language that left Africa 70,000 years back, or that it had not already changed by the time the Mundas reached the subcontinent. Retroflex consonants stayed. But words, and grammatical features, would have drifted apart, new mutations arising on their own, each strand ready to take its own direction.

About 9000 years ago there was a migration of farmers from the Zagros mountains in southern Iran, which showed up in the genetic record. These migrants settled in Mehrgarh, in what is now Balochistan, and came into contact with Munda people settled in the northwest. The 'Iranian farmers' were the people who interbred with the early Mundas and created a hybrid people, most probably the ones we now call the Dravidians.

But the Mundas living in the Gangetic plains were essentially left to themselves for long millennia, though Munda words trickling into Sanskrit speak of some degree of contact with the lands to the west.[58] The first big population influx to mix with the Gangetic Mundas was a bit before the entry of the Vedic men, about 4000 years ago, from Southeast Asia. This migration brought a large number of Austro-Asiatic men into the Gangetic plains, and they came into contact with Mundas who were already growing an indigenous variety of rice. At this time the entire Gangetic region, going all the way to the east, would have been full of Munda speakers: it is only later that the last speakers retreated into forest areas, and preserved their languages. When the Southeast Asian men came, there would have been many more Munda languages than there are today.

~

But just as I sat down and put my feet up after 'scouring the shire', ready to write peacefully about Austro-Asiatic men coming into India, marrying Munda women and going on to have little hybrid children, I found myself in the middle of another mess that had to be cleared up before the story could continue. Life is never easy for hobbits! All of a sudden, the same Mundas who had come to India in the first human migration out of Africa, the same Mundas who shared mutations of the M haplogroup with First Australians and no one else on Earth, were being labelled as Austro-Asiatic. Not *partly* Austro-Asiatic, on their paternal descent line, but simply . . . Austro-Asiatic. They had *not* reached India from Africa 65,000 years ago. There was another more compelling narrative: that the Mundas *themselves* had come to India much later from Southeast Asia and were not First Indians at all.

There is a bewildering amount of belief invested in a purely Austro-Asiatic origin for the Munda people, the kind of fervent faith that shakes one's trust in academia. There is a paper from 2011 on the National Institutes of Health, US, website titled 'The Austroasiatic Munda population from India and Its enigmatic origin: a HLA diversity study'. Unable to reconcile the genetic data with a mindset predisposed to see the Munda people as migrants from Southeast Asia, it ends lamely with:

> Our results do not favor either a scenario where the Munda would be representative of an ancestral Austroasiatic population giving rise to an eastward Austroasiatic expansion to Southeast Asia. Rather, their peculiar genetic profile is better explained by a decrease in genetic diversity through genetic drift from an ancestral population having a genetic profile similar to present-day Austroasiatic populations from Southeast Asia (thus suggesting a possible southeastern origin), followed by intensive gene flow with neighboring Indian populations.[59]

Mundas, by this reckoning, are Southeast Asians who got diluted by living too long in India.

There is also a 2019 paper titled 'The Munda Maritime hypothesis', by Rau and Sidwell, which takes us through all the possible explanations why Mundas are Austro-Asiatic, before citing a 2011 genetics paper by Gyaneshwer Chaubey et al., which says: 'Austroasiatic speakers in India today are derived from dispersal from southeast Asia, followed by extensive sex-specific admixtures with local Indian populations.'[60] In other words, the old-old story: migrant men who had children with local women:

> While Munda populations feature a considerable percentage of Southeast Asian heritage—over 60% of the Y chromosome variation is dominated at haplogroup O2a1-M95—their mtDNA (i.e. purely maternally inherited DNA) is virtually exclusively South Asian.[61]

In 2020 Chaubey himself got into the discussion of language in a paper, written with George van Driem, a Dutch linguist, titled 'Munda languages are father tongues, but Japanese and Korean are not'. They highlight the 'pronounced gender asymmetry of this linguistic intrusion', and while intrigued by the 'daring Munda maritime hypothesis', admit in the end that the linguistic data in that paper 'are gossamer [thin] and limited to a few lexemes',[62] which is exactly what had been bothering me all this while. Without a model to describe a linguistic hybrid like this, Chaubey and van Driem stick to the basic facts and merely confirm that the Austro-Asiatic component in Munda languages is solely in the vocabulary, the paternal line. That is precisely the sort of mixed language that this book is about, so their paper is very welcome.

Where, then, was the *linguistic* proof of wholly Austro-Asiatic origins? I searched the net looking for anything I could find by David Stampe, an American linguist specializing in phonology who had spent years working on Munda languages in India. I wrote to a friend in his department at the University of Hawaii at Manoa looking for him, only to hear that he had passed away. Then I found a paper he had written in 2002 with Patricia Donegan where they promised to show what the argument about Munda being Austro-Asiatic was based on.

Donegan and Stampe begin by admitting that the Munda family and the Mon-Khmer family of Southeast Asia are 'so exactly opposite at every level of structure that Sir George Grierson in his *Linguistic Survey of India* remarked that if they were descended from a common language, the language must have been adopted by people with opposite orders of thought'.[63] They list the typological oppositions between Munda and Mon-Khmer:[64]

	MUNDA	MON-KHMER
Phrase Accent:	Falling (initial)	Rising (final)
Word Order:	Variable – OV, AN, Postpositional	Rigid – VO, NA, Prepositional
Syntax:	Synthetic – subj/obj agreement on verb	Analytic – no inflectional morphology
Word Canon:	Trochaic	Iambic, monosyllabic
Morphology:	Agglutinative, Suffixing, Polysynthetic	Fusional, Prefixing or Isolating
Timing:	Isosyllabic or Isomoraic	Isoaccentual
Syllable Canon:	(C)V(C)	Unaccented (C)ə, accented (C)(C)V(G)(C)
Consonantism:	Stable, Geminate clusters	Shifting, Tonogeneric, Non-geminate clusters
Tone/Register:	Level tone (Korku only)	Contour tones or registers
Vocalism:	Stable, monophthongal, harmonic	Shifting, diphthongal, reductive

In other words, (to put it in less abstruse language and bring it back down to Earth), Munda and Mon-Khmer are different in every possible way. As different as Tamil and Chinese.

About vocabulary they accept that 'the evidence of the original linguistic unity of Munda and Mon-Khmer has rested, and still rests, mainly on lexical cognates', or the sort of lists Grierson had made of word resemblances in the *LSI*. These cognates are 'a magnitude smaller than the shared vocabularies of Indo-Aryan and Dravidian' in Munda, but Donegan and Stampe are satisfied.

> We have Austroasiatic cognates for the basic verbs and nouns relating to body, family, home, field, and forest, and for pronouns, demonstratives, and numerals. Agricultural vocabulary points to a very early SE Asian homeland (Zide & Zide 1976), but that does not prove that proto-Austroasiatic was of the analytic type now identified with 'South-East Asian'.[65]

An analytic language is one with short words and no endings, like Chinese. This was a major sticking point: how do languages with short words and tones change into something like Munda with complex morphology, lots of endings, and no tones? Donegan and Stampe wondered if it was the Mon-Khmer languages that had changed.

It is disturbing that they were ready to go through such contortions to shore up the position that Munda and Mon-Khmer had started out as a single language. How much academic scholarship has been tainted by this colonial speculation emanating from theories of 'race'! Grierson, Max Müller and the other colonial-era philologists were part of a tradition that looked only at *words* as an indicator of a substratum.

Linguistics is supposed to have moved on from that, though generally 'historical linguistics' has not. Instead, we see modern linguists turning cartwheels to endorse a position that had left even Grierson uneasy. What Donegan and Stampe should have done was reconcile the idea of 'father tongues' with vocabulary replacement. The University of Hawai'i at Manoa was the right place to do it, as it is well known for creole studies. Creoles are exactly the sort of mixed language that will take *all* their vocabulary from a 'father tongue' and paste it on to a grammar that looks nothing at all like the source language. There was no contradiction. All Donegan and Stampe ever needed to solve the enigma was the right model.

~

Spare a tiny thought for the Mundas 4000 years ago, who saw their lands overrun by intruders from Southeast Asia who came with japonica rice and proceeded to have children with their women. If no less than 60 per cent of the Y-DNA today in the remotest Munda tribes comes from Austro-Asiatic men, it doesn't take much imagination to see that these were not quiet, peaceful settlers. If that many Munda men were sidelined, one must wonder if they simply stepped aside with a smile. Were male-driven migrations something to celebrate, or were they just a milder form of the population replacement that happened all over Europe and Southeast Asia, where the First People, the 'orang asli', are now nearly extinct?

In a way, it was the japonica rice that did it. Before it came to India and mixed with our local rice growing in the Gangetic plain, multiplying the yields and making possible a much larger population, it had done precisely the same thing in Southeast Asia, and earlier in China. The population pressure that drove young men out from Southeast Asia to explore and conquer new lands had its source in a food supply that allowed the population to grow too big too fast. What is interesting is that this migration was absorbed by the Mundas, without India becoming a continuing extension of Southeast Asia. Behind each migration there is a story. And sometimes with a little imagination we can catch a glimpse of what it was.

~

Now let us get back to the model I sketched out in Chapter 1, and the main purpose of this book: which is to understand a particular type of language hybridization that we find again and again in the subcontinent, and how the different strands of lineage manifest in the new languages that get made. It is a refinement of the old creole model—which has also been dogged by misconceptions that have no basis in history, like the notion that creoles began as pidgins in an atmosphere of chaos. Our new model does not have pidgins but starts with a few local people who learn the newcomers' language well. The first approximation of the new language of power is not a pidgin, but a prakrit.

Our new creole model imagines a more plausible scenario of male explorers entering a new land, settling and having children with local women, children who first learn their mothers' languages, after which they graduate to the new languages of power brought by their fathers. The 'almost' varieties of the migrant men's languages learnt by the hybrid children, and elite local men who become interpreters for the migrants—with local touches, at first only in 'accent'—are prakrits. The little people, who stand aside from all the intermarriage, continue to speak their old languages for as long as they can. But eventually their efforts to adjust result in vocabulary transfer from the 'almost' variety, along with a few features that make sense to them, and they paste it all on to their old operating systems, the grammars of their old languages. Basic vocabulary. Words like 'hand' and 'foot', 'sun' and 'moon'. In the Extended Indus Valley Periphery it was not only basic vocabulary that went across. Every single affix or marker used in the new languages was adapted from the prakrit. It was like a coat of 'prakrit paint' on top of features that were not prakrit at all.

This produces a characteristic distribution of genetic traits, which in my previous book I called the Tiramisu bear model. A Tiramisu bear is the offspring of a male grizzly bear who has migrated north in a time of climate change and a female polar bear who, in other times, would not have been on land but on the sea perched on an ice floe. As polar males cannot migrate south—they can only walk on snow and ice—and female bears do not migrate at all, grizzly males and polar females are the only way to produce a Tiramisu bear.

And what would a Tiramisu bear offspring of Austro-Asiatic and Munda look like? Well, we don't know what Munda was like 4000 years ago, and we are not sure what part of the Austro-Asiatic language spectrum came to India, or what the languages of Southeast Asia were like back then. But going by our model, we would expect the hybrid to have the same highly agglutinative structure as present-day Munda, with long words and lots of agreement markers at the end of verb stems, and basic vocabulary from the men's language, along with the sort of grammatical features that can swim through the cell membrane into a creole. In Dakkhini and the western Indo-Aryan languages that was grammatical gender. But the Austro-Asiatic languages did not have grammatical gender. They had another feature that could 'migrate' with vocabulary: numeral classifiers. We can therefore say with reasonable certainty that the Munda-Austro-Asiatic Tiramisu bear would look a lot like the Munda languages we see today. It would have a Munda complex grammar and sound system, a lot of basic vocabulary from Austro-Asiatic languages, and numeral classifiers.

The Munda languages are 'Austro-Asiatic' in exactly the same way that Saramacaans and Ndjuka in the Amazonian regions of Suriname, South America, are 'English'. These are creole languages spoken by Africans who escaped the slave plantations of coastal Suriname and headed into the jungles of the interior way back in the mid-1600s. If you try, you can match a few English words with words that exist now in Saramacaans and Ndjuka, but there is a huge substratum from West Africa that defines the languages much better than English ever could, and a long history after the initial contact without slavery and the British in their lives. The Munda languages are creoles too: they are only *partly* Austro-Asiatic.

Mundas still trace back to First Indians, though there is more to their story. Just as you don't go calling Swahili in East Africa 'Semitic' because of all the Arabic vocabulary and genetic mixture from male Arab travellers, as it is structurally a Bantu language, you don't go calling First Indian languages 'Austro-Asiatic' with even less Southeast Asian vocabulary to show for it. To dismiss their entire maternal history and focus only on the men's languages that gave the hybrids some vocabulary and numeral classifiers in an encounter thousands of years ago is the sort of patriarchal thinking that linguistics should have got over long ago.

~

The onward journey for the Munda languages is clear, now that the hurdles are gone. There is a sense of déjà vu as we fast forward to the time when this chapter and the historical record begin. The rulers are different: they are no longer Austro-Asiatic men who came in from the east and took all the women for themselves. But one thing did not change: the educated and the powerful still behaved like outsiders, and still spoke like outsiders. This was, after all, Magadha, where time was cyclic. It was a land where Buddhists, Jains and Ajivikas imagined earlier lives, endless cycles of rebirth, and even a world without beginning or end.[66]

For the little people of the region, time would have continued as a span, punctuated by milestones that affected the elite more than anyone else. There must have been hiccups, things that led the tribes to reach out and take advantage of new opportunities, or to migrate out of harm's way, but we are unlikely to find them in the historical record, which is only about kings, empires and great religious movements. Munda speakers, with their new vocabulary and infusion of Southeast Asian genes, would have gone about their lives in a region where there would have been many more Munda languages than there are today.

The same questions arise that we faced in the west: how long did the little people go on speaking earlier languages? In Magadha the answer is different. Many still speak them, in the hinterland, and reading through Grierson's language samples in the *LSI*, I sense something achingly familiar. It is not only grammatical features, but words too: so much of Grierson's data feels like my Bhojpuri recordings from Trinidad that I can imagine time itself having slowed, and the transition from the Munda to the Māgadhan languages proceeding in a gentle trickle, with nouns, and even numeral classifiers, getting a fresh coat of paint from time to time. In the Māgadhan area each stage of the process is still there for us to see.

~

According to Suniti Kumar Chatterji, 'by the time Aryan speech had penetrated into what is now Bihar, *i.e.,* after 1000 B.C., some distinct tendencies in pronunciation were manifesting themselves in the eastern Aryan dialects, spoken by the non-Vedic Aryans.'[67] It is hard to imagine that the only steppe people who came to South Asia were the Vedic Ārya. Many groups of young men must have been on the move at that time. The Vedic Ārya were the ones who produced the Rig Veda, and whose nexus with kings and Kṣatriyas did the most to spread Indo-European language and culture over the north of the subcontinent. But there would certainly have been other related people who preceded and followed them, not always in well-defined groups, but sometimes numerous and influential enough to attract attention. One such group was the Vrātyas.

The Vrātyas had no hesitation in crossing the confluence into the Māgadhan lands. The Vedic Ārya referred to them as *outcasts*, or *riteless people*. 'The tract where these Vrātyas were the most numerous seems to have been Magadha. Their priests were probably bards as well . . . Vrātyas were Aryan in speech . . . and they *speak the language of the initiated* (i.e., into brahmanism), *although they are not initiated* . . . '[68] They were also known for their 'wild mysticism', and some of the anti-Brahman and anti-sacrificial ideas that developed in the Buddhists and the Jains later on probably go back to influence from these Vrātya priests. But not all Brahmans visiting the Magadha region were Vrātyas. The Bṛhadāraṇyaka Upaniṣad tells of Brahmans from the west travelling to Magadha to take part in philosophical debates, which they didn't always win.[69] The Māgadhans were never out of touch with the Ārya or Vedic knowledge.

Modern Marathi still uses the term *vrātya*, as well as its more Marathi-sounding version *vātaraṭ*, which now means a disobedient child, one who refuses to conform.[70] And modern Bengali has the term *brāttyo*, pronounced *brātto*, which has the same basic meaning of a 'disobedient child' as in Marathi.[71] Sumanta Banerjee in an email added that it now also refers to a 'fallen Brahmin, who doesn't wear the sacred thread, and who is engaged in manual labour (which is forbidden to Brahmins) . . . In later Bengali social discourse it was extended to describe dissidents from within the upper castes who were exiled from their communities, and excommunicated as "*brāttyo*". In modern Bengali literature, however, it has been stripped of its pejorative association, and is instead proudly adopted as a self-assertive term by dissenters who are rejected by the Establishment.'*

Could this 'disobedient child', the *vrātya/brātto*, be the source of the English word 'brat'?[72] That would make more sense than the other suggested etymologies, such as a Celtic word meaning 'coarse cloth' or 'rag'. Did the British get the idea of 'brats' when they first lived in Bengal?

And another thought: would the Vrātya, also from the Pontic Caspian Steppe, not have been genetically indistinguishable from the Vedic Brahmans? If the Dravidian ancestry of the Brahuis, south Indians and the present-day inhabitants of the

* Email on 28 February 2024.

Indus Valley region cannot be identified as either original to the IVC or a later migration from peninsular India by a genetic test,[73] wouldn't the Vedic Ārya and the Vrātya have looked genetically identical too? How much of the 'steppe ancestry' in South Asia actually goes back to people like the Vrātyas, who would have mingled more readily with the local population than the Vedic Brahmans? This is something to ponder.

~

This explains how the languages of the elite in Magadha have such an Aryan look to them, but that is not the whole story. Chatterji says that during the time of the Mauryas, and especially of Ashoka, 'standard East Indian' was the official language all over India, so much so that it exerted a strong influence on other forms of Prakrit and Middle Indo-Aryan. The discourses of the Buddha and Mahavira were originally in this Prācya speech, but later, after the time of Ashoka, Buddha's discourses were put into a western dialect. 'This Western dialect into which Buddha's teachings were translated came to be known as "Pāli", which simply means *texts*.'[74] The Jains, however, left Mahavira's teachings mostly in their original Western Prācya language.[75]

In other words, Ashoka, the Buddhists and the Jains, in the way they made Māgadhan Prakrit, Pali and Ardhamāgadhi, had tuned them not towards a local audience, but hoped that the elites of the larger empire would find them easy to follow. The little people of Magadha were never their intended audience. That probably explains why the various prakrits in the Ashokan inscriptions look so very alike: Ashoka *intended* them to show his realm as united.

Two travellers from China, Faxian in the fifth century CE and Xuanzang in the seventh century CE,[76] write about language in Magadha at the time when they visited. Chatterji says that Faxian tells of a 'flourishing in (Aryan) learning and culture, at least in the West and the North',[77] but tells of 'decay in Southern Bihar—the country had become jungly, and was sparsely peopled: and the reason of this decay is not known'.[78] Was Buddhist Magadha beginning to fray at the edges? Xuanzang in the seventh century, according to Chatterji, says that 'the Aryan language had been generally adopted by the people all over Bengal, and it had penetrated as far east as Western Assam, but it had not spread among the masses even in Northern Orissa.'[79] The *Encyclopedia Britannica*, however, presents a gloomier picture of what these two Buddhist monks had to say about their visits to India:

> Although Buddhist institutions seemed to be faring well under the Guptas, Chinese pilgrims visiting India between 400 and 700 CE discerned a decline in the Buddhist community and the beginning of the absorption of Indian Buddhism by Hinduism. Among these pilgrims was Faxian, who left China in 399, crossed the Gobi, visited various holy places in India, and returned to China with numerous Buddhist scriptures and statues. The most famous of the Chinese travelers, however, was the 7th-century monk Xuanzang. When he arrived in north-western India, he found 'millions of monasteries' reduced to ruins by the Huns, a nomadic Central Asian people . . .
>
> After the destruction of numerous Buddhist monasteries in the 6th century CE by the Huns, Buddhism revived, especially in the north-east, where it flourished for many more centuries under the kings of the Pala dynasty [of Bengal].[80]

Chatterji regards the Buddhist culture spreading into Bengal as 'Aryanization from the West', set in motion by Magadha, as Magadha was definitely to the west of Bengal. Ever since the time of the Atharva Veda, Magadha was fully Aryanized, as by then the Āryāvarta extended to the lands across the confluence. When Chatterji speaks of 'the people', he means the elite. The written record is always about the elite. But one can easily imagine the little people of Magadha continuing to speak the old languages, much more than today, with the transfusion of Middle Indo-Aryan vocabulary into the Munda languages going on slowly, new words from Indo-Aryan trickling in from time to time. We are still seeing this happening, this slow seepage, with Bhojpuri words all over Grierson's Santali samples in the *LSI*, which make them so familiar to me. The first millennium CE was not a time of turbulent change.

The cataclysms came later, in the twelfth century, when the last Buddhist kingdom, the Pālas of Bengal, finally fell. Chatterji blames it all on the 'Turks', though all over India that century was an age marked by change, with new players, and new languages, coming up from below into a position of leadership:

> During the time of the Pālas, who were professed Buddhists, Magadha seems to have flourished exceedingly. But the conquest of Bihar by the Turks in the last decade of the 12th century was fraught with disastrous results for the intellectual life and culture of the province. The story of the sack of Bihar, as preserved by Minhaj-i-Sirāj, in the Ṭabaqāt-i-Nāṣirī, is typical of what had happened all over Magadha. Catastrophes like these extinguished learning in the land. The learned men were slain, or else they fled to Nepal with such manuscripts as they could take with them . . . In Magadha, all indigenous literary culture was at an end . . . The desolation of the country favored the incoming from the South of the Musahāras and other non-Aryan (Kōl) tribes, who were partially Aryanized, and took up the Aryan speech from the Magadha people. All sense of connection with the past was lost, all knowledge of the glories of pre-Moslem

> Magadha . . . The masses were rude, and to a great extent, in the lower classes, recruited from aborigines. The new upper classes were Brahmans and Kṣatriyas as well as Kāyasths, mostly from the West: the original Brahmans, the 'Bābhans', took to agriculture and became degraded. The aristocratic communities spoke or affected Hindi (Braj-bhākha, and Awadhi) as well as Urdu.[81]

But that is only one side of the story. Sumanta Banerjee in *Unravelling the Bengali Identity* tells of local people's 'resistance to total assimilation within the Brahminical order of the *Āryāvarta*'.[82] Buddhism in Bengal had not vanished: 'the majority of the people stuck to an indigenous form of Buddhism which by the 10th-11th century was being pushed to the wall by the rising Brahminism of the ruling dynasties . . . Buddhism retreated into the shelter of a localized popular religious practice called "Dharma-puja" and followed mainly by the lower caste Bengali masses of pre-Aryan origins.'[83] The rituals of the Dharma-puja were described in a treatise called *Shunya-purana*. One section tells of how Brahmans imposed taxes on the people of Malda, and killed the 'Saddharmis', the followers of the Buddhist Dharma cult.

Because of this, the narrative continues, the god 'Dharma' (i.e. Vishnu) in his abode in Vaikuntha, got angry, and arrived on earth in the incarnation of 'Khode' (the god of the Muslims) . . .

> *Dharma hoilo Jaban rupi matheye tar kalo tupi*
> *Hatey shobhey triruch Kaman.*
> (Dharma assumed the form of a *Jaban*—a Muslim—with a black cap and a bow and arrow in his hand.)[84]

The poem goes on to describe how other members of the Hindu pantheon join Vishnu:

> *Brahma hoilo Mahammad, Vishnu hoilo pekambar*
> *Adampha hoilo Shulapani*
> *Ganesh hoiya gaji, Kartik hoilo kaji*
> *Fakir hoilya jato muni.*
> (Brahma became Muhammad, Vishnu the *paigambar*, Shiva became Adam, Ganesha became a *gaji* and Kartika a *kaji* and all the Hindu hermits became Muslim fakirs.)[85]

As in the Deccan, where the Sufis arrived a full century before the Sultanate forces, the people of Bengal came to know about Islam early. 'Arab traders and travellers had started visiting Bengal from the ninth-tenth century period. Muslim Sufi preachers arrived in Bengal in the eleventh century: Shah Sultan Rumi reached Mymensingh in the Barendrabhumi in 1053, to be followed by Baba Adam Shahid who reached Bengal at around 1119.'[86] The Sufis arrived in Bengal well in advance of the new rulers and encountered a restive population of Buddhists, unhappy with Brahmans and orthodox Hinduism and ready to turn to Muslims for protection:

> It seems that the followers of Dharma suffered much for their religious beliefs and practices from the Caste Hindus and when the Mahomedans entered Bengal as a conquering power the Dharmites took shelter under them . . . In fact, from the earliest available literature composed by Bengalis we find that it had been marked by a strong streak of anti-Brahminism.[87]

By the thirteenth century when the Muslims became rulers of Bengal, something very like modern Bengali had already taken shape, initially as separate regional dialects, and it was the language of the little people. The Hindu rulers and Hindu elites during the earlier period had not encouraged Bengali as a language of literature, preferring to stay with Sanskrit as their court language.

Literature in Bengali before the arrival of the Muslims had been limited to folk ballads, which had not been welcome in the courts of Hindu kings. Now, all of a sudden, these folk poets were being encouraged by Muslim rulers, who began to take an interest in local customs and literature.[88] The wish for change and self-assertion by the little people had found support from new rulers who had no intention of shoring up Sanskrit and the Brahman-king nexus that had dominated not just Magadha but the entire north of the subcontinent for more than a millennium. The great twelfth-century upheaval had begun. The little people and their languages were all set to shine again.

~

This is something we have been speculating about ever since we identified the period between the tenth and twelfth centuries as the time when the modern languages began to show up in the written record in South Asia. It had to be the end of a tired and unwieldy dispensation of elites spread across the north of the subcontinent who spoke closely related prakrits, and its replacement with new players who identified with the modern languages we know today. We always knew there had to be a major *event* that served as a catalyst for a flip of this magnitude. And in Bengal, where the history of the little people has been better remembered than in the rest of South Asia, we can see in detail how the end of the Buddhist era, popular resentment against Brahmans and elites, the entry of Sufis (followed by Muslim rulers), and the little people's pride in their own languages acted in concert to bring about change that was just short of revolutionary.

The early Muslim sultanates must be credited as the political force behind the emergence of all the modern languages of north India, including Dakkhini in the south. It is interesting to speculate on what South Asia would have been like had they not come when they did. From a linguistic point of view, we can imagine a continuation of a brahmanical era where Sanskrit and a family of prakrits united the land for the elites, while the languages of the little people remained below sea level, barely visible except as trade-related entries in merchants' ledgers. In the detailed story of this period in Bengal, we see exactly what made all the difference, what supported a change of this magnitude that unseated an old order and ushered in something new, with a totally new cast of local actors besides the foreigners who had taken over.

The early Muslim sultanates were the singular event that we were wondering about, that 'thing' that happened in the twelfth century that gave space for the new 'Indo-Aryan' languages to rise and grow. Even in faraway Maharashtra, an early sultanate in Ahmednagar and the sultanates in the Deccan gave a similar shot in the arm to Marathi, which was taking shape in the shadow of a written record still dominated by Sanskrit and prakrits. While Brahmans did not exactly go into decline—Maharashtra did see the rise of Shivaji and Brahman Peshwas later on—in many parts of India they never had the same kind of power over rulers as they had had over earlier kings. And this gives a tiny glimpse of why some Indians still choose to see the entry of Muslim rulers as the end of a glorious era.

~

It took something more than the little people's angst to change language in this era. The wish for a resurgence of local languages could only be spearheaded by new regimes with their own reasons to move on from the Sanskrit-Prakrit-Brahmans-Kings formula that had an immense amount of inertia behind it, having stood in place for centuries. Bengal here means both East and West Bengal: the huge hinterland of the East was more rural, and more drawn to the opportunities that the Muslim sultans offered.

And what did this new Bengali look like? In a region where time was cyclic, one does not need to wonder. What had happened millennia earlier when the Munda people faced an onslaught of Austro-Asiatic men, turning their languages into 'Austro-Asiatic' hybrids, repeated itself, with 'Indo-Aryan' hybrids coming up, not just in Bengal but all over the Māgadhan region. These were Tiramisu bears with grammars based mostly on earlier Munda languages and words drawn from the prakrits. All over the region these creole-type mixed languages had been coming up gradually for centuries, new words getting stabilized with regular use. These developments started out as local dialects, but as they turned literary, in places like Bengal, they quickly evolved standard forms. And in these Māgadhan languages, numeral classifiers, now an 'old' Austro-Asiatic feature in Munda, found a happy home.

Here is a family photograph of the Māgadhan languages, with Santali standing in for all the other Munda languages in the role of clan matriarch:[89]

Bhojpuri:	(*ham*)	*tīn-go*	*baṛā*	*gāi*	*dekh-l-ī*
Maithili:	(*ham*)	*tin-ṭā*	*paigh*	*gāi*	*dekh-l-āũ*
Bengali:	(*āmi*)	*tin-ṭe*	*baṛo*	*goru*	*dekh-l-ām*
Odia:	(*mū*)	*tin-ṭā*	*boṛo*	*goru*	*dekh-il-i*
Assamese:	(*moi*)	*tini-joni*	*dangor*	*goru*	*dekhis-il-u*
Santali:	(*iñ*)	*p-ea*	*maṛaŋ*	*gāi*	*ñei-ket'-ko-a-ñ*
	I	three-CL	big	cow	see-PAST-(3pl.O-finite)-1sg.S

'I saw three big cows'

All these languages have a numeral classifier, the verb agrees with the first-person subject, and there is no gender agreement between noun and verb, or between the adjective 'big' and the noun 'cow'. The Māgadhan languages have two verb markers, one for tense and one for subject agreement. Santali has four: tense, object agreement, finiteness and subject agreement. Assamese uses the classifier *joni*, normally used with female humans, with cow (*tā* would have suggested that *goru* was a bull). In the Māgadhan and Santali languages the subject pronoun is optional.

~

Map 12: Light grey: North Munda languages

Dark grey: South Munda languages

There is one other remarkable feature in the Munda languages that some linguists have noted, but which somehow has never been played up as significant: object marking. Northern Munda languages, Mundari, Santali, Ho, Birhor, Korku and Gorum, have markers on their verbs not only for subject agreement, but for object agreement too. Subject markers can roam around a bit, maybe even attach themselves to objects, but when they go on to verbs they come near the end. Object markers precede them. In the following examples the object markers, like the subject markers, show person and number agreement (singular-dual-plural), which links them to the objects, and are underlined and in bold. In these examples S is subject, O is object, sg and pl are singular and plural, and +trans is a transitive verb that can have an object:[90]

Mundari:

Soma	*hon-ko*	*lel-**ko**-ka-e?*
Soma	child-pl	see-**3pl.O**-3sg:S-Ques

'May Soma see the children?'

Santali:

(iñ)	*p-ea*	*maṛaŋ*	*gãi*	*ñei-ket'-**ko**-a-ñ*
I	three	big	cow	see-past-**3pl.O**-finite-1sg.S

'I saw three big cows'

Ho:

añ	*hapnam-ko-ñ*	*nel-le-ḍ-**ko**-a*
1sg.S	girl-pl-1sg.S	see-tense-[+trans]-**3pl.O**-finite

'I had seen girls'.

Birhor:

iŋ	*am-ke*	*lel-**me**-kan-a-iŋ*
1sg.S	2sg.O	see-**2sg.O**-cop-finite-1sg.S

'I am looking at you'.

Korku:

iñ	*gãw-en*	*sene-ba*	*badon*	*ḍi-ku-ke ḍo-**ku**-ba*
1sg.S	village-loc	go-non past	after	3-pl-O see-**3pl.O**-non past

'I will see them after I go to the village'.

Gorum:

e-niŋ	*laʔ-r-**iŋ**-gi*
ACC-1sg.	hit-tense-**1sg.O**-3pl.S

'They hit me'.

What these object agreement markers point to is something very old, fading out even in the Munda languages as one goes south, something that has echoes of the double marking that exists in Burushaski, Shina and the Andaman languages, where it is part of ergativity. In the northern Munda languages it is *not* about ergativity, but objects are clearly important too, and their presence needs to be marked on the verb.

The First Indian languages spoken by hunter-gatherer people in the early northwest have vanished, and so have the Indus Valley languages they made in fusion with the languages of the migrant men from the Zagros mountains. But could object marking in the Munda languages be a pointer to something that could have been a feature of the First Indian languages of the northwest? Could it have had something to do with the way split ergativity came up later, with objects taking on the starring roles in past tense sentences? Or is object marking the last glimmer of an early ergativity in exactly that place between the Karakorams and the Andamans that completes something of an arc?

What is intriguing about object marking is that it is both *like* and *unlike* the ergativity in the northwest. It gives a hint of something that may have dwindled in the Munda region, though not completely, while fencing off the Munda region as . . . different. And it dwindled further in the Māgadhan languages that came up later, which were fiercely non-ergative, though they traced their ancestry back to the Munda languages, which were not incompatible with the languages of the northwest.

~

What does this mean, the northern Munda languages having numeral classifiers as well as double marking, with both subject and object agreement on the verb? Add to this Grierson clearly stating that Munda languages also had a distinction between animate and inanimate nouns, something that amounts to a gender distinction. This is a heavy load for a language to carry. Languages either have gender, or numeral classifiers.[91] The northwest Indo-Aryan languages have grammatical gender, and the Māgadhan languages have numeral classifiers. But here in the northern Munda languages we see signs of both.

This is an indicator of transition. A language family that once had something like gender has become a classifier language, because migrant men from Southeast Asia who married local Indian women 4000 years ago spoke languages with numeral classifiers. The old animate-inanimate distinction is also clearly fading. Subject and object markers on verbs tell us things like **3plO** and **1sgS**: first/second/third person, singular/dual/plural, but not whether the subject or object is animate or inanimate. Instead, numeral classifiers now give us this information, the way in Bengali *-ṭā* tells us that the thing being counted is non-human, while *-jon* tells us that it is human.

The picture we get from this is of a Munda family that once had gender and double marking like we see in Burushaski and the Andaman languages. But when it came under the influence of Southeast Asian classifier languages, and adopted these classifiers, its animate-inanimate distinctions in nouns began to fade out.

And that may be why the languages east of the confluence today differ sharply from the western Indo-Aryan languages. We may have found the moment when the divide began, and the reason why it began. Before the Austro-Asiatic men came, it is quite likely that *all* the languages across the north of the subcontinent had some form of 'gender', and maybe even ergativity, or at the very least subject and object marking on their verbs.

It is rare, in the study of evolution, to happen upon a missing link. But the persistence of a fossilized form of gender in Munda languages, a class distinction between animate and inanimate nouns, tells us that things were not always as they are now. There had been an older system, which the numeral classifiers eclipsed.

Could it really be that simple? That once upon a time, back in the time-before-time, when it was only First Indians in this land, because no other people had yet left Africa, there was something closer to a seamlessness in the form of the languages we spoke? Not in the words, but in the sounds and the notions of grammar? Something that fit in with what we find in the languages of the Andamans and the First Australian languages to this day? Were all the languages from the Indus Valley region through the Gangetic plains to the Andaman Islands languages that had some form of 'gender' (or different 'noun classes'), subject and object marking on verbs, and maybe ergativity too? Was the Māgadhan region not an outlier in this region until the Austro-Asiatic men came, and the Munda tribes began the shift to being speakers of classifier languages, in the Southeast Asian way?

Did we just get a glimpse of primordial unity?

~

The genetics of the new Māgadhan region was less 'Indo-Aryan' than the languages, as the forces that had selected the prakrits as the lexifier languages were more political than genetic. The prakrits were not the 'father tongues' the Austro-Asiatic lexifier languages had been, with actual fathers contributing their Y-DNA to the Munda population. But the linguistic fusion was the same, in fact, even more skewed towards the Indo-Aryan. The 'maternal strand' in the languages sank below sea level to reside mostly in the substratum, while the vocabulary layer drawn from prakrit shone brightly on top, even as these new hybrid languages displaced the actual prakrits the words had come from.

Bengal was the epicentre of this activity, with huge swathes of formerly Buddhist territory becoming Muslim and new languages coming up to replace Sanskrit and the prakrits, and quickly turning into a stable literary variety. In Assam and Odisha, standard languages emerged a bit more slowly, but in the west, the former Māgadhan heartland, this process was cut short. Bhojpuri, Magahi and Maithili, while they became literary quite early, never had their literature supported by those in power. In that sense, Maithili evolved into something of a bridge between the fully fledged new languages of the east and the two dialects in the west. Bhojpuri and Magahi took on the subordinate role we began this chapter with, of little people east of the confluence speaking in a host of little Māgadhan dialects, each version representing a tiny village.

These dialects did not evolve standard varieties, as the elites in western Magadha (once again) chose to align with the language west of the confluence, and Hindi became the language of literacy and schooling. Standardization, and the ability to reach out and embrace all spheres of life, is something that only seems to happen when a language develops its own literature. Bhojpuri and Magahi instead turned into grafted varieties, like Alphonso mango trees, where a trunk with sturdy local rootstock adapted to the climate is lopped off part way, and a cutting of an exotic variety strapped on as a graft to feed off the local roots and yield flowers and fruit from a different land. Bhojpuri and Magahi remained stuck as languages of small children, rural people and the poor, and the literate sector lived and worked in Hindi.

~

We are back in present times, after a long journey into the remote past, in a part of South Asia where some of that past is still alive, and where the little people's history has been documented better than anywhere else. Thanks to geneticists, we could reach back and find the story of the Munda tribes, the first humans to have migrated out of Africa, who settled in the subcontinent 65,000 years ago. We also found that the 'orang asli' aboriginal people of the Malayan Peninsula were their close cousins from that migration, and that the Baiga and Birhor tribes in India share important genetic mutations on the M haplogroup with First Australians that tell of a parting of ways 55,000 years ago.

The first significant contact that the Gangetic Munda people had in their long millennia in the subcontinent was with a group of men from Southeast Asia who brought japonica rice with them and created a hybrid variety with indigenous Indian rice, while also sharing their genes with Munda women in India, a mixing geneticists were able to detect 4000 years later. This link to Southeast Asians was something old philologists in colonial times also suspected, after they found close matches between Munda words and words in Austro-Asiatic languages, leading them to suspect that the Munda people themselves were not aboriginal, but recent migrants from Southeast Asia. This belief persists in academia, where the Munda people and their languages are still routinely referred to as 'Austro-Asiatic'.

What we found was that the meeting between the Southeast Asian men and the Munda people had produced mixed languages, the kind of hybridization we have seen time and again in South Asia, where words from a new language of power get pasted on to an operating system that is a continuation of older local languages. That is the model this book is about, a revised creole model, where almost all basic vocabulary comes from the 'father tongue', while the 'maternal side' gets hidden away in the sound system and the grammar, though a few features of the 'father tongue' are able to slip across into the new language with the vocabulary. The presence of all this basic vocabulary does not mean that we are dealing only with the original language of the migrant men: this is the expected pattern you find in creole languages. In the Munda languages, the Southeast Asian feature that crossed with the vocabulary was the numeral classifiers—the *go*, *ṭā*, *ṭi* and *jon* we now find after numbers in all the Māgadhan languages—but 4000 years ago it would have been older avatars of these markers, which used Munda or Austro-Asiatic words, and maybe not exactly the same rules.

Was this new vocabulary incorporated into the Munda languages all at once, in an atmosphere of chaos and disruption, or was it more gradual, as more and more of the Munda people met the newcomers and adjusted to a life of plentiful rice, thanks to the new hybrid variety with its higher yields? It had to have been gradual, because it is hard to imagine an influx of men having a sudden impact over a large area in a time when there were forests all over that part of India and travel could only have been on foot, and at a walking pace. It also looks as if the Southeast Asian words that remain in the Munda languages are mostly nouns—just like the Sanskrit words in Malayalam and Persian words in Urdu, a relatively light footprint, considering how heavy the Austro-Asiatic stamp was on the paternal DNA of the Mundas.[92] Compare that with how Indo-Aryan prakrits replaced every single word or marker of the substratum languages without leaving anything like that sort of genetic imprint on the population of the north, and how English is still spreading in South Asia long after the British are gone. It is tempting to speculate that 4000 years ago a migration like this would not have resulted in a far-flung empire with new rulers and a need for people to adopt their language, even if the Austro-Asiatic men did manage to seed a lot of progeny in the new land.

But when numeral classifiers enter a language family that has 'gender', they set up a contradiction that needs to be resolved. Are the Munda languages 'gender' languages, or classifier languages? In the end the Munda languages opted to be classifier languages, and the old system of gender based on an animate-inanimate distinction began to fade out. What was left was a tectonic fault line separating the lands to the west of the confluence from the lands to the east. To the west were gender and ergativity, and to the east there was only a sliver of grammatical gender in the animate-inanimate distinction, and no ergativity, only a residual object marking on verbs that faded out the farther south one went, and a new Southeast Asian feature: numeral classifiers.

The next milestone in the history of the region coincides with the start of the historical record, and the emergence of a Māgadhan culture full of Buddhism, Jainism and the Ajivikas. While the rulers of Magadha thought of their region as different from the Āryāvarta lands to the west of the Ganga-Yamuna confluence, they and the Māgadhan elites were never out of touch with Vedic culture and knowledge. From that time (if not before) there was a cultural and linguistic gap between the Māgadhan elite and the little people, who would still have been speaking the old tribal languages, while the elites spoke Māgadhan Prakrit, Pāli and Ardhamāgadhi, and probably other prakrits that drew their vocabulary from Indo-Aryan.

The languages spoken by the little people must have absorbed vocabulary from the elite prakrits gradually, over centuries, so it is not easy to say when their spoken vernaculars reached their present shape. That is why we speak of the tenth to twelfth centuries as the period when the tide began to turn, and we begin to see these new languages in the written record. There had to have been a long run-up phase, new languages getting into place, before it all came together as a decisive flip. History was repeating itself: creole languages were again opening their newborn eyes, with vocabulary from the prakrits combined with grammar and sounds from earlier languages of the little people. Amid popular discontent on the margins, an old unwieldy Buddhist empire was still on its feet, but its vital signs were slowing.

It would take a new set of rulers coming into the area for the brittle structure of old Magadha to crack and crumble. That happened in a constellation of events in the twelfth century that brought down the last Buddhist kingdom, the Pālas of Bengal, which ruled an area where Brahmans from the west had happily set up shop. The divide between the new Brahman elite and the little people of Bengal who continued with Buddhism in clandestine cults, was total. All it took was the entry of Islam, first in the form of Sufis and then, a century later, in the form of a Muslim sultanate, for the popular angst against the old order to find common cause with the interests of the new leadership. The little people turned to the Muslim rulers for protection, and the Muslim rulers in turn lent their support to the local language, Bengali, in preference over the Sanskrit that had defined the earlier Brahman culture. Bengali, which had earlier been a language of folk ballads, blossomed into a fully fledged language of literature.

What happened in the Māgadhan region is the same as what happened in the western Indo-Aryan zone, except it had a Māgadhan flavour, as the Māgadhan languages became a separate family from the western Indo-Aryan group, with Bengali, Assamese and Odia as well as western dialects like Bhojpuri, Magahi and Maithili. An age of prakrit-speaking elites connected over the north of the subcontinent segued into a time of smaller more compact regions, with new languages drawing vocabulary from the very prakrits they replaced, and keeping grammatical operating systems from the older local languages. It was a repeat of the pattern of old, father tongues giving a top veneer to a much older motherland, except that the 'fathers' this time were a political group in power, and not actual parents.

This is not unlike the situation we find ourselves in right now: South Asia today once again has an elite connected over the entire land mass through English, another originally foreign language brought by conquerors, while our hinterland is full of local languages that are still, for the most part, alive and well.

We are again at an inflection point, in a land where time has always been cyclic, where what happened ages ago tends to happen again, but with a bit of a twist. Already our languages are drinking in English words, the way the Māgadhan and western Indo-Aryan languages lapped up prakrit words, and we are seeing new mixed varieties like Hinglish—Hindi-English—coming up, with counterparts in languages all over South Asia. It is not for historians or linguists to predict the future, but because we see trends, we get glimpses of what may just be around the corner. And if we are headed for a brighter future, it is in spite of all our mistakes, and not because we have been wise.

In the next chapter we move on to another region, which is not as trapped in the endless cycle of rebirths that Magadha sought to escape. In another journey into the remote past we will try to find out about the Dravidian people who went on to the south, and their encounters with the tribes already living there, and how they shaped each other's languages.

6

The Dravidian Dreamtime

. . . to those who've traveled through.

The Silence of a Candle, Paul Winter

The Dreamtime is an idea that comes from First Australians, fellow travellers of our ancestors, the First Indians, on the first ever migration of Homo sapiens out of Africa 70,000 years ago. It is a time-before-time when our ancestral spirits roamed the land, and all living things felt connected, and our ancestors made the living environment out of their dreams. What we are reaching for now is another origin story, and for that we will need all the old ones' imagination and ability to join pinpoints of distant light to stretch our minds back thousands of years to another Dreamtime, where we discover how the Dravidian people came to live in the south of India.

To stand on the edge of this Dravidian Dreamtime is like a moment of pause before diving into a vast lake. The longer we stand and look, the more we can see into its depths, and the less bewildering it looks. Soon we realize that while the lake is vast, we can at times see clear to the bottom, and the place begins to take on a familiar look. We have seen something like it before. If we dive in, we will not get lost.

The word 'Dravidian' is not a south Indian word. It comes from late Sanskrit, and dates back to a classification in the *Skandapurāṇa*, compiled sometime around the start of the first millennium CE. The original mention was about Brahmans, and a distinction between five groups of *Gauḍa* Brahmans in the north and five groups of *Draviḍa* Brahmans south of the Vindhyas. The word Draviḍa itself evolved from the word 'Tamil', with the *m* becoming a *v* and the final *l* becoming *ḍ*, an alternation we see in the first two verses of the Rig Veda.[1] Madhav Deshpande says that 'the term Draviḍa appears in some relatively late Dharmaśāstra works and in some poetic works, and the word Damiḷa is also found in some late Pali texts'.[2]

So the word Draviḍa itself is not old. It is not part of the early Rig Vedic Sanskrit of the time when the Vedic people first came into contact with the people who remained from the Indus Valley Civilization. It does not refer to the earlier inhabitants of the Indus Valley region. But the British liked the term and adopted it as a racial category to make a distinction between north and south Indians, as south Indian languages seemed to belong to a different family: their vocabularies had a different source from the languages of the north, which had taken all their vocabulary from local prakrits (and, in that sense, were linked to Sanskrit). 'Dravidian' languages were different, because they did not seem to be related to the Indo-European Sanskrit that so fascinated the old Western philologists.

But when we say that the people of the Indus Valley Civilization were 'Dravidian', and that the present-day people of south India are 'Dravidian', what do we mean by that? What exactly is a Dravidian?

Dravidian is not a useful term for referring to a population group, as all South Asians, barring the Andaman Islanders, are the result of a mixing of earlier and later migrant groups. It is only useful for identifying *languages* with Dravidian vocabulary, and when we say that people are 'Dravidian', we only mean that they are native speakers of one of these languages. But anyone can pick up any language: you do not need to be from a particular group to adopt its language. We need to get past these old racial labels. We are all the result of mixture.

About 9000 years ago there was a migration of farmers from the Zagros mountains of southern Iran into Mehrgarh, in what is now Balochistan. These migrants, like all migrants, would have been mostly male.[3] They came into contact with First Indians, hunter-gatherers settled all over South Asia and in the Indus Valley region too, and created mixed families as they settled down and had children with local women, and produced languages using the characteristic two-step process we have been observing since the start of this book. An early generation of children would have learnt their 'father tongue' well, but with a 'local accent', after which local people, not related to the migrants, would have adopted new words, slotting them into their old grammars. This is the same thing we saw in Chapter 5, where Indo-Aryan words slowly slipped into the Munda languages essentially without the old grammar changing.

In time, this mixed population set up the Indus Valley Civilization, and theirs would have been a language (or, more likely, a language *family*) that drew most of its words from the languages of the migrant men, while nesting them into an operating system essentially preserved from earlier local languages. The Indus Valley is too vast a terrain for there to have been just one language, especially back in those times, when connectivity between different parts of the region would have been poor. If this scenario is accurate, it would mean that the languages that we now call 'Dravidian', when they first appeared in the Indus Valley, would have been our familiar Tiramisu bear hybrids, with a strong component of earlier local languages in all but their vocabulary. That would also account for why specifically 'Dravidian' languages are not to be found outside of South Asia. Later migrants into the Indus Valley area would have followed this pattern, creating more mixed families that included local wives and half-local children. As a result, features of the First Indian languages, like retroflexion, the most iconic sound contrast in South Asia,[4] and many basic notions of grammar passed on into every new language that came up in the area. This common First Indian substratum explains why there is, to this day, a general sameness in the bedrock underpinning almost all our languages in South Asia.[5]

A 2019 genetics paper, 'The Formation of Human Populations in South and Central Asia', ventures a bit of clarity on who exactly the Dravidians might be:

> Our findings also shed light on the origin of its second-largest language group in South Asia, Dravidian. The strong correlation between *ASI* ancestry and present-day Dravidian languages suggests that the *ASI*, which we have shown formed as groups with ancestry typical of the *Indus Periphery Cline* moved south and east after the decline of the IVC to mix with groups with more *AASI* ancestry, most likely spoke an early Dravidian language. A possible scenario combining genetic data with archaeology and linguistics is that proto-

> Dravidian was spread by peoples of the IVC along with the *Indus Periphery Cline* ancestry component of the *ASI*. Non genetic support for an IVC origin for Dravidian languages includes the present-day geographic distribution of these languages (in southern India and southwestern Pakistan), and a suggestion that some symbols on ancient Indus Valley seals denote Dravidian words or names. An alternative possibility is that proto-Dravidian was spread by the approximately half of the *ASI's* ancestry that was not from the *Indus Periphery Cline*, and instead derived from the south and the east (peninsular South India). The southern scenario is consistent with reconstructions of Proto-Dravidian terms for flora and fauna unique to peninsular India.[6]

AASI refers to First Indians, the very first hunter-gatherer peoples of South Asia. *ASI* means ancestral south Indians, a mixed group, as almost all the modern populations of South Asia are the result of mixture between First Indians and later migrant groups.

Geneticists, then, have not made up their minds whether south India was settled by Dravidians only after the collapse of the Indus Valley Civilization about 4000 years ago, or whether there was a distinctive Dravidian presence in south India much before the Indus Valley Civilization went into decline, started by earlier migrants from the northwest who had met and married a different set of First Indians in the south. Was there just one Dravidian group that spread 'south and east' only after the collapse of the Indus Valley Civilization, or was there more than one group, one in the northwest, and other Dravidians already well established in the south long before the Indus Valley Civilization came apart? Did Dravidian diversity go back well into Indus Valley times, or is the Dravidian presence in the south a more recent development, which (like the Austro-Asiatic migration in the east, and the entry of the Vedic people in the Indus Valley) is exactly on the familiar 4000-years-ago milestone?

~

Let us return for a moment to the model we have been using as a compass all through this book, of migration as an activity that is male-driven, with women very unlikely to be part of an early group of explorers. We accept, because of genetic evidence, that early migrants in general tend to be male, but why is this so? Why did so many young men throughout history migrate to new lands leaving their mothers, sisters and other female family behind?

In 2023, on a visit with my family to Masai Mara in Kenya, I saw a group of gazelles, all of them young males, with horns. Our guide, Peter Kiyaa, calmly told us that this was a 'bachelor herd'. Minutes later we saw another herd where all the gazelles were female, without horns, except for one large alpha male at the centre of the herd standing guard, and one almost full-grown male already at the fringes.

'He is soon going to be driven out of the herd,' our guide announced.

The only prospect for a surplus 'bachelor' was either to defeat and replace the alpha male of his original herd, or to move on and join a new herd as its alpha male. Alpha males are powerful, but they come and go. The continuity of the herd rests in its females. There is nothing strange about young surplus males leaving the herd and moving on to new territory, and nothing strange about females staying put in their original lands.

In the Rig Veda I 32.9 there is the story of Vritra, a 'demon' that Indra slays, as he guards the 'cows' and blocks the Vedic men's access to 'wealth, prosperity and progeny'.[7] The image of Vritra is strikingly similar to the alpha male in Masai Mara who was the sole custodian of the herd of female gazelles. Had many of the other Indus Valley men moved on, heading south, leaving behind a social formation where they were not actually needed?

And immediately I remembered stories I had heard of the younger sons of nobles in Europe, not the heirs but the 'spares', with no prospect of inheriting the family property, setting out to capture new estates, replacing the lords there and marrying their widows or daughters to consolidate their status. How many of the British who came to India would have been younger sons with no prospects in Britain? And let us not forget the Namboodiri Brahmans of Kerala, among whom by tradition only the eldest son may stay in his family *īḷam* and marry a Namboodiri woman: the younger sons all have to look outside the community for partners in order to have children. In many communities around the world it has been quite standard for younger sons to move on, or go abroad: this sort of migration is no aberration brought on by hard times. And when these young males migrate, they marry local women in the new lands they settle in and create new communities.

The point here is that it would not require the fall of a civilization in the Indus Valley for its menfolk to start exploring other parts of India. Young men could have been moving on from the Indus Valley and heading south without women long before things in the northwest began to go sour, simply to get more living space for themselves, especially if the tightly knit order in the IVC had begun to show signs of fraying. Others would certainly have put off moving until climate change made the IVC unsustainable, but most of the population would have stayed back, living more modest lives. Many of us, their descendants, are still in the Extended Indus Valley Periphery region to this day, speaking new languages.

There is something that had worried me when I was thinking about the mostly male migrations from Central Asia while I was working on the story of Urdu for my earlier book, *Wanderers, Kings, Merchants*.[8] The suggestion that young Uzbek men were fleeing to India during the time of the Delhi Sultanate because of the danger posed by Changez Khan, leaving their mothers and sisters behind, just did not ring true. Wouldn't they have been just as afraid for their womenfolk as for themselves? Were they comfortable leaving them to fall into the hands of invaders? Not likely.

A more plausible scenario is that there was a population surge in mature Harappan times, a sign of prosperity, not of disaster, and that would have rekindled the age-old desire in young men to migrate and settle in new lands. We saw this later with the Vedic men and the Central Asians: but what about our earliest migrant group on record, the farmers from the Zagros mountains of southern Iran who started coming to Mehrgarh 9000 years ago? Farmers are unlikely migrants. Did they merely want more room for themselves? They too seem, from the genetic record, which tells of mixture with First Indian hunter-gatherer women, to have been mostly men. It is precisely because of the 'mostly male' character of almost all the migrations into South Asia that we have a bedrock of First Indian women in the South Asian genome.

In short: young men migrate, seeking living space, and they travel in 'bachelor herds'.

~

Why does it matter whether Dravidian language and culture all arrived in south India only after the Indus Valley Civilization had collapsed, as geneticists suggest, or whether the Dravidian presence in south India goes back to an earlier time? It matters because while the modern languages of the Indus Valley Periphery and the Extended Indus Valley Periphery are still *structurally* very similar to the Dravidian languages of south India (as we saw in Chapter 4), there is one feature that we have noted as unique to the Extended Indus Valley Periphery, and found nowhere else in South Asia: ergativity. Or split ergativity, only in the past tense. *By-me food-eaten* instead of *I ate the food.* Something in the old Indus Valley languages seemed to like ergativity. A whole mature Dravidian civilization on the move would likely have kept a feature like ergativity if it had relocated lock, stock and barrel.

The IVC languages, because of their ergativity, gave importance not only to subjects, but also to objects, in their verb marking. A feature like this exists in Burushaski, a 'double-marking ergative language' that is still spoken in the Hunza Valley, deep in the Karakoram Mountains of Pakistan. What this means is that verbs in Burushaski not only take endings to agree with their 'agents', but also prefixes that link them to their objects, and in all tenses.[9] *He woman (feminine agreement)-sees-(agreement with 'he')*, which translates as 'he sees the woman'. The verb 'sees' has to 'agree' with both 'woman' and 'he'.

And the northern Munda languages in the Māgadhan lands, tribal languages that are still alive for us to see, while not ergative, also have double marking where verbs take not only a final marker that agrees with the subject, but one before it that agrees with their object. In the Andaman Islands too, the tribal languages that date back to the very first humans who left Africa 70,000 years ago, and which have been out of touch with the South Asian mainland for about 60,000 years, are 'double-marking ergative languages', where verbs must agree with both objects and subjects.[10] Could double marking and ergativity have been common in many of the oldest languages of South Asia? Was it present in the languages of the early hunter-gatherer people of the northwest, and retained in the

Dravidian languages they made with the Zagros farmers in the Indus Valley?

Double marking in northern Munda languages still exists, but it fades out as one goes south, with the central and southern Munda languages having only subject agreement, just like the modern Dravidian languages of the south and the Māgadhan languages of the east.[11] Was this feature already missing from the languages of the southern tribes by the time the Indus Valley Dravidians began their long march south?

~

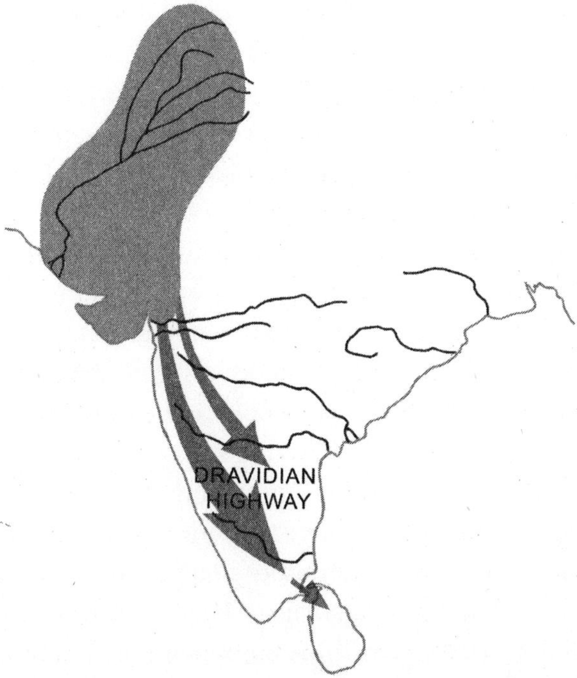

Map 13: The likely route south taken by settlers originating in the Indus Valley

Let us try to imagine those early journeys to the south. In our mind's eye are images of young men from the Indus Valley, speakers of Dravidian languages, travelling in small groups, intent on exploring and, if things go well, settling down in new lands. There isn't much of a language problem for a while, since much of the territory as far as Maharashtra is already part of the Extended Indus Valley Periphery. There will be a few people along the route who know the languages of the northwest. But part way into the journey through Maharashtra, there is a change. The people are new, and so are their languages.

The people they meet in these new lands are First Indian hunter-gatherers. This puts our Indus Valley men at an advantage, as they are part of the Bronze Age, with new skills and technology to offer. They know farming, and some of them know about working metals. This makes it easy for them to find wives and settle down, as they have not come empty-handed: they will be desirable son-in-law material. If the First Indian people they meet have not yet developed agriculture, the region will have a low population density, which means there will be much land available for settling.

How do they manage to talk to each other, the people living at the southern edge of the Extended Indus Valley Periphery and the hunter-gatherer tribal people to the south? That would not have been a problem. Populations in contact have a way of smoothening these things out, and these groups would have been in contact for a huge amount of time. By then they would have understood each other's languages, or would have developed ad hoc trade languages. People who need to be in touch do not live long with incomprehension. These two very different groups would have made the north-south borderlands feel almost as seamless as the onward linguistic journey to the end of the Indian peninsula, a smooth continuum of small dialects, with vocabulary changing slowly as one got farther and farther from the Extended Indus Valley Periphery. Our young men migrating south from the Indus Valley would not have had too hard a time communicating with the new people they met.

If the contact was only about men from the hunter-gatherer people picking up bits of a Dravidian language for trade, what would first have arisen could have been a pidgin, a rough and ready code destined to go no farther into the hunter-gatherer community. Pidgins, after all, are male languages, and intended as temporary stopgaps. But when travellers like our young IVC men crossed the periphery and started settling in the south, marrying local women and having families, words from their language, already known from trading, would begin to leak into the languages of the larger First Indian population, and soon all the young people would be using these new words. These words at first would be mostly nouns, but that is enough for essential communication. New vocabulary always comes from powerful migrant groups, who create new social formations larger and more hierarchical than the small tribal groups of old. The arrival of our young IVC men would soon bring a surge in the size of the group, partly by a new cohesion among the tribes, and partly from more food production, more sedentary living, a new generation of hybrid children, and more efficient tools and technology.

This is exactly how it happened in the Māgadhan area 4000 years ago, as we saw in Chapter 5, where there was an influx of Austro-Asiatic men into the Munda tribal lands. Hybrid people, and a high-yielding hybrid variety of rice—a mixing of local Lahuradewa rice and the japonica rice brought by the migrant men—which in turn led to a population surge and a phase change.

So the first port of call outside the IVC would have been in what we now call Maharashtra. Maharashtra in those days would have been nothing like the unified state it is now. In fact, there are many who say that to this day it is still only superficially united: there is much variation in the Marathi spoken in the different districts, evidence of a diverse group pulled together through literacy and made to align with the parts of Maharashtra that have the most cultural clout. And back in those days, before the south had become Dravidian territory, the borderland that we spoke of in Chapter 2 would have been farther north in Maharashtra, inching its way south over time like a cooling lava flow, transforming the bedrock as it went.

Who are the 'hunter-gatherers' that lived in the Maharashtra area, just beyond the Extended Indus Valley Periphery? The term 'hunter-gatherer' suggests primitive people, but were First Indian hunter-gatherers actually all that primitive? Think for a moment of the 12,000-year-old petroglyphs found in Ratnagiri, in the south of Maharashtra near the coast.[12] They are 3000 years *older* than the Indus Valley Civilization, which at the very earliest goes back to the influx of farmers into Mehrgarh, Balochistan, 9000 years ago. In *The Dawn of Everything: A New History of Humanity*,[13] David Graeber and David Wengrow caution us not to underestimate hunter-gatherers who opted not to take the plunge into cultivation and settled living. About 11,000 years ago the people of Göbelki Tepe in south-eastern Turkey produced 'monumental architecture . . . pillars, at least 200 in total', each one 'a unique work of sculpture, carved with images from the world of dangerous carnivores and poisonous reptiles':

> The main source of puzzlement is a group of twenty megalithic enclosures, initially raised there around 9000

> BC, and then repeatedly modified over many centuries . . . The creation of these remarkable buildings implies strictly coordinated activity on a really large scale . . . But the larger question remains: who made them? While groups of humans not too far away had already begun cultivating crops at the time, to the best of our knowledge those who built Göbelki Tepe had not. Yes, they harvested and processed wild cereals and other plants in season, but there is no compelling reason to see them as 'proto-farmers', or to suggest that they had any interest in orienting their livelihoods around the domestication of crops.[14]

And here is what Graeber and Wengrow had to say about the early Britons who built Stonehenge:

> Still more striking, the people who built Stonehenge were not farmers, or not in the usual sense. They had once been; but the practice of erecting and dismantling grand monuments coincides with a period when the peoples of Britain, having adopted the Neolithic farming economy from continental Europe, appear to have turned their backs on at least one crucial aspect of it: abandoning the cultivation of cereals, from around 3300 BC, to the collection of hazelnuts as their staple source of plant food. On the one hand they kept hold of their domestic pigs and herds of cattle, feasting on them seasonally . . . the builders of Stonehenge seem to have been neither foragers nor herders, but something in between.[15]

In other words, the transition to farming in the IVC probably had more to do with the culture of the migrants from the Zagros mountains than First Indian hunter-gatherers, north or south, being in any way less . . . 'evolved'.

The southward journey of our hypothetical IVC men is way back in the remote past, but we can still see traces of their early linguistic contacts with the First Indian peoples beyond the IVC Periphery. When we get below the surface homogeneity of modern Marathi and see how Marathi is actually spoken in the southern parts of Maharashtra, we begin to see the end of the Extended IVC Periphery, where the grammatical feature we are interested in abruptly vanishes. In the Marathi of Solapur, in southern Maharashtra, not far from Ratnagiri, which is near Mumbai, there is no ergativity. Instead of saying *by-him chilli-pepper-eaten*, in Solapur you would say *he ate the chilli-pepper*, and instead of saying *by-him/her book-read*, you would say *he/she read the book*:[16]

Standard Marathi:	*tyāne mirchī khāllī* [ergative]
Solapur dialect:	*to mirchī khāllo* [non-ergative]
Standard Marathi:	*tyāne pustak vāchle* [ergative]
Solapur dialect:	*to pustak vāchlā/tī pustak vāchlī* [non-ergative]

In the first example *khāllī*, 'eaten', is feminine to agree with *mirchī*, 'chilli-pepper', but in the second example it is *khāllo*, masculine to agree with *to*, 'he'. And in the next example we have *vāchle*, the past participle 'read', with a neuter ending to agree with *pustak*, 'book', which is neuter in Marathi, though in Solapur we would get *vāchlā* (masculine) or *vāchlī* (feminine) depending on whether the subject is 'he' or 'she'.

The important point here is that these are not native speakers of Kannada struggling with gender in Marathi. These are native speakers of Marathi who get Marathi genders right, but do not have ergativity. They are, in this sense, on the same wavelength as the Dakkhini speakers we met in Chapter 2, who have Urdu-style grammatical gender but no ergativity. Think back to the Hyderabadi man in Chapter 2 who was foxed by the northerner who said *āpne namāz paṛhī*? ('by-you namāz-done?'), with *paṛhī* feminine to agree with *namāz*, instead of *āp namāz paṛhe*? ('did you do namāz?') where *paṛhe* is masculine as its 'subject' is a man. Ergativity is missing in Dakkhini, but grammatical gender is alive and well!

The actual 'twilight zone' between north and south, in Maharashtra as in the Deccan, is a region with *stable* languages that have grammatical gender but no ergativity. It is only south of the twilight zone that grammatical gender disappears, though natural gender remains in the he/she/it distinction in Kannada, Telugu and Tamil. Think of the distinction in Tamil between the three natural genders marked by these verb endings:

avan sāpaḍarān	he eats
avaḷ sāpaḍarā	she eats
adı sāpaḍadı	it eats

Gender, it seems, did not rankle Dravidians all that much, not the way it bothered the Māgadhans, who simply ignored all calls for gender agreement, be it on verbs or adjectives. The start of the twilight zone must have been farther to the north 4000 years ago, but there was still an unmistakable 'border' to be crossed between the Extended IVC Periphery and the south, and it was a border defined by ergativity, not by the look of present-day Marathi, with all its Indo-Aryan vocabulary. The southern Maharashtrians, who to this day speak Marathi without ergativity, call to mind the children of our young IVC men who married First Indian women and settled south of the 'border'.

If this is an accurate picture of the Dravidian settlement of the south, what it says is that there would have been a *further* hybridization of the Dravidian population, similar to the earlier one that occurred when the men from the Zagros mountains of southern Iran came to the Indus Valley and mixed with First Indians to make what we now call Dravidian people. This time it was Dravidian men from the IVC, themselves hybrids from an earlier mixing, travelling south and settling down to have children with new groups of First Indians, people whose languages would have differed in a few significant ways from the languages spoken by the First Indians who met the Zagros farmers in the Indus Valley a few thousand years before. In South Asia, it seems, time travels in circles, the past repeating itself over and over again. What happens next in this land is almost always a story that we have heard before.

~

Ever since the geneticists got into the game, there has been no doubt that the people of the IVC Periphery and the people of the south have the same lineage: in short, they are both Dravidian.[17] But what the geneticists have not yet been able to say is *when* the Dravidians of the IVC first reached the south. There have been no reports of ancient DNA from burial sites that could give us a date when people from the IVC first arrived in the south.

Does it matter whether Dravidians reached the south before the fall of the IVC, or whether some (or many) of them headed south a mere 4000 years ago? Could things have turned out the same regardless of whether Dravidian migrants reached the south before—or after—the fall of the IVC?

It all depends on whether we imagine the migrants to have been mostly men, or whether we imagine them as families uprooted and transplanted, with all their memories and languages intact, into the soil of south India, many of them not mixing with locals at all. Did only men go, or did women and families go too? If the migration from the IVC to the south was male-driven, it does not matter when they left the IVC. When men migrate alone, they marry local women or they go extinct, and their languages change, subtly at first, as their children have different 'mother tongues'. But when women migrate, old communities revive to live again, with scarcely a hiccup.

When Indian migrants to the Caribbean were only men, in the early days, any children they could have had would have been with local women, and these children would have been absorbed into the local African communities their mothers belonged to.[18] These men were not explorers, or conquerors, out to change the world: they were just little people fitting in as best they could. But when Indian *women* began to migrate as indentured labour, after the 1860s, even when most of them travelled without husbands, but maybe with children, an Indian community emerged, a remake of the Indian world they had left behind in their villages in India. The right question to ask, then, is not *when* Dravidian migrants started heading south, but whether the migrants were at least at first almost all male, or whether they were refugees, a mix of men and women. Women will always be a smaller proportion of any migrating group, but a reasonable mix capable of perpetuating an old way of life would be 20 to 30 per cent women.[19]

Women do go, but later, after the dust has settled and there is a new world in place, with a core of pioneers who settled there first. The founders. There is a term linguists use: 'founder effect'. It means that those who get there first set the tone and get to decide what the language will be. It doesn't matter how many others follow later on: the founders are the ones who leave their stamp, the first men, who travelled light and married the local women. Families from the IVC probably headed south later, with women and children, once the news got back that there was land there, and opportunity. But these newcomers would have had to change their ways to fit in with a new frontier society.

And it is not only women who need a new world up and running before they migrate. Many men too would find themselves at a loss in a world of explorers and pioneers. Artists. Intellectuals. Men who could only find a niche in a complex urban society. Goldsmiths. If we go by Bahata Mukhopadhyay's understanding of the Indus Valley seals,[20] goldsmiths played a central role in the economic life of the IVC. They not only made jewellery in gold, silver and copper, but were also linked to a system of licences, permits, assaying metals for purity, hallmarking and taxation, and possibly currency too. While some goldsmiths, like my great-great grandfather, left India for a less-than-urban outpost like the Caribbean sugar estates in the 1870s, most would not have been ready to leave a running set-up like the IVC, even in decline, until they had a sense that the new settlements in the south were ready for business.

An urban civilization with families migrating in response to a climate emergency would have preserved some nostalgic memories of an earlier urban existence, though small groups of rugged male pioneers would probably have been less inclined to keep looking back as they went. There is enigmatic mention in Old Tamil literature, dating back to the second century CE, of Vēḷ chieftains who had migration memories of Gujarat, and of a city, Araiyam, which means a city divided into two sections, and calls to mind the layout of the IVC cities.[21] There is also medieval Tamil commentary that refers to the Vēḷ chieftains as migrating south from Gujarat and introducing agriculture and irrigation to the deep south.

~

Was there a link between metalwork in the IVC and in the south? Were there archaeologists looking for correspondences? In Bangalore I met an archaeologist, Sharada Srinivasan, who was investigating excavations in the Nilgiris with gold and high-tin bronze artefacts that went back as far as 1000 BCE.

In her paper, 'Ancient Nilgiri Metallurgy: the Nilgiris in the Iron Age',[22] she looks at the 'long-standing continuities' between present-day crafts in the Nilgiri area and jewellery items recovered from the Nilgiri cairns, and sees a link to the goldsmithing style of the IVC:

> The prehistory of the Nilgiris is intriguing, having yielded some of the earliest surviving specimens of gold jewellery from the subcontinent in the post-Harappan period. The rich but rare finds of gold jewellery from some Nilgiri cairns, demonstrating skills of stone setting, filigree, and granulation . . . may date from the early or mid-first millennium BCE to CE, according to some commentators such as Knox (1985). The gold granulation technique in some of the earrings from the Nilgiris, where tiny gold spheres were formed due to surface tension, may suggest Hellenistic influences, and is found, for example, in jewellery discovered in Taxila. However, the use of gold micro-beads was also noted at much earlier Harappan sites such as Lothal and Mohenjo Daro.[23]

Is there evidence of collaboration between goldsmiths in the IVC and in the south that goes back to an earlier time, closer to the last days of the IVC? There could be, but we have not found it yet. Nevertheless, the signs of IVC influence in the south 3000 years ago, and the thought of IVC craftsmen sharing their skills with tribal goldsmiths in the Nilgiris, suggest a continuing trickle from the northwest to the south.

And as if on cue I suddenly got a message from Sharada Srinivasan with a link to an article about a habitation-cum-burial site in Mayiladumparai, Tamil Nadu, where radiocarbon dating confirmed that iron was used in Tamil Nadu as early as 4200 years ago, a time when the IVC was still in its mature phase. She was about to analyse some of the iron artefacts. According to the article, 'the excavations have led to three major findings – that the Iron Age in Tamil Nadu has been identified as early as 2172 BCE; that the late Neolithic phase (or the last part of the Stone Age) has been identified before 2200 BCE; and that black-red pottery [common in the IVC] was introduced in the late Neolithic phase itself and not in the Iron Age.'[24] Was there wheel-made pottery from the IVC in the south before their craftsmen had begun to work with iron? Or was it pottery made on potters' wheels in the south, using a new technique brought from the IVC, and shared with local craftsmen? Was this sharing of skills something that went in tandem with a sharing of IVC genes?

A year earlier 'findings from archaeological excavations in Sivakalai, Thoothukudi district indicated that there was possibly a city civilization in South India as long back as 3,200 years ago', and 'that these findings could potentially establish a connection between the Indus Valley Civilization and Tamil civilization'.[25]

Iron has been known in the tribal lands of Bastar since time immemorial. It was not only mined but also smelted and worked by tribal craftsmen who had nothing to do with the IVC. But iron found in the deep south is generally seen as a marker of urbanization. Was the south already beginning to urbanize, and full of craftsmen well placed to collaborate with metal smiths from the IVC who came as settlers? Intriguingly, Sharada Srinivasan in a conference lecture mentioned a word she heard from a colleague in Sindh, Pakistan, the local Sindhi name for a vessel she knew from south India, and which was very close to the name for it in Tamil Nadu in the Chola era.

> The word in Tamil and Malayalam for this vessel is *olaveṭṭu* or *talaveṭṭu*. And I found *veṭṭil* was mentioned in a Chola inscription. What intrigued me was that the term *veṭṭu/veṭṭil* is similar to a Sindhi word *waṭṭau*, which I came across when a Pakistani showed a similar-looking vessel on Facebook and I asked what it was called.[26]

Could this similarity point to an old connection between the south and the IVC, an old Tamil name, *veṭṭil/veṭṭu*, that goes back to IVC times? Yes, and maybe no. I have no doubt that a huge number of words in Tamil and the other southern Dravidian languages, including these two, *veṭṭil/veṭṭu*, trace back to the IVC. That is precisely what we have been tracking in this chapter: words and other features from IVC languages travelling south with migrants around the time that the IVC was going into decline. If words like *veṭṭil/veṭṭu* existed in Old Tamil, they must go back to similar words in IVC languages.

But the similarity with a modern Sindhi word is a surprise, too good to be true. Sindhi, after all, is in touch with Brahui, a Dravidian language of Balochistan that some think of as a possible relict IVC language, and others see as a relative newcomer in the area, brought by a Dravidian group from peninsular India migrating north long after the IVC languages had disappeared. Was *waṭṭau* a word that had come into Sindhi from Brahui? I dashed off a WhatsApp message to Nazir Shakir Brahui, director of the Brahui Research Institute in Pakistan. Had he heard this word before?

'Yes,' he replied. 'This word or vessel is an important part of Brahui culture. Because the Brahui live in the mountains, there is no concept of jug and glass, therefore we eat and drink water or curry in it. Basically in Brahui it is called *vaṭo*.'[27]

So here, in Brahui, is a word no longer used in modern Tamil, a memory from the Chola era. A word for an *olaveṭṭu* that, Sharada

Srinivasan says, is very much the preserve of the Kammalar community, an old community of hereditary craftspeople in Tamil Nadu that is essentially Hindu.[28] In the Brahui community in Pakistan, however, the *vaṭo* was not traditionally made of bronze. According to Nazir Shakir Brahui, in early times they were made of stone, and later of wood. It is only recently that they are being made of bronze. Time, in the subcontinent, is truly circular, and the bronze *vaṭo* is back where it belongs.

~

Map 14: Dark grey: tribal Dravidian languages

Light grey: mainstream Dravidian languages

When we look at the languages of southern India today, we find them divided into tribal Dravidian languages and mainstream Dravidian languages like Telugu, Kannada, Malayalam and Tamil. How are these two groups different? Is there something particularly 'tribal' in the structures or vocabularies of the tribal languages that sets them apart from Telugu, Kannada, Malayalam and Tamil? Are they, in some sense, *less* Dravidian than the mainstream Dravidian languages? More like the Munda languages of the north? I looked far and wide, and asked every linguist I knew who worked on Dravidian languages to tell me, but I was met with a deafening silence. The most those in the know would say is that tribal Dravidian languages differed in having no scripts of their own and no literature. Every article I read seemed to go no further than listing the languages in each category, stopping short of giving me any *linguistic* reason why they might fall into two separate groups. The only differences between the Dravidian languages ever mentioned seemed to be geographic.

In desperation I turned my attention to the largest tribal Dravidian language, Gondi. What made Gondi a 'tribal' language and not just another Dravidian language? And so I chanced upon a very lucid write-up about the Gonds and their language in an article online from *World Culture Encyclopedia*, Vol. 4: People of India:[29]

> Little is known about the origins of the Gonds. They belong to the strata of aboriginal peoples of India who pre-date the Aryan and Dravidian speakers of the country. They are usually classified as Proto-Australoids by race. As their language is Dravidian, the Gonds may have passed through lands to the south where the Dravidian languages are found. DNA evidence suggests they might have branched off from early Proto-Australoids who

> apparently traveled from Africa to Australia along the coastal margins of India. But Gond migrations before they reached their present homeland remain shrouded in the mists of time. Scholars believe that the Gonds settled in Gondwana between the 9th and 13th centuries AD. The core region of Gondwana can be considered to be the eastern part of the Vidarbha region of Maharashtra, the parts of Madhya Pradesh immediately to the north of it, and parts of the west of Chhattisgarh.

This article recognizes the enigma: a group that seems to be First Indian speaks what is unequivocally classed as a Dravidian language. The mismatch between the Gonds' ethnicity and the genetics of their language leads the author to speculation not very different from the thoughts that had been going through my head:

> Gondi is the mother tongue of the Gonds. It belongs to the Dravidian family of languages and is closely related to Tamil and Kannada. Clearly, the Gonds are not physically related to the Dravidian-speaking peoples of India, thus at some time they must have abandoned an earlier language in favour of Gondi. There is, however, no evidence of what this language might have been. It is the Gondi language, as much as anything else, that lends a sense of cultural uniformity to the diverse tribal groups that make up the Gonds. Even so, many Gonds are bilingual or trilingual, speaking Hindi, Marathi, or Telugu as well as their mother tongue. Some Gond groups have totally abandoned Gondi and speak the language or dialect common in their locality.

On the face of it, this is not strange at all. You and I are now having our conversation in English, though we probably have no genetic link to the English people. We both picked up their language second-hand. This happens all the time, when powerful groups spread into new lands and change the politics, making it necessary (or simply desirable) for local groups to learn their languages, after which their own earlier languages often fall by the wayside. Genetic heritage often correlates with language loyalties, but it is not the only way a new migrant language can spread.

In 2023, I travelled in East Africa where a local language, Swahili, had come up in the wake of male-driven Arab migration to coastal East Africa. The name Swahili comes from an Arabic word, *sāḥil*, which means 'coast'. As on the Malabar coast of India, Arab men had been coming for centuries in their dhows for trade and had set up families with local women, converting the group to Islam later, after the time of the Prophet Muhammad. Swahili was never seen as a version of Arabic: it was always classed as a Bantu language, though many of its nouns, and some other words, had been drawn from Arabic.

On a walking tour through Stone Town in Zanzibar, we had a guide who was excited about history, and full of information about early times. Arab men *had* come and set up families with local matriarchs, going on to have hybrid children who spoke Swahili, but these were not the only Africans who converted to Islam and had Swahili as their native language. A sizeable number of Africans with no Arab ancestry also became Swahili-speaking Muslims.

According to our guide, these two groups did not really merge. The Arab influx into East Africa had had one dismal side to it: slavery. While the 'Arab' families were safe from the slave traders, African Muslims who had no Arab ancestry were not. Africans, even Swahili-speaking African Muslims, were often trafficked to the Middle East, where the men lived out their lives as eunuchs in Arab households.

The difference between the two groups, then, was not in their religion or language. It was a lingering ethnic division that kept one group conscious of having once been a target while the other lived in relative safety. Could this be something like our continued separation of Dravidian languages into 'tribal' and mainstream? Had the early Dravidian men migrating south from the IVC mixed their genes with only *some* of the First Indian people of the south, while other tribal groups on the sidelines had to absorb their influence indirectly?

~

Santoshi Markam, a journalist from Abujhmad, Chhattisgarh, who writes in Gondi, shared with me her insider view of the relationship between Gondi and Dravidian languages like Tamil and Telugu. She did not talk of 'mainstream' and 'tribal' Dravidian languages. Instead, she saw them as Dravidian languages of the plains, and Dravidian languages that had been pushed aside to occupy hilly regions that were thickly forested. Gonds had memories of having once lived in the plains, and of a confluence of rivers that was still sacred to them.

Which languages were the older ones? She thought it was just possible that languages like Gondi were older. While Gondi had more grammatical features in common with Telugu, its closest neighbour to the south, it seemed to have more words in common with Tamil. Her partner, Venkat Kishan Prasad, a native speaker of Telugu, said that there were a number of Gondi words that had once been common in Telugu, but had since fallen out of use, though they were still used in Tamil. This gave the impression of Gondi being in recent contact with Tamil, which it actually was not.

Gondi is not exactly like the mainstream Dravidian languages. Like Munda in the north, Gondi also has a retroflex *ṛ*, often in free variation with plain *r*, which the mainstream Dravidian languages do not have, and the aspirated stop consonants *kh, ćh, ṭh, th* and *ph*.[30] It also has two natural genders, masculine and 'non-masculine', which combines feminine and neuter.[31] Kannada, Tamil and Malayalam have three natural genders in their third-person pronouns: masculine, feminine and neuter. But Telugu also only has two, according to K.V. Subbarao, when you get past the old prescriptive grammars that yearn for a sameness in all the Dravidian languages. Telugu, like Gondi, has only masculine and non-masculine, 'based on subject-verb agreement', which makes Gondi all of a sudden look like less of an outlier.[32] And Malayalam, for its part, has no subject-verb agreement at all.

These two natural genders, as in all Dravidian languages, only affect verb agreement, never nouns and adjectives. Finite verbs take 'a person-number-gender agreement suffix . . . The agreement is between the pronoun (subject) and the final suffix on the verb', with gender differences only showing up in third-person forms:[33]

Subject	Object	Verb stem (past)	
nannā	*mal-d-un*	*sūḍ-t-ōn*	'I saw a peacock'
maraṭ	*mal-d-un*	*sūḍ-t-āṭ*	'We (incl.) saw a peacock'
mommoṭ	*mal-d-un*	*sūḍ-t-ōm*	'We (excl.) saw a peacock'
(v)ōr	*mal-d-un*	*sūḍ-t-ōr*	'He saw a peacock'
ad	*mal-d-un*	*sūḍ-t-a*	'She/it saw a peacock'

The pronouns in Gondi also feel like familiar Dravidian words. Grierson lists *nannā* for I, and *ōr*, he, 'corresponding to Tamil or Malayalam *avar*, Kannarese *avaru*'. The neuter form is *ad*, she or it, corresponding to *adı* in Tamil and 'Kannarese'.[34] But there are enough other words from the north in Gondi that I recognize for me not to feel lost when I go through Grierson's sample texts of Gondi in the *Linguistic Survey of India*, Vol. IV. Over millennia the rough edges between our languages have smoothened, just as young fold mountains grind down over time to become gentle hillocks.

Gondi has other Dravidian words, like the numbers from one to seven: *undi, rāṇḍ, mūṇḍ, nālūṅg, saiyūṅg, sajgi* and *yeṛūṅg*. The same numbers in Tamil are *ondrı, iraṇḍı, mūndrı, nāṅgı, aiṇḍı, ārı* and *ēzhı*.[35] Gondi must be very old, since *nālūṅg*, four, has both the *l* of Malayalam *nālı* and the *ṅg* of Tamil *nāṅgı*. Also *yeṛūṅg*, which is *ēzhı* in modern Tamil, raises the question whether the *zh* in Tamil and Malayalam, found nowhere else in India and pronounced as *ḷ* in many colloquial varieties of Tamil, is not, perhaps, a recent innovation.

This is not as heretical as it sounds, the thought that Tamil is not 'old'. It is just an observation that smaller languages off the great highway are often good repositories of forms that mainstream languages may have moved on from, or chosen not to adopt, during their evolutionary journey. Just as Gondi has been open to new influences over the ages, so has Tamil, which is why linguists are cautious about calling any language 'the oldest'. When, in its long innings, did a language reach its present shape? And what, in all the shape-shifting, can we declare to be its present shape, especially with Tamil, which has so much variety? We cannot even take for granted that the languages of the Andamans, which we imagine to have been free of outside influence for as many as 60,000 years, are exactly the same as they were when they left the Horn of Africa 70,000 years ago. To be alive is to adapt, whenever the need arises. Only the dead cease to change and have to be 'preserved'.

~

The picture that emerges is of a Dravidian people who first came into existence in the northwest of the subcontinent as a hybrid group, when First Indian hunter-gatherers met and interbred with farmers who came as migrants from the Zagros mountains of southern Iran, starting 9000 years ago. That is probably the best explanation for why, as Grierson says, 'with regard to the Dravidian languages the attempt to connect them with other linguistic families outside India is now generally recognized as a failure, and we must still consider them as an isolated family'.[36] The fusion of words from the Zagros mountains on to the highly agglutinative structure of First Indian languages, with retroflexion as a distinctive feature of the sound system, created a chimera with no obvious relatives outside of South Asia.

The story of Dravidian settlement in the south seems to be the same as all the other migrations into South Asia and within India: there was probably an advance party made up of young men who explored and settled in lands beyond the Extended Indus Valley Periphery, first in what is now Maharashtra and the Deccan. Some of these men would have left the Indus Valley region only after the Indus Valley Civilization had begun to decline, when its urban infrastructure was in disarray, but it is hard to imagine that the exploration had not begun earlier, as young men are wont to strike out for new lands just to get a bit more living space for themselves. In either case, if the first migrants were young men, as they always seem to be, the first Dravidians to settle in the south would have found themselves wives from among the local population, and this would have brought a second hybridization, as an already hybrid Dravidian population from the northwest met and further mixed their genes with a different set of First Indians in the south, with signs of the new contact being recorded in the languages they made.

But genetic mixture was not the only way the Dravidian languages of the northwest spread in the south. There were groups of First Indians in the south, tribes that did not mix with the Dravidian migrants, but who absorbed their languages second-hand, resulting in a large number of 'tribal Dravidian languages'. These were not substantially different from the four mainstream Dravidian languages, Tamil, Malayalam, Kannada and Telugu, but the tribal Dravidian languages were spoken by groups that were fully First Indian in terms of their genetic heritage.

The existence of all these tribal Dravidian languages tells us that the Dravidian culture may have been strong enough that even tribal groups not related to the migrant men felt a need to learn their languages. This does not suggest small, isolated groups of migrant men, but a large and far-reaching Dravidian presence capable of transforming a tribal south into a homogeneous networked place where the languages of older groups were eventually lost.

Or maybe the tribal and the mainstream Dravidian languages look alike because both have a substratum of local First Indian languages. Did the new 'frontier' Dravidian languages of the south already incorporate most of the features of the local First Indian languages? Was it the same sort of situation as we found in Chapter 2 where Dakkhini looked a lot like northern Urdu, but differed because it had a southern substratum? In both cases we are looking at the same feature, ergativity, which defines the Extended Indus Valley Periphery languages, but which goes starkly missing in the south. Did the mainstream Dravidian languages of the south evolve as more 'tribal' in their grammar, while the tribal languages became more 'Dravidian' as they replaced old vocabulary with words from the newcomers' languages? It could have been as simple as that.

So were the Dravidians a 'peaceful' migration? It would be nice to think so. Even the descendants of Indo-Aryans in the north like to project themselves as good people who somehow managed, despite that, to leave their linguistic stamp on three-quarters of South Asia. But the kind of clout that the Indo-Aryan and the Dravidian migrants wielded indicates a ruthlessness and military might that people of our times find uncomfortable to contemplate. Indeed, the very existence of large language families in those early days tells of a transition from small and diverse tribal groups to something more like kingdoms, and the start of a centralization of power and language that continues into our present age.

What does this make the Dravidian languages of the south? How close would they be to the languages of the IVC? At a guess I would say: very close, as close as Dakkhini is to northern Urdu—another case of an advance party of northern men migrating south, marrying local women and losing ergativity. This would make southern Dravidian languages Tiramisu bear hybrids, new languages with a few details different from the IVC languages, things that did not matter in the First Indian languages of the south that could have been lost. But there seems to be a core of features, and even words, that take us back to the first Dravidian languages of the IVC. Every time we hear the words for numbers, and pronouns, that sound alike in the different Dravidian languages today, our antennae should tingle, because we are probably in the presence of something very old. We cannot prove this—there were probably as many languages in the IVC family as there are Dravidian languages in south India today—but it is a possibility I would happily bet on. It may just be that something close to Language X is alive and well in south India.

In the next chapter we complete the four-cornered journey this book takes, looking as far back as we can see into the languages of the northwest, the north-east, the south and now the northern edge of South Asia, where Nepali combines features of east and west that we have up to now thought incompatible. Could there be a linguistic duck-billed platypus, so to speak, a language that lays eggs but is still a mammal? In the Kathmandu Valley of Nepal and in Darjeeling and Sikkim to the east, the Nepali language defines another edge of the cooling lava flow into the subcontinent as Indo-Aryan pushes its way northwards into Tibetan language space.

7

A Chimera on the Northern Rim

. . . a peaceful balance to be found, just beyond . . .

The Silence of a Candle, Paul Winter

Nepali is a language that has always felt familiar to me. I am a speaker of Bhojpuri, the Indian language whose territory lies directly south of Nepal, so there are many words in Nepali that call up memories and take me back to my childhood. Nepali is also written in Devanagari, which allows me to follow the signs, in more than one sense, and find my way.

At first I didn't think about its grammar, beyond noting that it seemed to have gender, and ergativity, the thing that in some Indo-Aryan languages turns sentences around in the past tense and makes verbs suddenly agree with their objects. If Nepali lined up with Hindi, I reasoned, it could not be a Māgadhan language like Bhojpuri or Bengali, however familiar the vocabulary sounded, because Māgadhan languages do not have gender and ergativity.

But on a visit to Darjeeling and Sikkim, in West Bengal, I heard familiar endings on numbers that reminded me of classifiers in Bengali and Bhojpuri, and they stopped me in my tracks. I would get whiffs of people saying *euṭā*, meaning one, or *duīṭā*, *tinṭā*, two, three. And I also heard *ekjana*, or *ek-dzana*, one-person, which we would also hear in Bhojpuri folk tales before *jana* fell out of use.

Were they speaking Bengali? No, it was Nepali, but with an almost Bengali touch in the numbers. Was it only Darjeeling and Sikkim that had these Bengali-sounding numbers, or were they also used in Nepal? I checked. Yes, numbers like these existed in Nepal too. There was no doubt about it. Nepali had numeral classifiers.

Numeral classifiers are the endings, common all over East and Southeast Asia, that we found in Chapter 5 in the Māgadhan languages of eastern India and Bangladesh. These languages make a distinction between numbers in a mathematical sense, like 'two plus two equals four', and separate countable items, like two separate glasses of water, as opposed to the total quantity of water in the two glasses. When numbers refer to separate countable items, they must be followed by a classifier. In Bengali the classifier used with 'things' is *ṭā*, with a diminutive *ṭi*. In Bhojpuri it is *go*, with a variant *ṭho*. In Maithili, another Bihari language spoken just south of Nepal, it is *goṭā*. And in the Nepali of Nepal it is *woṭā*, with variants *ṭā/ṭi/goṭā/oṭā*. 'One' in Nepali is *euṭā/ek-woṭā*, 'two' is *duīṭā/duī-woṭā*, and 'three' is *tinṭā/tīn-woṭā*.

~

What is strange is that grammatical gender and numeral classifiers are normally not found in the same language.

Grammatical gender and numeral classifiers have a largely complementary distribution in the languages of the world.[1] Recall how, in Chapter 5, we found the importance of the old inanimate-animate gender distinction fading when the Munda languages became classifier languages. Languages in South Asia either have grammatical gender or numeral classifiers, making Nepali one of those rare 'cross-linguistically complex systems',[2] with numeral classifiers, grammatical gender *and* ergativity.

A linguistic duckbill platypus, as it were: a language that has a beak and lays eggs but is still a furry mammal.

Nepali is supposed to go back to a migration, about 500 years ago, of people known as the Khasas who travelled eastwards from the Karnali-Seti river valley of western Nepal and settled down in the lower valleys of the Gandaki River and started rice cultivation.[3] Nepali was actually once known as Khaskura. The Khasas were speakers of an old language related to Kumaoni and Garhwali, Pahari languages spoken in Uttarakhand in the Indian Himalayas, with grammatical gender and the split ergativity found in the north-western Indo-Aryan languages. In the eighteenth century, Prithvi Narayan Shah raised an army and conquered the foothills of the Himalayas and made his kingdom there, with Gorkhali, the language of the Gorkhas, as his official language, and began the unification of Nepal.[4] The Gorkhali language later came to be known as Nepali.

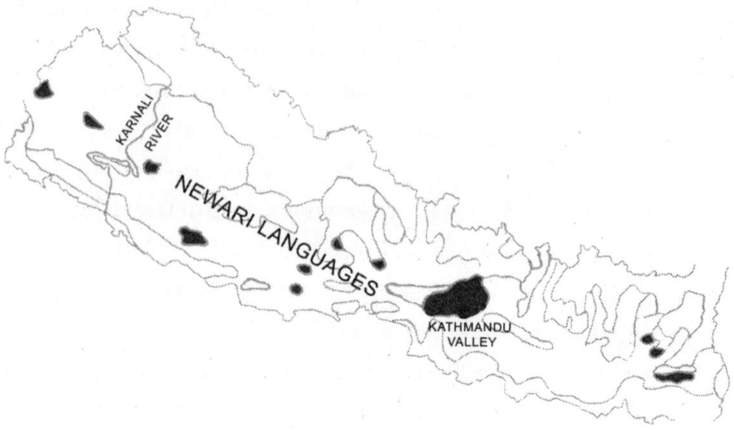

Map 15: Dark grey: Newari languages

Note the concentration of Newari speakers in the Kathmandu Valley

This is a familiar tale: a powerful group with knowledge of farming migrates into an area and makes it their home. But the place they choose is not an empty land: there are people already living there, people not taken into account when this sort of history is written. Again and again in South Asia we find migrants, mostly men, entering sparsely populated regions and settling down with local women. Then comes a population surge, because of cultivation, a more sedentary population, mixed children and new mixed languages, initially almost identical to the migrants' language, but with new features appearing as more locals join in. The 1500s is a bit late for an origin story. Shouldn't there, in Nepal, have been earlier inhabitants, maybe tribal groups that spoke Tibeto-Burman languages?

When I looked for numeral classifiers in Tibetan, the language family in northern Nepal, I drew a blank. Tibetan seemed to be the only language group in an Asia that included China, Japan, Korea and Southeast Asia that did *not* have numeral classifiers.[5] So where had the numeral classifiers in Nepali come from?

When I shifted my attention to Newari, a Tibeto-Burman language of Nepal, it was like a break in the clouds. The Newar[6] are an indigenous people of Nepal who have lived in the Newar kingdom of Nepal Mandala since prehistoric times. Early on, the Newar embraced Buddhism, and about 10 per cent of them are still Buddhist.[7] Newari has three main dialects: Dolakhā Newari, Pahari and Kathmandu Newari, all with numeral classifier systems very similar to Nepali. There had also been early contact between the Newar of Kathmandu and the Māgadhan lands in India. The Malla, a Newar dynasty that ruled Kathmandu from the thirteenth century, had patronized Maithili, a Māgadhan language from Mithila in Bihar, just south of Nepal, inviting Maithili Brahman priests and their families to settle in Kathmandu. Before the Khasas travelled east 500 years ago, the main inhabitants of the valley were either the Newar or their progenitors.[8] The Newar were the local people the Khasa rice farmers had met when they arrived as settlers in the Kathmandu Valley.

What is special about Newari is that it has a numeral classifier system that 'consists of perhaps fifteen common classifiers that are chosen based on inherent semantic features of the noun, such as a salient one-, two- or three dimensional nature, being round or flat, animate, inanimate or plant'.[9] This is about the same as the number of numeral classifiers in Nepali's expanded list, but both Newari and Nepali, like most languages with a numeral classifier system, have a general or generic classifier that can be used in place of other specific classifiers.[10] In Newari these are *gu*, used with inanimate nouns, and *mhā*, for animate nouns. In Nepali *woṭā/ṭā* is used with non-humans, and *jana/dzana* is used for humans. A similar, though not identical, distinction:

Newari:	*ni-gu saphū,*	*ni-mhā sālā*	two books, two horses
Nepali:	*duī-ṭā kitab,*	*duī-dzana manche*	two books, two men

This opens up a load of questions. First: how is Newari the only early language in Nepal to have numeral classifiers when none of its neighbours has them? Apart from modern Nepali, only two languages in all of Nepal, Newari and Meche,[11] have full-fledged numeral classifier systems.[12] The Kiranti languages, spoken in eastern Nepal, do have a few numeral classifiers, but they do not play a prominent role, and seem to be falling out of use.[13] The other Tibeto-Burman languages that are Newari's neighbours, like Lhasa Tibetan, Sherpa, Chepang and Kagate, do not seem to have even the simplest form of the numeral classifier construction.[14] Why is Newari so different? Are numeral classifiers in Newari a new thing? According to Kazuyuki Kiryu:

> In old manuscripts, there are instances of numerals directly attached to the noun that is the target of counting. The oldest manuscript written in Newari is a palm leaf of *Tāḍapatra* (Rudravarnṇa Vihāra tāḍapatra, Ukhu-bāhā, Patan, NS 235 (AD 1115)). Malla [a Nepali linguist] claims that Newari at this time had not 'developed any classifier system for enumeration of nominals' (Malla 1990: 17), which is quite right . . . When I examined the transliteration of the palm leaf manuscript given in his paper, I found seven instances of enumeration, among which there are no sortal classifiers.[15]

But in *Gopālarājavaṃśavalī* [GV], another palm leaf manuscript, a chronicle of the Gopāla kings that contains an account of some 332 years from 1057 to 1389, he finds a large number of numeral classifiers:

> If they are counted based on the appearance of classifiers per sentence, there are ten sentences that contain sortal classifiers while there are four sentences that do not contain any classifiers. Therefore, the percentage of sentences that contain classifiers is 71.4 per cent, hence in the GV the use of sortal classifier, although not yet obligatory, was active. Interestingly, there is no instance found where an inanimate item is counted with a classifier. All the instances of classifiers in the GV are in counts of animate beings.[16]

He then adds that while in modern Newari the number always comes before the numeral classifier, *ni-mhā manu*, 'two men', in the GV manuscript it was often the other way around. The number came *after* the classifier in seven out of the ten examples. It only came before the classifier in three of the examples, in a line that recorded an event in 1377 CE. Since the last date in the GV is 1389 CE, the text in question must have been written in the late fourteenth century:

> Close examination of the last half of the manuscript reveals that the classifier used for counting days, *nhu* [which also means 'day'], appears very often with a numeral before it . . . In other instances, the word *dina* 'day' [an Indo-Aryan loanword] is used and it is followed by the numeral . . . There is no instance of *dina* preceded by numeral, but the word *nhu* 'day' is always preceded by numeral.[17]

Kiryu formulates, from this evidence, a few rules that govern the occurrence of numeral classifiers in old Newari. First, numbers *precede* classifiers when what are being counted are days, or human subjects of a sentence. Also, numbers *follow* the classifier when they are in lists of items, or when the nouns are the 'object of verbs with killing and giving, or subjects of verbs that mean die'.[18] Not the most elegant set of rules.

Had Newari really not developed numeral classifiers by 1115, or had they simply been suppressed by the Maithili Brahmans writing the texts? Remember how one Maithili scribe had suppressed all the Maithili numeral classifiers from the *Linguistic Survey of India* (leading many linguists to imagine that they had never been there in Maithili at all).[19] Modern Newari, however, seems to have a much more robust numeral classifier system than what was there back in the eleventh century. It has also extended its ambit from only referring to humans, and items in lists, to making fine distinctions between living things and all sorts of objects, depending on their appearance. There also seems to be a general shift in word order from the classifiers not having any fixed location to them consistently coming *after* numbers, as they do in the Māgadhan languages of India and Bangladesh. In modern Newari the phrase with the number now comes *before* the noun, *ni-gu saphū*, 'two books', just like in Māgadhan languages like Bhojpuri, *du-go pothi*, Maithili, Bengali, Odia and Assamese, and modern Nepali.[20]

Can we go even further back in time? Can we identify the wild seed that found an ideal patch of ground to grow and spread and make the Newari language we know now, with lots of numeral classifiers? Was it Meche, with its well-developed numeral classifier system, that nourished Newari from deep inside the ground? There was clearly a live current that ran from Meche to Assam, where it is also known as Bodo, shining on Assamese in exactly the same way that Newari shone on Nepali. Numeral classifiers in Nepali and Assamese are the most elaborated in the Indo-Aryan family, and they look similar too. This was a current that went beyond numeral classifiers to even more enigmatic features like ergativity in both the languages.

If you match up Nepali and Newari, and get past the differences between the Tibeto-Burman and Indo-Aryan vocabularies, the two languages line up so well together in the way they do their numeral classifiers that we can't help but see them as mother and child. Nepali had to have got its numeral classifiers from Newari, its 'maternal' heritage, holding on to the more prestigious Indo-Aryan vocabulary that the Khasas brought with them from the lands to the west.

From Indo-Aryan (probably Maithili) we get the *form* of the numeral classifiers in Nepali, while the idea behind them came from its substratum language, Newari. The mixing process brought not only Khasa vocabulary into the new language, but, as with the other Indo-Aryan languages, it replaced every single marker that didn't sound Indo-Aryan with a marker that seemed to hark back to the language of the more prestigious parent.

This is why, as numeral classifiers got adopted in early Nepali, they took familiar forms, like numeral classifiers in the Māgadhan languages. The Newari marker *gu* became *ṭā/ṭi/goṭā/woṭā*, which call to mind *ṭā/ṭi* from Bengali, and *goṭā* from Maithili, which in turn calls to mind the Bhojpuri marker *go* in tandem with Bengali *ṭā*. And *woṭā* sounds like *goṭā*.

So in that sense there must have been influence from the Māgadhan languages: Maithili Brahmans had been living in the Kathmandu Valley for a long time. But even if they hadn't, it was on the cards that numeral classifiers would have an Indo-

Aryan look, the way classifiers used with numbers above ten do now even in the Munda languages of India.[21]

~

Newari conforms to the expected pattern of a language with numeral classifiers *not* having grammatical gender.[22] In other words, gender in Nepali cannot have come from Newari. It has to have come from Khasa, which was an Indo-Aryan language.

But while Nepali does have two genders, masculine and feminine, it is an 'attenuated' gender system, with feminine agreement markers restricted to female humans, 'optional or loose even then, and greatly reduced in semantic scope'.[23] Nouns agree in gender with both adjectives and verbs, as they do in western Indo-Aryan languages like Hindi, but if a noun is inanimate, non-living, in Nepali it must take masculine agreement markers (even if the same noun would be feminine in the Indo-Aryan languages of the northwest):

a.	*mero*	*keto*	*nepālī*	*boltsɔ*
	my.Masc	boy	Nepali	speak.PRS.3SG.Masc
b.	*merī*	*ketī*	*nepālī*	*boltse*
	my.FEM	girl	Nepali	speak.PRS.3SG.FEM
c.	*mero*	*kitāb*	*yahā̃*	*tsɔ*
	my.Masc	book	here	be.PRES.3SG.Masc[24]

In example *c.* above, *kitāb*, an inanimate noun, has masculine gender agreement with 'my' (*mero*) and the verb (*tsɔ*). But in the western Indo-Aryan languages *kitāb* is feminine. *Kitāb* in Nepali is masculine simply because it is inanimate. Could the Khasa language, the other parent of Nepali, also have had an attenuated gender system?

Khasa no longer exists, but Garhwali, from Uttarakhand, India, is a close relative. And in Garhwali *kitāb* is feminine, just as in the other north-western Indo-Aryan languages. The verb 'to be' in Garhwali, *cha*, does not have gender agreement:

d.	*merū*	*beṭā*	*gaṛhwāḷī*	*boldū cha*
	my.Masc	son	Garhwali	speak.Masc.PRES.3SG
e.	*merī*	*beṭī*	*gaṛhwāḷī*	*boldī cha*
	my.FEM	daughter	Garhwali	speak.FEM.PRES.3SG
f.	*merī*	*kitāb*	*yekh*	*cha*
	my.FEM	book	here	be.PRES.3SG

The gender system in Nepali is different from what it must have been in early Khasa. Did gender in Nepali evolve differently because its substratum language, Newari, does not have grammatical gender? If full grammatical gender in early Khasa has dwindled to natural gender in Nepali, it is significant. And not a surprise: 'there is considerable areal variation in Nepali with regard to the presence and expression of gender.' Even within Nepal native speakers of Newari tend to treat all nouns as masculine in spoken Nepali: *ma'am āyo!* (ma'am is here) has a masculine ending, *-o*, on the verb āyo, 'came'.[25] And gender is also missing in varieties of Nepali spoken in Darjeeling and Sikkim, where the majority of the speakers come from Tibeto-Burman family backgrounds.[26]

We have already seen, in borderland languages like Dakkhini, grammatical gender surprising us by being present. In the north-western Indo-Aryan languages too, grammatical gender was retained from the early prakrits (though in most languages it was pared down to two genders from an original three). Gender, we decided, was a grammatical feature that could 'swim' through a porous cellular membrane around a new language under certain conditions. Here again we have an example of gender marking itself present, even as it limits its scope to suit the substratum language that it emerged from.

But Nepali was up against a law of nature, as it were. Languages with numeral classifiers are not supposed to have grammatical gender: it is too heavy a load. So what we find in Nepali is a choice being made. Nepali became a classifier language with a half-hearted show of natural gender, which looks enough like grammatical gender to let it pass.

Perhaps the correct animal analogy was not the duckbill platypus. It should have been the zebra. Is a zebra black, or white? There is an answer to this question. Even though zebras have white stripes, they are actually black. The white fur is because of an absence of melanin: white is not a pigment. White stripes are pigment being denied, so black is the zebra's default colour.[27] Likewise, Nepali is a numeral classifier language, with natural gender stripes.

~

That leaves ergativity, not as fraught a topic as gender. There is no one out there loudly proclaiming that a language with numeral classifiers should not have ergativity. But still, if we were expecting to see anything similar to, say, Hindi in Nepali ergativity, we are in for a big surprise.

My first glimpse of ergativity in Nepali was in a class I was teaching, where we were exploring how different languages of South Asia expressed ergativity. A student from Nepal came to the board and started writing down sentences. They seemed to be following rules I had never seen before, with a few subjects being marked with the ergative ending *le*, but the verbs agreeing with them anyway, and not with the objects. What also struck me as unusual was the way he stopped to think about each example separately, using his instinct to tell him whether it sounded right with *le*, or whether it was better to leave it out.[28]

A paper on the semantics of ergativity in Nepali by Tikaram Poudel shows the ergative marker *le* coming in past-tense sentences, present-tense sentences, intransitive sentences (without objects), but *not* occurring in one sentence where Hindi would have had it (if it were in the past tense). PT means past tense, and NPT means non-past tense:

us	*le*	*mero*	*nām*	*mā*	*ujur*	*gar*	*-yo*
3.SG	ERG	my	name	LOC	complaint	do	-PT.3.SG.M

He made a complaint against me.

jyotisi	*le*	*cinā*	*her*	*-chan*
astrologer	ERG	horoscope	see	-NPT.3.PL

Astrologers see horoscopes.

goru	*le*	*mut*	*-yo*
bull	ERG	urinate	-PT.3.SG.M

The bull urinated.

ma	*shodhpatra*	*lekh*	*-chu*
1.SG	research paper	write	-NPT.1.SG

I will write a research paper/I write research papers.[29]

It is a daunting task reading through academic papers on ergativity in Nepali, as it is precisely the sort of complicated scenario that sends linguists into abstruse technical jargon. But, simply put, what they find is that Nepali is 'different'. There are many more reasons besides past tenses for sentences to be ergative in Nepali. It could be whether the nouns are animate or inanimate, 'living' or 'things'. It could also have to do with the verbs: there is a long list of verbs that *can* be in ergative sentences (like 'bloom', 'boil', 'break', 'twinkle', 'fall' or 'stay') and a list of verbs that *cannot* (like 'bathe', 'beg', 'crawl', 'fly', 'dance' or 'play').[30] The subjects of some verbs are ergative in all tenses, but with other verbs this is optional in some tenses, obligatory in others. And speakers also often disagree about whether the ergative marker *le* should be there or not.

Or as the linguist Chao Li puts it, 'Nepali is neither a fully ergative language nor a simple split-ergative language conditioned by tense/aspect.' Instead, when subject nouns are inanimate, 'the language is ergative; elsewhere, neither ergative nor accusative is readily applicable'.[31]

Where could Nepali have got this unusual sort of ergativity? We do not have to look far for the answer. Scrolling through a paper about verbs in Newari, I chanced upon a list of eight sentences with ergative subjects. Here ERG means ergative marker. PC means past conjunct; Q means question marker; NPC means non-past conjunct; PD means past disjunct. Newari has only two tenses, past and non-past, and verbs do not take person markers.[32]

ji-ī	*khāpā*	*tin-ā*
I-ERG	door	close-PC

'I closed the door'

cha-ā	*khāpā*	*tin-ā*	*lā?*
You-ERG	door	close-PC	Q

'Did you close the door?'

ji-ī	*khāpā*	*khan-e*
I-ERG	door	open-NPC

'I will open the door'

cha-ā	*khāpā*	*khan-e*	*dhal-ā*
you-ERG	door	open-NPC	say-PD

'You said you will open the door'

wa-ā	*khāpā*	*til-a (~tit-a)*
he-ERG	door	close-PD

'He closed the door'

ji-ī	*khāpā*	*til-a (tit-a)*	*lā?*
I-ERG	door	close-PD	Q

'Did I close the door (accidentally)?'

wa-ā	*thva*	*jyā*	*yā-i*
he-ERG	this	work	do-NPD

'He will do this work'

ji-ī	*thva*	*jyā*	*yā-I lā?*
I-ERG	this	work	do-NPDQ

'Should I do this work?'

While there is probably more to ergativity in Newari than this, such as lists of verbs that take ergativity and verbs that don't, what we are seeing here is a neat and elegant system that looks unlike anything we find in Indo-Aryan languages, and which calls to mind fully ergative languages of the far north like Burushaski and Shina, where ergativity exists in all tenses, and verbs have 'subject agreement' with nouns that carry ergative markers.[33] Ergativity in Newari can occur in any tense, not just the past. Newari has no person markers on verbs, though one imagines that if there were person agreement in Newari, it would be with subjects, just like in Nepali. Ergativity in Newari is without a doubt the parent of ergativity in Nepali.

~

If Nepali were the only Indo-Aryan language to have emerged from a Tibeto-Burman substratum with ergativity, it would still be an interesting stray example of ergativity coming into an Indo-Aryan language from a different source. But it isn't the only example. Assamese has an ergativity that looks identical to what we find in Nepali, in all tenses, and following rules that look exactly like the Nepali rules. Compare these sentences in Assamese and Bodo, a Tibeto-Burman language spoken in the same parts of Assam as Assamese:[34]

Assamese:

Ram pore /poribo /poril[35]
Ram fall-PR-3 /fall-FUT-3 /fall-PST-3
'Ram falls/will fall/fell'

*Ram-**e** doure /douribo /douril*[36]
Ram-ERG run-PR-3 /run-FUT-3 /run-PST-3
'Ram runs/will run/ran'

*tɛõluk-**e** kukur-tu=k bhat dile*[37]
3.PL-ERG dog-CLF-ACC rice give-PST-3
'They gave rice to the dog'

Bodo:

*Ram-**ma** əŋkham za-bai*[38]
Ram-ERG rice eat-PST
'Ram ate the rice'

*Sitha-**ja*** *phərai-jə*[39]
Sita-ERG read-PR
'Sita reads'

jəi *əŋkham* *tsoŋ-nai*[40]
Mother rice cook-FUT
'Mother will cook'

Map 16: Bodo and Assamese

Both Assamese and Bodo have ergativity, just as Nepali and Newari do. In Assamese, like in Nepali, the verb agrees with the 'subject' regardless of whether there is an ergative marker or not. In Assamese, too, tense doesn't seem to have much to do with ergativity. What matters is the class the verb belongs to. What is clear is that the ergativity in Nepali, Newari, Assamese and Bodo are essentially identical. It is also radically different from the split ergativity that came up in the modern Indus Valley Periphery lands.

What we have found at the end of this journey is not a total surprise to me. Just as the other Indo-Aryan languages in South Asia emerged as Tiramisu bears from migrant fathers and local mothers, with grammars that include features unknown in the old prakrits, I could not imagine Nepali being an exception to this pattern. What I expected, before I started, was that Nepali would have a substratum of Tibetan. But when Tibetan turned out not to have numeral classifiers, that trail went cold.

Newari, however, a Tibeto-Burmese language quite different from Tibetan, turned out to be the maternal line we were looking for. Newari had been the language in the Kathmandu Valley in contact with the Khasa migrants from the very start, and Newar women were the locals who had married the Khasa men and given them the chance to continue their line. Newari is also the best explanation for the rare constellation of features in Nepali: numeral classifiers, and a sort of ergativity that only superficially looks like the split ergativity found in the Extended Indus Valley Periphery.

Nepali follows the same trajectory as the other languages in this book, though there are a few twists and surprises. We started out with the enigma of a language that seemed to have grammatical gender and ergativity, and strangely numeral classifiers too. We do not expect to see numeral classifiers in a language that has gender and ergativity.

The story of Nepali starts with a familiar Tiramisu bear encounter: a mostly male group, the Khasas, migrating into the Kathmandu Valley about 500 years ago. Why do we think the Khasas were male? Because migrants in South Asia have almost always been male. These men came into contact with speakers of Newari, a Tibeto-Burman language, who had been living in the area since prehistoric times. The result was intermarriage between the early Khasa men and the Newar women, from which emerged hybrid children and a hybrid language, initially called Khaskura, with structural features from its maternal side and vocabulary from its father tongue.

Newari did not have gender. How, then, did Nepali get it? Well, we are used to seeing gender 'swim' through the cellular barrier from a father tongue into a hybrid offspring: this is what happened with Dakkhini. But still, the three features together, gender, ergativity and numeral classifiers, was unusual.

Nepali turned out *not* to be a western Indo-Aryan language that had picked up numeral classifiers. Numeral classifiers were actually basic to the language. They had not come from the Māgadhan family, but from Newari, a Tibeto-Burman language that differed from Tibetan languages in having these classifiers. The numeral classifiers in Nepali neatly line up with the numeral classifiers in Newari, about fifteen in each language.

Ergativity too was not what it had seemed at first glance. While Nepali had an ergative marker *le*, it behaved very differently from the marker *ne* in western Indo-Aryan. First, it seemed to be linked to the semantics of certain verbs: it would occur in sentences that had those verbs, and only sometimes with other verbs, with a lot of leeway for speakers to make up their own minds about what sounded better: with *le*, or without it. And when they did use *le*, the verb agreed with the 'subject' as if the ergative marker were not there. It didn't 'realign' to agree with the object as it did in western Indo-Aryan languages.

Ergative sentences in Nepali and Newari also looked exactly like ergative sentences in Assamese and Bodo, whose story mirrors that of Nepali and Newari.

When we looked at gender in Nepali, it turned out not to be the grammatical gender we were expecting. While there were indeed masculine and feminine nouns, which agreed not only with verbs but with adjectives too, it was actually natural gender. Male humans were masculine, and female humans were feminine, but *things* were always masculine. Even things that would have been feminine in western Indo-Aryan languages. Gender in Nepali, called 'attenuated' gender by some linguists, was the add-on.

What we had first thought to be a western Indo-Aryan language with an add-on of numeral classifiers turned out, on closer examination, to be an Indo-Aryan language with a Tibeto-Burman substratum that had retained numeral classifiers and a Tibeto-Burman version of ergativity, adding a sort of natural gender that looked, superficially, like the grammatical gender in western Indo-Aryan languages, where nouns agreed with verbs and adjectives too.

~

Where Nepali, as a modern Indo-Aryan language, runs true to type is in the way it has managed to spread out and bring under its sway a huge expanse of territory, so much so that it is now another major force for the centralization of culture in South Asia, just as Nagamese is now evolving into a link language in India's north-east.[41] That is what mixed languages *do*. They are the linguistic side of the political change that has drawn together communities that previously lived their separate lives, making them live as a region with a standard language, literacy, a new mainstream religion and a market, replacing the old worlds of isolation and subsistence that preceded the age of empires and governments.

Nepali is now spreading northwards, capturing previously Tibetan spaces not only in Nepal, but in Darjeeling and Sikkim too, where it replaces older languages like Lepcha, Rai, Gurung,

Sherpa, Tamang and other languages from the Tibetan family. In its second avatar, Nepali is no longer reinventing itself to fit in with its new environments. It is now behaving like the prakrits of old, accessible enough for new communities to learn it easily. There are little local variations, words and accents that acknowledge its new speakers, but it holds its shape this time as a language of literacy.

So what we have, as with Sanskrit, and Hindi, and English, are two distinct phases in the life of an 'invasive' language. Nepali's initial phase was 500 years ago, when it was coming to life as a Tiramisu bear, with much of its structure being decided by its maternal parent, and its vocabulary and a few other features passed on by a paternal group that entered a new place and forever changed its politics. Then, when it was in place as an accepted link language, it began to expand its terrain and replace the other languages in the neighbourhood, mainly languages that were not related to it at all. This was easy, because it is not linguistic resemblances that decide whether a new language is easy to learn. It is whether the new language is needed in a changed economic climate. As long as people feel that their children will be better placed to get jobs if they speak these link languages, languages like Nepali, Nagamese, Hindi and English will find their way into our lives. And we will phase out the old languages, which help us less and less as the world moves on.

Once again, we are in the midst of an old, old story, and time is back to being cyclical. That is not to say that it is a law of nature that languages will inevitably cluster together in this way, 'thinning the row' so that the 'hardiest plants survive'. What we are seeing, again and again, is a tough invasive species coming in and capturing new spaces, interbreeding with the native life forms, such that these old flora and fauna do not die but are merely 'domesticated'. As these languages spread, native peoples learn new languages of power and shift their loyalties in that direction, abandoning their old identities and languages.

We are at a point in the story where tiny streams and tributaries from the uplands are flowing down to the valley below, guided by gravity, as the glaciers that once held them back to nourish the highlands are almost gone. It is the story we see not only all over South Asia, but all over the world. The little dark corners we played in as children are suddenly exposed to the glare of the midday sun, and we ourselves are being drawn into the big world, pushed by our families who want 'the best' for us. Let us leave this story, while the road ahead is still open, and pull together the threads of our journey up to now.

8

The Return of the Tiramisu Bear

Stillness that resounds . . .

The Silence of a Candle, Paul Winter

And in the end we are back where we started, with the reason why I wrote this book. In my earlier book, *Wanderers, Kings, Merchants*, as I plunged into the story of India's languages, I kept stumbling over bits of underbrush that hadn't been properly cleared. Some parts of the trail were easy to see, and they kept me going, but the model itself needed work. Were the very mixed languages in South Asia[1] creoles? If they were creoles, and the classic model I was following was a pidgin-creole model, how was it that we never found any pidgins at all?

Had there been no pidgins in South Asia? Had there been no pidgins even in the Caribbean? When I tried to find the source of the claim that creoles had come from pidgins, ad hoc languages that would come up in encounters between groups that had no language in common, I found that the earliest contact languages spoken between European traders and African merchants on the West African coast had not been pidgins at all. According to Salikoko Mufwene, the African traders who had had business dealings with the Europeans coming in their big ships back in the time of the Atlantic slave trade had essentially learnt the European languages well.[2] Between the sixteenth and the nineteenth centuries, Europeans trading for slaves on the West African coast had used these local traders as interpreters, along with the children they themselves had with African women, who knew both local and European languages well.

'Well' is an interesting term: it doesn't mean 'exactly'. There would have been local touches, mostly in accent and expression, that did not violate the rules of the European languages, though they did reflect a different environment. Think of the elite colonial varieties of English, or French, that we speak now which, in written discourse, are hard to dismiss as not English or French, though hearing us talk using unfamiliar sounds can be unsettling at times to speakers in the metropole. In these early one-on-one encounters it was perfectly feasible for a motivated learner to acquire a reasonable version of the new European language. Salikoko Mufwene calls these 'local varieties' and says that on the early slave estates of the New World, which had been small homestead farms, African slaves had spoken these varieties, and not creoles.[3] These 'local varieties' are what we, in this book, call 'prakrits'.

When we look at this sort of language contact in South Asia we find the same sequence of events. It starts with a migration of men, with essentially no women. The first locals to meet the powerful newcomers are elite local men, who pick up a 'prakrit' variety of the newcomers' languages, and the local women the newcomers have children with. These prakrits were not pidgins. They were local varieties that differed mostly in accent, and a few features that did not really go against the rules of the language as spoken by the newcomers. But when everything is done orally, what really stands out is the accent, that thing that best identifies a speaker as 'us' or 'them'. The important point here is that prakrits were not something midway between the newcomers' languages and the local languages, and they were definitely not the languages of the little people. The first prakrits were close approximations of the newcomers' languages by the local elites, differing mostly in accent.

Creoles did not actually emerge on slave plantations until much later. Mufwene says they came up when the plantations adopted industrial-scale production, where the ratio of African slaves to European planters changed dramatically. There were now huge numbers of new Africans who seldom interacted directly with Europeans, picking up their words from earlier slaves who spoke the 'prakrit' varieties of the European languages.

It would have been a gradual process. On the slave plantations there would, however, have been a sense of never going back, and a need to come to terms with the new language environment. In South Asia there was probably less pressure, as the local people who found themselves occupied by powerful settlers had not actually left home. So the mixed languages would have emerged more slowly, with the old languages surviving much longer. This is something we still see happening in the tribal Munda lands in eastern India, words from Indo-Aryan dialects trickling in, giving the tribal languages a familiar feel to some of us who know those local dialects. But in the end, there would have been enough environmental change for 'Tiramisu bears' to start appearing, languages where almost all the vocabulary came from the prakrits, while much of the 'operating system', or grammar, was preserved from the old local languages. These new mixed languages would have come to life slowly, with new words trickling into the old languages over centuries in a long gestation until they were 'viable', ready to be 'born', and the old languages they grew out of ready to fade away. All this while, in the written record, the only things visible were Sanskrit and the prakrits, the languages that were still being used by rulers and the elites.

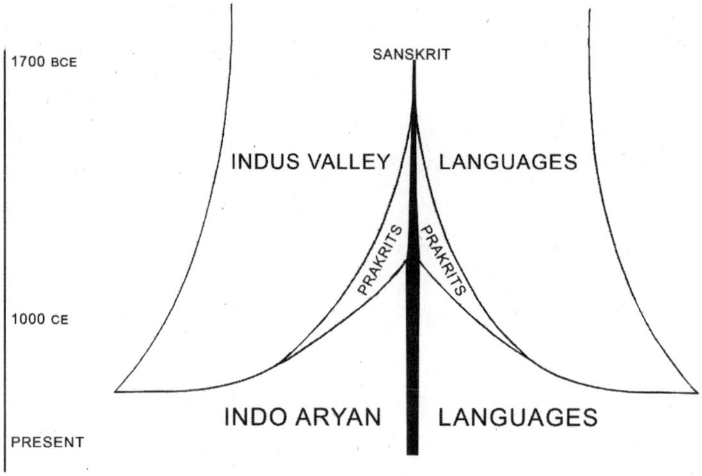

Map 17: The revised model, starting with a landscape of earlier local languages, the entry of a settler language, the formation of elite prakrits around the settler language, and the much later emergence of mixed language. This model, using Sanskrit as an example, presupposes a huge presence of Indus Valley languages at the time of Sanskrit's entry, and surviving till around the eleventh century. It also imagines Sanskrit and prakrits, as elite languages, having had relatively few speakers.

The prakrits were the settlers' languages swallowed whole, as it were, words and grammar together, like the English we are having this conversation in now.

To make the creoles, new words were taken into older local languages, spoken by little people who were not in direct contact with the original settlers. It may be helpful to see the grammar of these creole languages as coming from deep roots, like an old tree: a *vertical* transmission. And to see the words as the pollen that spreads from tree to tree: a *lateral* transmission. This lateral transmission would respond to changes in the local environment. There is a new power group in charge, and it is adaptive for the little people to pick up the words of their language, starting with nouns, but ultimately going on to replace all their words and grammatical markers.

Then, in the twelfth century, the prakrits were swept out of power by a wave of newcomers, and political change that brought in a new elite language, Persian. This change was the entry of rulers from Central Asia who set up the Delhi Sultanate, and sultanates in other parts of the subcontinent. They recognized and elevated the creole languages of the little people to the status of regional standard languages, and set up a new dispensation where their official language, Persian, replaced Sanskrit and the prakrits at the top.

So our new creole model does not start off fast and furious, full of incomprehension and a scrambling together of the two language streams. It is a calm two-step process. The first thing to appear is a prakrit, a 'local variety' of the settlers' language, spoken 'well' by elites and the settlers' own half-local children. Then as the environmental changes set in and become permanent, the little people make the transition from only including new words into their old languages to replacing their entire vocabulary and all the grammatical markers, especially when they begin to write, keeping the essence of their old grammars (though at times bringing in new features of the language of power).

A model is essentially a map, to help you venture into unknown spaces without getting lost. Before you can use a model with confidence, you need to test it, test it on things you *can* see, before you use it as a guide to things you *can't* see. The first thing we did was test it out on a language mixture situation in India that had happened recently enough for there to be historical records and written literature in the language that could tell us if we were on track. There was such a thing: Dakkhini, a mixed language spoken in the borderland area between north India and south India, where an influx of Central Asians in the fourteenth century had created a local community with a new religion and a new language. Was this the process that had brought Dakkhini to life?

What we see with Dakkhini is two starting points, separate but close in time. There is the 'Dakhni' spoken by the actual migrant men who brought the Dehlavi dialect from the north and passed it on to their local wives and half-local children. And there is the Dakkhini that is full of calques from Telugu, literal translations that tell us about the earlier language spoken by the little people who converted to Islam quickly and in large numbers, and populated the new sultanate. There is much evidence that these little people were first exposed to northern languages *not* by the elite migrants and their families, but by wandering Sufis, mystics who adapted the message of Islam to local imagery and a proto-version of the new language, Dakkhini. What is interesting is that the presence of these Sufis *predates* the arrival of sultanate forces, by a full century, raising the question of whether the Dakkhini of the little people could have come up before the elite 'Dakhni' was in place. Could a huge number of local people have managed to convert before there was a system in place to convert to? There are reports of conversion starting early in the fourteenth century, with whole castes such as weavers opting to join the new religion. There are consequently two Dakkhinis: an elite one known as 'Dakhni', with the second vowel missing, following northern sound assimilation rules, and the other called 'Dakkhini', or 'Dakkani', with kk and no h, which sounds more southern. The model worked.

Could the model work in reverse? If we knew the present-day languages, could we triangulate backwards to extract the essence of a language that had vanished? If there was enough structure remaining in the modern languages, could we find the old language in it?

So we got ready to look inside the blackest box of all, the vanished languages of the Indus Valley Civilization. We did not expect to see 'flesh', which would have been the first thing to melt away, but we knew we would find ancient 'bones'. And we didn't want to see words anyway, as they would only have confused us: words are the things that differ the most from language to language, the things that keep changing in each language over time. What we wanted to do was choose grammatical features, the 'bones' in the present-day languages of the Indus Valley Periphery region, that did *not* look like Sanskrit and the prakrits, and use them to arrive at an X-ray image of our hypothetical Language X. We would look not only at the main Indo-Aryan languages of the area, the Tiramisu bears, but also at two others: Burushaski, a language isolate spoken in the Hunza Valley in the Karakorams, and Brahui, a Dravidian language spoken by tribes in the Balochistan desert. If Burushaski had been brought into the region by the usual settlers—men—it stood to reason that these men would have found wives locally, and this could have brought in some features that went back to a time before Sanskrit. And given the buzz around Brahui, which many insisted was an original Indus Valley language, there was no way we could exclude it.

The first feature we looked at was retroflexion, which is something that goes back all the way to the first successful human migration out of Africa, where dental sounds ***t d n l***, the palato-alveolar ***ś*** and retroflex sounds ***ṭ ḍ ṇ ḷ ṣ*** are in phonemic contrast. Changing ***t*** to ***ṭ*** will make it a totally different word, like *dānt* (tooth) and *ḍāṇṭ* (a scolding). The retroflex sounds ***ṭ ḍ ṇ ḷ*** are not unique to the South Asian mainland. They are found in First Australian languages too, and two of them, ***ṭ*** and ***ḍ***, are found in the languages of the Andaman Islands and the central New Guinea highlands, people who have been out of touch with the South Asian mainland for at least 55,000 years. All the modern languages in our sample had retroflexion, but the actual sounds differed. Most had ***ṭ ḍ*** and usually ***ṇ***; Punjabi also had ***ḷ***; and the ones farther north, like Sindhi and Pashto, had the ***ṣ*** that we also find in Sanskrit, and Pashto and Burushaski even had retroflex affricates like ***tṣ*** and ***ḍẓ***.[4]

The proof that Burushaski had been influenced by the early languages of the Indus Valley area is that it, too, had retroflexion: in fact, the same retroflex sounds as Pashto. There was no way that the first Burusho migrants who came with their language could have had this South Asian feature in their sound system. That was the earliest validation of our decision to include Burushaski in our list.

The most interesting feature we found was ergativity, which set the Extended Indus Valley Periphery apart from the rest of South Asia. In the modern languages this showed up as split ergativity, verbs in the past tense agreeing with their objects, and not their subjects, the famous *by-me food-eaten* structure. What we found was that a simpler, more basic kind of ergativity must have existed in the region earlier, not only in the past tense but in all tenses, something still found in Burushaski, Shina, and in the languages of the Andaman Islands and the First Australian languages. (Nepali and Assamese also have something like this full ergativity, though its sources are in the Tibeto-Burman family.) In these languages verbs had 'agents' that did the action: what other languages expressed as subjects these languages put into *by-me* type expressions. This full version of ergativity, in all tenses, more user-friendly than the modern split ergativity, was very likely a feature of Language X. Had this been the spur that pushed the prakrits, the modern languages of the region and, indeed, later Sanskrit too, to reimagine their past tenses as *by-me-food-eaten* instead of *I ate*, as it had been in earliest Sanskrit?

The biggest surprise was that Burushaski turned out to be the closest to Language X in terms of the test features we selected, followed by Brahui. Tamil and Punjabi tied for third place, followed by Bhojpuri, representing the Māgadhan zone. Then, with eight points of difference, came Sanskrit, far and away the least similar to Language X. The other languages looked like close family, while Sanskrit was like a foreign guest that had come to visit.

Tamil and Punjabi only seemed a bit less like Language X because they were modern and had picked up honorifics and compound verbs (the *ho gaya* as distinct from *huā* forms) that were unlikely to have been there back in those times: Burushaski and Shina did not have them. But it was easy to imagine both languages without honorifics, especially as the highest level of honorific (*āp* in Punjabi for 'you' and *taŋgaḷ* in Tamil, spelt as '*thangaḷ*') feel like recent inclusions in those languages. In fact, Language X came across as a Dravidian language with a typical agglutinative structure and full ergativity, which made it sound almost like a cross between Tamil and Punjabi.[5] After all, the Indus Valley Civilization had been Dravidian, and Harappa was in west Punjab. One could almost hear the words that would fill in our reconstructed outline.

Brahui was close too, but any Dravidian language would have been. The problem with Brahui was that it did not have ergativity or gender, not even the *he/she/it* natural gender in southern Dravidian pronouns, which made it seem more like Balochi, an Iranian language sharing space with Brahui in Balochistan, than a pristine Dravidian language. Natural gender and ergativity seemed to be important in Language X. Could Brahui have been part of the original Indus Valley family, hiding all these millennia in the mountains of Balochistan, and in danger of extinction only within the last fifty years? Or was it something like Kurukh, a tribal north Dravidian language whose lands might have been located closer to the northwest a few centuries ago, and which it resembles in many ways? The Brahuis have the same genetics as other Pakistanis, so that doesn't tell us anything. Almost all Pakistanis, regardless of what they speak now, trace back in large measure to people who lived there in IVC times. It would take nothing less than a breakthrough, with better evidence, and better models, to say if Brahui is part of the original IVC family, or if it is not. We are way past the time when the Brahui issue can be decided by wishful thinking.

After Language X, our journey continued east across the Ganga-Jamuna confluence and into the Māgadhan lands, going back through the ages to seek out the story of the Munda tribes, First Indians who had lived there since earliest times. And there too, about 4000 years ago, we found another Tiramisu bear story. There had been an influx of men from Southeast Asia who had interbred with local Munda women, leaving their genetic imprint in the paternal DNA of at least 60 per cent of the Munda population, along with a number of words of

Vietnamese and Burmese origin in the Munda languages. That migration did not turn into a long-term colonial presence, and the Munda languages did not begin to look like Vietnamese or Burmese, with short words, scant morphology and East Asian tones. They remained the agglutinative languages they had always been, with the addition of some words and numeral classifiers: the *ek-ṭā kukur* (one dog) we now find in Bengali and the Māgadhan languages. Is this enough to reclassify all Munda languages Austro-Asiatic? I don't think so.

A closer look at the northern Munda languages reveals an interesting anomaly. These languages still have a distinction between animate and non-animate nouns, which, in other words, is a gender system. At the same time, the Munda languages, after the influx of the Austro-Asiatic men 4000 years ago, became classifier languages, with numeral classifiers, and there is a contradiction between being a gender language and a classifier language. This contradiction was resolved by gender in the Munda languages fading out to be just a vestigial presence, creating an almost tectonic divide between the Extended Indus Valley Periphery languages west of the Ganga-Yamuna confluence, which had grammatical gender and ergativity, and those to the east, which essentially had neither (though the northern Munda languages continued to have both subject and object agreement on their verbs). This dates the great divide between the western and eastern languages of the north to the time when the Austro-Asiatic men came.

In other words, before that migration, 4000 years ago, the entire north of the subcontinent must have been one continuous belt of languages with gender and, if not exactly ergativity, something very much like it. When we peeled away the layer of grammar that the Austro-Asiatic men had added to Munda, we arrived at an age of primordial unity.

Two features of the time-before-time, when there were only First Indians in this land, stand out prominently: retroflexion and ergativity. Both form a geographical arc going all the way from the Horn of Africa to Australia, with South Asia bang in the middle. As it happens, in south-west Ethiopia, 'phonemically distinctive retroflex consonants are found in Bench and Sheko, two contiguous, but not closely related Omotic languages'.[6] Was retroflexion more widespread in that part of Africa when the first human migration out of Africa took place? Amharic, spoken in Ethiopia, does not have ergativity as such, but the same sort of object marking we find in our northern Munda languages, where verbs can agree with both subjects and objects.[7] A sort of 'ergativity lite'. Earlier we wondered if object marking in the northern Munda languages was something very old, and linked to what we suspected was an arc of ergativity that spread all the way from the Indus Valley to Australia. Could object marking in Ethiopia, and retroflexion, be the western pot of gold at the end of an old, old rainbow?

When we traced the story of how the Munda languages segued into early Māgadhan dialects, gradually pulling in words from local prakrits since Ashokan times, we saw how these new languages, in the Māgadhan region and all over the north of the subcontinent, managed to replace the prakrits by the twelfth century and become the standard languages of large regions. They had to have had political support to topple a crumbling regime where local prakrits still ruled, but where had this support come from? As it turns out, this change coincided with the arrival of Central Asians from what is now Uzbekistan, who brought Persian as their language of governance, and had no interest in sustaining the old prakrit-linked leadership. These sultans gave recognition to the new languages in preference over the old prakrits.

Did south India have a Tiramisu bear story too? It seems so. Once it was clear that the Indus Valley Civilization had been Dravidian, it was logical to wonder how Dravidian languages came to be associated almost exclusively with south India. We know how the Dravidian languages of the northwest got eclipsed under a coat of prakrit vocabulary when the IVC declined and the Vedic people arrived. But when had the Dravidian people moved south? Was it after the IVC had gone into decline, or had a trickle of migrants, probably men, started even earlier? If the first Dravidians to reach south India had been men, would they have found wives among the First Indian people living there and created a frontier society? Were the Dravidian people in the south a case of *double* hybridization, first a mixture between men from the Zagros mountains and First Indians in the northwest, and then their progeny again mixing with a different group of First Indians in the south? Or were there substantial numbers of families, refugees with vivid memories of the IVC, heading south to a better life with women and children?

There do not seem to be many differences between the Dravidian languages of the IVC and the ones now in south India, but one feature in the western Indo-Aryan languages today is strikingly different: ergativity. Ergativity came up in all the modern languages of the Extended Indus Valley Periphery, and nowhere else, which raises the question whether there had been a basic ergativity in the Dravidian languages of the IVC which is not there in the Dravidian languages of the south. This is like the object agreement in Munda verbs, which fades out as one goes south, even within the Munda family. Ergativity seems to end, like a cooling lava flow, just before the southern districts of Maharashtra, and it isn't there in Dakkhini at all. It is almost a geographical thing: beyond this point there is no ergativity. That is what brought my question: did the first Dravidian migrants to the south go as single men without any women? Is this sea change in language towards the south of Maharashtra the work of the First Indian wives of these migrant men, whose languages did not have anything like ergativity, and whose children made the new Dravidian languages without it?

There is a sense of discontinuity in the south, an absence of the buildings that call to mind the IVC, and all its linkages to other old cultures from Egypt to Mesopotamia, and the sense of being something truly grand. It feels like a fresh start in a new frontier universe, like waking up with only glimmers of a past life in the IVC hidden in the languages you brought, until linguists, archaeologists and geneticists could bring this all to light.

The end of this book's journey takes us back to the north, to explore a strange enigma in Nepali, which seemed to be at the same time a western Indo-Aryan language, with gender and ergativity, and a Māgadhan language with numeral classifiers. Which was it, or could it actually be both? Nepali turned out to be something else again: an Indo-Aryan language whose substratum was Tibeto-Burman. Nepali was formed in a fusion between the Khasas, migrant men from the Indian Himalayas who spoke an Indo-Aryan language, and the Newar people who had lived in the Kathmandu Valley since earliest times.

Once again, it turned out to be true that a language could either have grammatical gender or be a 'classifier language'. And Nepali was a classifier language, with a kind of ergativity that was Tibeto-Burman, and nothing to do with the ergativity in the northwest, and a simplified natural gender behaving, outwardly, the way gender did in the northwest, affecting verbs and adjectives, but with its nouns being either biologically female, or not. Nepali was yet another Tiramisu bear, but one with a different 'mother' from another part of the north of the subcontinent. And Nepali was not alone in this: there was a clear echo of the Nepali story in Assamese, which has the same sort of ergativity as Nepali, and about as many numeral classifiers. Assamese also has a Tibeto-Burman substratum, an earlier language of the area, Bodo, which is related to Newari.

~

What these Tiramisu bear situations have in common is the way they took things to a higher pitch, pulling large regions together into a single unit the way modern governments, markets and literacy do. Each of the languages we have looked at in this book has replaced the languages and dialects that little people spoke before, drawing them into mega systems that need to be managed and governed in the manner of empires.

It is tempting to say that this is merely evolution at work, and that this is the natural path for languages, and people, to take. But, in truth, these were not your everyday migrants who come in unassumingly and blend into existing cultures, content to live out their lives in peace with new neighbours. These were settlers on steroids, so to speak, the sort of people whose motors were running faster. These were groups of people possessed of great certainty who brought in their wake irreversible change.

And yet . . . there was a certain inevitability about the way things turned out, because the strong always do seem to prevail over the ones who are quiet, the ones who just want the world to continue smoothly without strife and disruption. Where it is open country with no natural barriers like the high mountains that kept the Burusho in seclusion, or the Daṇḍakāraṇya forests that shielded the Munda people, or the deep oceans that kept the Andaman Islanders out of our reach for millennia, the little people get overrun and reorganized in ways that suit powerful newcomers, who know how to make 'better' use of their resources, and in time local people have no choice but to adapt to the new identities thrust upon them. Many of us are from communities that are watching our ethnic languages die, and the scale of the extinction is now at a point where it has become an endemic feature of this age.

~

Still, old habits die hard. We don't see ourselves as those people. We have learnt to think of ourselves as just one thing, the victorious parental side that gave us our vocabulary, and our name. So the north Indian languages are known as 'Indo-Aryan', ignoring the huge amount of grammatical structure that goes back to the ancient women who have lived in this land since the first human migration out of Africa. And Munda languages are 'Austro-Asiatic', because of a migration of men that it took geneticists researching ancient rice to uncover, with linguists in colonial times finding Vietnamese and Burmese words that matched Munda words and concluding that they had all been 'one race'. But the Munda and Mon-Khmer languages are, as Grierson put it, 'so exactly opposite at every level of structure that . . . if they were descended from a common language, the language must have been adopted by people with opposite orders of thought'.[8] And now that the geneticists have told us about the Zagros farmers, we have ardent Dravidianists proudly claiming the Zagros men as their ancestors, disregarding the ancient women who interbred with them to create what are now known as the Dravidian people, a hybrid group that built the Indus Valley Civilization and which has no known relatives outside of South Asia. Each step of the way we have downplayed the Indian component in our ancestry, the maternal line that has brought an underlying stability and continuity to the languages of the subcontinent.

Sanskrit and English are very much a part of this story. We looked at both these languages in my earlier book, *Wanderers, Kings, Merchants*, where we saw them as two more invasive species that had built empires and prevailed at the cost of local languages that had lived here for an eternity. And we found Nagamese, a relatively new language of the north-east, which looks as if it will one day replace the small tribal languages on the hilltops that lived their separate existences. In Nagaland this has not yet happened, but elsewhere we have to think hard to stand outside the selves we have become and remember earlier lives, and all the good things that those other selves have lost.

It was never about language itself. Language was only the reflection of all the larger forces acting on our society and natural environment, which is how we have been able to view so much of our history by looking at the way our languages have evolved, or vanished. If we want to preserve our languages, as artefacts distinct from the other things happening in our lives, we are not thinking about living languages, which will keep adapting and changing as things in the outside world impact us. Only dead languages cease to change and need to be preserved. And even if we do manage to hold on to them, the way the world works now we will end up not using them anyway, and they will vanish, when there are no children who know them as their first languages.

~

Our most important takeaway from this book should be that, against all odds, there is something that lingers on when the living form of language fades away. We might not know our great-grandparents, or their parents, maybe we don't even know who they were, but deep within us in the way we think and speak our history lies preserved. There is much that we can never know, old words that we can only imagine. But from the languages that are still here with us, we can glimpse an inner structure, ancient bones, that give a sense of continuity over a huge expanse of territory where languages are related like family and tell a story of people who met and mingled over long millennia.

This journey we have just taken together has, on the face of it, been about language, and a few things that geneticists, archaeologists and historians have found. Like language, it has depended crucially on an inner architecture that calls for imagination, a readiness to venture into new spaces, make bold connections, and ask questions even when we cannot find the answers. The facts by themselves need a binder, a model, which will hold them in place like cement so they can serve as a floor. This journey has also been about waiting, being comfortable with *not* knowing, because it is only when we step off the beaten path and experience the void that new ideas get a chance to float up into our range of vision.

Maybe after this time together, we will start to see ourselves in a new light: outwardly different, full of variety, but with a shared inner core that goes back to ancestors who were curious enough to cross a stretch of water or venture through a mountain pass because they thought there was something interesting on the other side. That reaction is precious: excitement at expecting something new, and a wish to engage with it. When we lose our sense of wonder at the diversity of life around us and yearn only for a dull sameness that holds no challenge, the road before us begins to close. This is a thought to keep in mind as we watch ourselves hurtling towards a dismal future, spurred on by those with a short-term vision, who see only profit in the destruction of our living environment and people who are part of the mosaic of our shared history. It has taken much manipulation to get us into this spot where we believe that this is the logical outcome of our great journey. It is not.

In *The Dawn of Everything* Graeber and Wengrow speak of the Greek notion of *kairos*, 'one of those occasional moments in a society's history when its frames of reference undergo a shift . . . and, therefore, real change is possible'.[9] These are moments that recur, time and again, in our long journey, when the road we are on seems to hold no future. Is it possible that we have reached a moment of *kairos* again?

A Note on Spelling

To write the different languages in this book in the Roman script I have used a number of phonemic symbols:

Vowels: short

a pronounced like the *u* in the English word ***cut***
Hindi e.g. *kaṭ* (get cut) अ

i pronounced like the *i* in ***it***
Hindi e.g. *piṭ* (get beaten) इ

u pronounced like the *u* in ***put***
Hindi e.g. *pul* (bridge) उ

e pronounced like the *ai* in ***wait***
Hindi e.g. *le* (take) ए

o pronounced like the *o* in ***boat***
Hindi e.g. *gol* (round) ओ

Vowels: long

ā pronounced like the *a* in the English word ***calm***
Hindi e.g. *mār* (kill) आ

ī pronounced like the *ee* in ***feet***
Hindi e.g. *pīṭ* (beat) ई

ū pronounced like the *oo* in ***root***
Hindi e.g. *phūl* (flower) ऊ

ṛ	pronounced like the *ri* in ***rig*** in north India pronounced like the *roo* in ***roof*** in Gujarat and Maharashtra Sanskrit e.g. *Ṛgveda* ऋ
ã ẽ ĩ õ ũ	the tilde symbol indicates nasal vowels, as in Portuguese *pão* (bread) Hindi e.g. *hā̃* (yes) हाँ

Retroflex: with the tip of the tongue curled upwards to touch the front of the palate
(Retroflex sounds essentially exist only in the Indian subcontinent, and have a '*hoṭ poṭaṭo* in the mouth' sound, also referred to as 'r-coloration')

ṭ	pronounced like an English *t* with r-coloration Hindi e.g. *kāṭ* (cut) ट
ṭh	pronounced like an English *t* with r-coloration and a following *h* Hindi e.g. *ṭhīk* (okay) ठ
ḍ	pronounced like an English *d* with r-coloration Hindi e.g. *ḍaṇḍā* (stick) ड
ḍh	pronounced like an English *d* with r-coloration and a following *h* Hindi e.g. *ḍhona* (to bear weight) ढ
ṇ	pronounced like an English *n* but with r-coloration Malayalam e.g. *veṇam* (is required) ण
ṣ	pronounced like the *sh* in English ***shout*** but with a whooshing sound Sanskrit e.g. *ūṣā* (dawn) ष
ḷ	pronounced like an English *l* but with r-coloration Marwari e.g. *puḷ* (bridge) ळ
ṛ	pronounced like a *ḍ* but with the tongue flapping forward Hindi e.g. *baṛā* (big) ड़

Dental: with the tip of the tongue behind the top front teeth

t pronounced like the Spanish *t* in ***toro*** (bull)
Hindi e.g. *tārā* (star) त

th pronounced like the Spanish *t* but with a following *h*
Hindi e.g. *thālī* (a round tray) थ

d pronounced like the Spanish *d* in ***Dios*** (God)
Hindi e.g. *devtā* (deity) द

dh pronounced like a Spanish *d* but with a following *h*
Hindi e.g. *dhonā* (to wash) ध

D pronounced like a Spanish *d* but with a yawning sound
Arabic e.g. *RamaDan* (the month of Ramzan) Perso-Arabic ض

Palato-alveolar: between the ridge behind the top front teeth and the dome of the mouth

ś pronounced like English *sh* as in ***ash***
Hindi e.g. *āśā* (hope) श

ć pronounced like English *ch* as in church
Hindi e.g. *ćor* (thief) च

Alveolar: with the tip of the tongue touching the alveolar ridge, midway between dental and retroflex positions

ṯ pronounced exactly like the English *t* in ***top***
Malayalam e.g. *ṯinnun̲n̲u* (eat)

n̲ pronounced exactly like the English *n* in ***no***
Malayalam e.g. *ṯinnun̲n̲u* (eat)

In languages like Assamese and Nagamese which have no retroflexion, plain *t th d dh n* and *l* are alveolar, as in British or American English 'put' or 'dog'.

ü pronounced like *ee* but with the lips rounded, like the *ue* in French ***rue*** (street)
Chaghtai e.g. *sekkizyüz* (eight hundred)

ö pronounced like *ay* but with the lips rounded, like *œ* in French *sœur* (sister)
Turkish e.g. *Özbek* (Uzbek)

ı pronounced like *oo* but with the lips spread flat, a bit like the *i* in English *third*
Chaghtai e.g. *onıkı* (twelve); Tamil/Malayalam *adı* (it)

kh pronounced as a guttural hiss, a single continuant sound
Uzbek/Urdu e.g. *khātūn* (honorific with female name)
Perso-Arabic خ

gh pronounced as a guttural gurgle, a single continuant sound
Uzbek/Urdu e.g. *Farghana* (a city in Uzbekistan)
Perso-Arabic غ

q pronounced like English *k*, but farther back in the mouth
Urdu e.g. *diqqat* (difficulty) Perso-Arabic ق

zh pronounced like an English or American *r*, with the tongue more retracted
Tamil/Malayalam e.g. *pazham* (fruit) Malayalam ഴ

The apostrophe ' (ع) stands for the *ain* sound in Arabic, in *'ālam* (world), and it is simply omitted in Persian and Urdu.

Acknowledgements

When I wrote my earlier book on Indian languages, *Wanderers, Kings, Merchants*, it felt like I was clearing a path through a jungle and taking readers along with me as I went. There were a number of things I didn't properly resolve, but I was happy enough to get a glimpse of answers to my questions about the past. I knew that if I thought further, I could come to better conclusions about how things had happened. I needed to look at why I found no pidgins in our history in South Asia, but instead lots of prakrits.

Salikoko Mufwene had been asking precisely this in the context of Caribbean creole languages. When he shared his work and thinking with me, it was a much-needed reassurance that I was on solid ground with these radical thoughts. K.V. Subbarao also mentioned in passing that Dakkhini was full of *calques* from Telugu, which immediately made it sound like creole. He put me in touch with Harbir Bano Arora, who gave me a copy of her dissertation on Dakkhini and answered questions about the language as I wrote. Sajjad Shahid and Shagufta Shaheen of Hyderabad also shared their writings and thoughts about 'Dakhni' and its history.

Madhav Deshpande, my Sanskrit professor, was always an email away when I had questions about Sanskrit, the prakrits or

Marathi. Probal Dasgupta kept up a lively theoretical discussion with me as I wrote, and introduced me to Arun Ghosh, who generously shared his data from different Munda languages. Probal also generously went through the entire manuscript twice with a fine-tooth comb. Sumanta Banerjee gave me the answer to the burning question of what exactly happened in the twelfth century to bring all these new languages into the sunlight. Chinmay Dharurkar gave me information on the Marathi spoken in the southern districts of Maharashtra, where the split ergativity of the north ends. Noburo Yoshioka sent me his dissertation on Burushaski. Masato Kobayashi sent me his dissertation on Brahui. Nazir Shakir Brahui, director of the Brahui Research Institute of Pakistan, was in constant touch as I wrote. Sharada Srinivasan shared her work on the archaeology of the South and its implications for a Dravidian journey south from the Indus Valley. Karan Pillai gave me information about the Vēḷ chieftains who had memories of a northern origin. Santoshi Markam and Venkat Kishan Prasad told me about Gondi and its history.

Friends and students gave me data as I needed it—Amita Paul (Punjabi), Santosh Adhikari and Aayushma Adhikari (Nepali), Anwar Khairi (Pashto), Nilim Datta (Assamese), Devdutt Pattanaik (Odia), Mangla Negi (Garhwali) and Unnati Mishra (Maithili). Imrana Qadeer told me about the Dakkhini-speaking girls from Hyderabad who, in the 1950s, would go to Aligarh to write their final high school exams.

Ruchi Varma made the maps and diagrams.

Karthik Venkatesh of Penguin Random House India walked the long journey as my commissioning editor. Aparna Abhijit copy-edited the book. Aakriti Khurana designed the cover.

And Dinesh Mohan's insights and advice still keep me on track.

Bibliography

23andMe blog. 2009. https://blog.23andme.com/articles/direct-genetic-link-between-australia-and-india-provides-new-insight-into-the-origins-of-australian-aborigines

'Australian Aboriginal languages: Linguistic characteristics'. *Britannica*. https://www.britannica.com/topic/Australian-Aboriginal-languages/Linguistic-characteristics

Abbi, Anvita. 1997. 'Languages in contact in Jharkhand: A case of language conflation, language change and language convergence'. In Anvita Abbi (ed.), *Languages of Tribal and Indigenous People of India: The Ethnic Space*. Delhi: Motilal Banarsidass.

Abbi, Anvita. 2013. *A Grammar of the Great Andamanese Language: An Ethnolinguistic Study*. Leiden: Brill.

Abbi, Anvita. 2018. 'Echo formations and expressives in South Asian languages'. In *Non-prototypical reduplication*. Aina Urdze (ed.). (Studia typologica 22). Berlin: De Gruyter Mouton, pp. 1–33, https://www.academia.edu/37286095/NON_PROTOTYPICAL_REDUPLICATION

Abbi, Anvita. 2020. *Reduplication in South Asian Languages. An Areal, Typological and Historical Study*. New Delhi: Allied Publishers. https://www.researchgate.net/publication/347914129_REDUPLICATION_IN_SOUTH_ASIAN_LANGUAGES_AN_AREAL_TYPOLOGICAL_AND_HISTORICAL_STUDY

Abbi, Anvita. 2021. *Voices from the Lost Horizon: Stories and Songs of the Great Andamanese*. Delhi: Niyogi Books.

Alkhateeb, Firas. 2014. *Lost Islamic History: Reclaiming Muslim Civilization from the Past*. London: Hurst Publishers. Excerpt reprinted as 'Do you know how Islam spread in the Indian subcontinent?' in *Egypt Today*. 29 May 2017, pp. 2–3. https://www.egypttoday.com

Amritavalli, R. and Partha Protim Sarma. 2002. 'A case distinction between unaccusative and unergative subjects in Assamese'. *Snipp.ets*. Issue 5, pp. 6–7. https://www.ledonline.it/snipp.ets/allegati/snipp.ets5001.pdf

Anderson, Gregory D.S. 2006. *The Munda Verb. Trends in Linguistics. Studies and Monographs (TILSM)*. The Hague: Mouton de Gruyter.

Anderson, Gregory D.S. (ed.). 2008. *The Munda Languages*. Oxfordshire: Routledge.

Arora, Harbir K. 2004. *Syntactic convergence: The case of Dakkhini Hindi-Urdu*. University of Delhi Publication Division.

Avtans, Abhishek. 2022. 'Beyond the binary: Gender in Southasian languages'. *Himal SouthAsian: Crossborder Dialectal*. https://www.himalmag.com/dialectal-beyond-the-binary-language-gender-2022/

Baker, Mark C. 2016. 'On the Status of Object Markers in Bantu'. *Semantic Scholar*. https://sites.rutgers.edu/mark-baker/wp-content/uploads/sites/199/2019/07/status-of-OMs-in-Bantu-paper.pdf

Balochi Dictionary: Grammar. Copyright Upp.sala University 2019. https://www.webonary.org/balochidictionary/language/grammar/#:~:text=Balochi%20has%20no%20gender%20distinctions%20in%20the%20noun%20system (accessed 4 April 2023).

Banerjee, Sumanta. 2020. *Unravelling the Bengali Identity: Sub-Nationalism and Nationalism in Nineteenth-Century Bengal*. Kolkata: Purbalok Publication.

Barz, Richard K. and Anthony V.N. Diller. 1985. 'Classifiers and standardization: Some South and South-East Asian comparisons'. In David Bradley (ed.), *Language policy, language planning and sociolinguistics in South-East Asia*. Canberra: Pacific Linguistics, pp. 155–84. http://www.sealang.net/sala/archives/pdf8/barz1985classifiers.pdf

Bhandari, Bhabendra. 2008. 'Tense and aspect in Meche'. *Nepalese Linguistics*. Volume 23, pp. 1–14. https://www.academia.edu/43616070/Nepalese_Linguistics

Bhat, D.N.S. 1973. 'Retroflexion: An Areal Feature'. *Working Papers on Language Universals*. No. 13, Stanford University, California, Committee on Linguistics, pp. 27–67.

Bhatia, Tej K. 1993. *Punjabi: A cognitive-descriptive grammar*. New York: Routledge.

Bhatta, Toya Nath. 2008. 'Complex aspects in Meche'. *Nepalese Linguistics*. Volume 23, pp. 15–24. https://www.academia.edu/43616070/Nepalese_Linguistics

Bloomfield, Leonard. 1933. *Language*. New York: Holt, Rinehart and Winston.

Bray, Denys De S. 1909. *The Brahui Language: Part 1, Introduction and Grammar*. Calcutta: Superintendent Government Printing, India.

Bronkhorst, Johannes. 2007. *Greater Magadha: Studies in the Culture of Early India*. (Handbook of oriental studies, Section two, India). Leiden: Koninklijke Brill.

Butt, Miriam. 2003. 'The Light Verb Jungle'. In G. Aygen, C. Bowern and C. Quinn (eds), *Harvard Working Papers in Linguistics*. Vol. 9, Papers from the CSAS Dudley House Workshop on Light Verbs, pp. 1–49.

Butt, Miriam and Aditi Lahiri. 2013. 'Diachronic pertinacity of light verbs'. *Lingua*. 135: 7–29.

Chandra, Pritha. 2017. 'Optional ergativity with unergatives in Punjabi'. *Taiwan Journal of Linguistics*. Vol. 15.2: 1–35. http://tjl.nccu.edu.tw/main/uploads/TJL_15.2_.1_.pdf

Chandra, Pritha (ed.). 2023. *Variation in South Asian Languages: From Macro to Micro Differences*. Singapore: Springer Verlag.

Chandra, Pritha and Roberta D'Alessandro. (preprint pdf, submitted in 2022). 'Ergativity, agreement and alignment shift in Western Indo-

Aryan'. https://www.researchsquare.com/article/re-2288028/latest.pdf

Chandra, Pritha and Gurmeet Kaur. 2020. 'Braj in the Ergativity Hierarchy'. https://www.researchgate.net/publication/339100329_Braj_in_the_Ergativity_Hierarchy

Chatterji, Suniti Kumar. 1926 (reprinted in 1985, 1993, 2017). *The Origin and Development of the Bengali Language*. Calcutta: Calcutta University (Delhi: Rupa).

Chaubey, Gyaneshwer, Mait Metspalu, Ying Choi et al. 2011. 'Population Genetic Structure in Indian Austroasiatic Speakers: the role of landscape barriers and sex-specific admixture'. *Molecular Biology and Evolution*. Vol. 28, Issue 2, pp. 1013–24. https://academic.oup.com/mbe/article/23/2/1013/1220271

Chaubey, Gyaneshwer and George van Driem. 2020. 'Munda languages are father tongues, but Japanese and Korean are not'. *Evolutionary Human Sciences*. 2. E19: 1–17. https://www.cambridge.org/core/journals/evolutionary-human-sciences/article/munda-languages-are-father-tongues-but-japanese-and-korean-are-not/9F302F4A80E691B05F424312CA03BCDE

Chaudenson, Robert. 1992. *Des Iles, des Hommes, des Langues: Essais sur la Créolisation Linguistique et Culturelle*. Paris: L'Harmattan.

Chaudenson, Robert. 2001. *Creolization of language and culture*. London: Routledge.

Chawla, Janet. 1994. 'The Mythic Origins of the Menstrual Taboo in the Rig Veda'. *Economic and Political Weekly*. Vol. 29, No. 23 (22 October 1994), pp. 2817–27.

Dahl, Eystein and Krzysztov Strońsky. 2016. 'Ergativity in Indo-Aryan and beyond'. In *Indo-Aryan Ergativity in Typological and Diachronic Perspective*. John Benjamins Publishing Company, pp. 1–37. https://www.researchgate.net/publication/303946707_Ergativity_in_Indo-Aryan_and_beyond

Das Gupta, Shashibhushan. 1946 (1962). *Obscure Religious Cults*. Calcutta: Firma K.L. Mukhopadhyay.

Dash, Siniruddha. 1977–78. 'Classifiers and quantifiers in Oriya'. In *Bulletin of the Deccan College Post-Graduate and Research Institute*. Vol. 37, Nos. 1–4, pp. 15–21. https://www.jstor.org/stable/42936566

DeLancey, Scott. 2011. '"Optional" "Ergativity" in Tibeto-Burman Languages'. *Linguistics of the Tibeto-Burman Area*, Volume 34.2: 9–20. http://sealang.net/archives/ltba/pdf/LTBA-34.2.9.pdf

Delfarooz, Behrooz Barjasteh. 2020. 'Two Brahui texts with Glossary and Grammatical Analysis'. *Iranian Journal of Applied Language Studies.* Vol. 12, No. 1, pp. 89–122. http://ijals.usb.ac.ir

Deshpande, Madhav M. 1979. 'Genesis of R̥gvedic Retroflexion: A Historical and Sociolinguistic Investigation'. In Madhav M. Deshpande and Peter Edwin Hook (eds). *Aryan and Non-Aryan in India.* Ann Arbor: The University of Michigan Center for South and Southeast Asian Studies.

Deshpande, Madhav M. and Peter Edwin Hook (eds). 1979. *Aryan and Non-Aryan in India.* Ann Arbor: The University of Michigan Center for South and Southeast Asian Studies.

Deshpande, Madhav M. 2010. 'Pañca Gauda and Pañca Draviḍa: Contested Borders of a Traditional Classification'. In Klaus Kartunnen (ed.), *Anantaṁ Śāstram: Indological and Linguistic Studies in Honour of Bertil Tikkanen. Studia Orientalia.* Vol. 108. Helsinki: Finnish Oriental Society, pp. 29–58.

Dharurkar, Chinmay. 2022. 'The Uncanny Sisterhood of Deccan's Languages'. Wire. 30 July 2022. https://thewire.in/society/the-uncanny-sisterhood-of-deccans-languages https://m.thewire.in/article/society/the-uncanny-sisterhood-of-deccans-languages?utm=authorlistpage

Dige, Stefan. 2022. 'Rosetta Stone: The race to decipher Egypt's hieroglyphs'. Live TV. https://amp.dw.com/en/rosetta-stone-deciphering-mysterious-egyptian-hieroglyphs/a-63268251

Donegan, Patricia Jane and David Stampe. 2002. 'South-East Asian Features in the Munda Languages: Evidence for the Analytic-to-Synthetic Drift of Munda'. *Berkeley Linguistic Society (BLS)* 28S: 111–20. http://www.ling.hawaii.edu/austroasiatic/AA/bls2002.pdf

Drechsel, Emanuel. 2014. *Language Contact in the Early Colonial Pacific: Maritime Polynesian Pidgin before Pidgin English.* Cambridge: Cambridge University Press.

Ebert, Karen H. 1994. *The Structure of Kiranti Languages: Comparative Grammar and Texts.* Zurich: ASAS, Universitat Zurich.

Elfenbein, Josef. 2012. 'BRAHUI'. *Encyclopedia Iranica.* IV/4, pp. 433–43. https://www.iranicaonline.org/articles/brahui

Emeneau, Murray B. 1956. 'India as a Linguistic Area'. *Language.* Vol. 32, No. 1, pp. 3–16.

Encyclopedia Britannica: Nepal https://www.britannica.com/place/Nepal/Economy (accessed 9 September 2023).

Encyclopedia Britannica: *Sino-Tibetan languages.* https://www.britannica.com/topic/Sino-Tibetan-languages?Use-of-noun-classifiers (accessed 9 September 2023).

Farmer, Steve, Richard Sproat and Michael Witzel. 2004. 'The Collapse of the Indus-Script Thesis: The Myth of a Literate Harapp.an Civilization'. *Electronic Journal of Vedic Studies (EJVS)* 11–2, pp. 19–57. http://www.safarmer.com/fsw2.pdf

Ghosh, Arun. 1994. *Santali: A Look into Santali Morphology.* (Language, Linguistics, Tribal Studies, References). Delhi: Gyan Publishing House.

Graeber, David and David Wengrow. 2021. *The Dawn of Everything: A New History of Humanity.* Great Britain: Penguin Random House.

Grierson, George A. 1904 (Indian reprint in 1966). *Linguistic Survey of India*: *Volume* 2: Mon-*Khmer and Siamese-Chinese Families* (*including Khassi and Tai*). Delhi: Motilal Banarsidass.

Grierson, George A. 1904 (Indian reprint in 1966). *Mon-Khmer and Siamese-Chinese families. Linguistic Survey of India*, *Vol. 2.* Delhi: Motilal Banarsidass.

Grierson, George A. 1906 (Indian reprint in 2017). *Linguistic Survey of India, Volume IV: Munda and Dravidian Languages.* Calcutta: Government of India. (Reprinted in Delhi by Kalpaz Publications).

Grierson, George A. 1919 (Indian reprint in 2017). *Linguistic Survey of India*, *Vol. VIII, Indo-Aryan Family, North-Western Group. Specimens of the Sindhī and Lahnda.* Calcutta: Government of India. (Reprinted in Delhi by Kalpaz Publications).

Gumperz, John J. and Robert Wilson. 1971. 'Convergence and Creolization: A Case from the Indo-Aryan/Dravidian Border in India'. In Dell Hymes (ed.), pp. 151–67.

Haig, Geoffrey. 2015. 'Ergativity in Iranian'. https://www.academia.edu/15321950/Ergativity_in_Iranian

Hardy, Peter. 1979. 'Modern European and Muslim Explanations of Conversion to Islam in South Asia: A Preliminary Survey'. In Nehemia Levetzion (ed.), *Conversion to Islam in South Asia.* New York: Holmes and Meiers.

Hook, Peter Edwin. 1973. *The Compound Verb in Hindi.* Ann Arbor: The University of Michigan Center for South and Southeast Asian Studies.

Hook, Peter Edwin. 1991. 'The Compound Verb in Munda: an Areal and Typological Overview'. *Language Sciences.* Volume 13, Number 2, pp. 181–95. https://deepblue.lib.umich.edu/bitstream/handle/2027.42/29571/0000659.pdf?

Hymes, Dell (ed.). 1971. *Pidginization and Creolization of Languages: Proceedings of a Conference Held at the University of the West Indies, Mona, Jamaica, April 1968.* Cambridge: Cambridge University Press.

Hyslop, Gwendolyn. 2016. 'Newar Classifiers: A Summary of the Literature'. https://www.researchgate.net/profile/Gwendolyn-Hyslop/publication/228545953_Newar_Classifiers_A_Summary_of_the_Literature/links/57214fd008ae82260fab40db/Newar-Classifiers-A-Summary-of-the-Literature.pdf

India Mapped: Languages in India. http://www.indiamapped.com/languages-in-india/sikkim-nepali-language (accessed 9 September 2023).

John, Asher. 'Ergativity in Punjabi'. http://asher.john.weebly.com/uploads/3/1/5/3159130/ergativity_in_punjabi1.pdf

Joseph, Tony. 2018. *Early Indians: The Story of Our Ancestors and Where We Came From.* New Delhi: Juggernaut Books.

Kansakar, Tej Ratna. 2005. 'A historical development of the numeral classifier system in Newar'. In Y. Yadav (ed.), *Contemporal Issues in Nepalese Linguistics.* Kirtipur: Tribhuvan University, pp. 101–16.

Kansakar, Tej Ratna. 2005. 'Classical Newar verbal morphology and grammaticalization in Classical and modern Newar'. *Himalayan Linguistics* 3, pp. 1–21.

Karim, Piar. 2011. 'Light Verbs and Noun Verb Agreement in Hunza Burushaski'. In *Pakistaniaat: A Journal of Pakistan Studies.* Vol. 3, No. 3 (2011).

Kilarski, Marcin and Marc Tang. 2018. 'The coalescence of grammatical gender and the numeral classifier *wota* in Nepali'. *Proceedings of the Linguistic Society of America.* 3: 56–65. https://hal.science/hal-02529164/document

Kiryu, Kazuyuki. 2009. 'On the rise of the classifier system in Newar'. In Yasuhiko Nagano (ed.), *Issues in Tibeto-Burman Historical Linguistics.* Osaka: National Museum of Ethnology, pp. 51–69.

Knox, Robert. 1985. 'Jewellery from the Nilgiri Hills: A Model of Diversity'. In Janine Schotsmans and Mauricio Taddei (eds), *South Asian Archaeology.* 1983, pp. 523–33. Naples: Instituto Universitario Orientale, Dipartimento di Studi Asiatici (Series Minor XXIII).

Kolichala, Suresh. 2016. 'Dravidian Languages'. In De Gruyter, *The Languages and Linguistics of South Asia: A Comprehensive Guide*, pp. 77–105. https://www.academia.edu/33656818/Dravidian_in_The_Languages_and_Linguistics_of_South_Asia_A_Comprehensive_Guide

Korn, Agnes. 2009. 'The Ergative System in Balochi from a Typological Perspective'. *Applied Language Studies.* 1: 43-79. https://hal.science/hal-01340943/document

Kramer, Ruth. 2011. 'Object Markers Are Doubled Clitics in Amharic'. In *Morphology at Santa Cruz: Papers in Honor of Jorge Hankamer.* UC Santa Cruz, pp. 41–54. https://escholarship.org/content/qt6n7023wb/qt6n7023wb.pdf?t=lrgu3p

Krishnamurti, Bhadriraju. 2003. *The Dravidian Languages.* Cambridge: Cambridge University Press.

Kulkarni-Joshi, Sonal. 2016. 'Forty years of Language Contact and Change in Kupwar: A Critical Reassessment of the Intertranslatability Model'. *International Language of South Asian Languages and Linguistics*, pp. 147–74.

Kumar, Satish, Rajasekhara Reddy Ravuri, Padmaja Koneru, B.R. Urade, B.N. Sarkar, A. Chandrasekar and V.R. Rao. 2009.

'Reconstructing Indian-Australian phylogenetic link'. In *BMC Evolutionary Biology* 9, Article number 173. https://bmcecolevol.biomedcentral.com/articles/10.1186/1471-2148-9-173

Li, Chao. 2007. 'Split Ergativity in Nepali and Its Typological Significance'. *U. Penn Working Papers in Linguistics.* Volume 13.1:169–81. https://core.ac.uk/download/pdf/76381732.pdf

Malla, Kamal P. 1990. 'The earliest dated document in Newari: The palmleaf from Uku Bāhāh'. NS 235/AD 1114. *Kailash* 16, pp. 15–25.

Masica, Colin P. 1979. 'Aryan and Non-Aryan Elements in North Indian Agriculture'. In Madhav M. Deshpande and Peter Edwin Hook (eds), *Aryan and Non-Aryan in India.* Ann Arbor: The University of Michigan Center for South and Southeast Asian Studies, pp. 55–151.

Masica, Colin P. 1991. *The Indo-Aryan Languages.* Cambridge: Cambridge University Press.

Masood, Talat. 2021. 'Light Verbs in Pashto: Traditionally and Generatively'. *Pakistan Social Sciences Review.* Vol. 5, No. 4, pp. 652–64.

McAlpin, David. 1979. 'Linguistic Prehistory: The Dravidian Situation'. In Madhav M. Deshpande and Peter Edwin Hook (eds), pp. 175–1889.

Misra, Bibhu Dev. 2018. '12,000-Year-Old Petroglyphs in India Show Global Connections'. In Ancient Inquiries: Rediscover the Past. *New Dawn Magazine.* Issue 172. https://www.bibhudevmisra.com/2018/10/12000-year-old-petroglyphs-in-india.html?m=1

Mohan, Peggy. 1978. *Trinidad Bhojpuri: A Morphological Study.* Doctoral dissertation, the University of Michigan, Ann Arbor. University Microfilms.

Mohan, Peggy and Paul Zador. 1986. 'Discontinuity in a Lift Cycle: The Death of Trinidad Bhojpuri'. *Language.* Vol. 62, No. 2, pp. 291–319.

Mohan, Peggy. 2007. *Jahajin.* New Delhi: HarperCollins Publishers India.

Mohan, Peggy. 2021. *Wanderers, Kings, Merchants: The Story of India through Its Languages.* Gurgaon: Penguin Random House India.

Montaut, Annie. 2009. 'Ergativity and Pre-ergative Patterns in Indo-Aryan as Predictions of Localization: A Diachronic View of Past and Future Systems'. In A.R. Fatihi (ed.), *Language Vitality in South Asia.* Aligarh: Aligarh Muslim University, pp. 295–325. https://www.researchgate.net/publication/49135290_Ergative_and_Pre-ergative_Patterns_in_Indo-Aryan_as_Predications_of_Localization

Mufwene, Salikoko S. 2008. 'Creole Languages'. In *Encyclopedia Britannica.* https://www.britannica.com/topic/creole-languages (accessed 11 September 2022).

Mufwene, S.S. 2014. 'The case was never closed: McWhorter misinterprets the ecological approach to the emergence of creoles'. In *Journal of Pidgin and Creole Languages.* 29:1, pp. 157–71.

Mufwene, S.S. 2015. 'Pidgin and Creole Languages'. In James D. Wright (editor-in-chief) *International Encyclopedia of the Social & Behavioral Sciences.* 2nd edition, Vol 18. Oxford: Elsevier, pp. 133–45.

Mufwene, S.S. 2020. 'Creoles and pidgins: Why the latter are not the ancestors of the former'. In Evangelia Adamou and Yaron Matras (eds), *The Routledge handbook of language contact,* pp. 300–24.

Muhammad. 2019. 'Pashto Language Blog'. https://blogs.transparent.com/pashto/ergative-construction-in-pashto/

Mukhopadhyay, Bahata Ansumali. 2019. 'Interrogating Indus inscriptions to unravel their mechanisms of meaning conveyance'. *Palgrave Commun.* 5, 73. https://www.nature.com/articles/s41599-019-0274-1

Mukhopadhyay, Bahata Ansumali. 2021. 'Ancestral Dravidian Languages in Indus Civilization: Ultraconserved Dravidian Tooth-Word Reveals Deep Linguistic Ancestry and supports Genetics'. In *Nature: Humanities and Social Sciences Communications.* Article No. 193. https://www.nature.com/articles/s41599-021-00868-w

Mukhopadhyay, Bahata Ansumali. 2022. 'Crucible-Blowpipe Symbol for Gold and Ratti-Seed Symbol Signifying "Indian

Karat" Engraved on Mohenjo Daro's Gold Assaying Needles: Rosetta Stones for Decoding Indus Script?' https://ssrn.com/abstract=4198499

Mukhopadhyay, Bahata Ansumali. 2023. 'From Structural Analysis to Rosetta Stones: A Multidisciplinary Paradigm of Decoding the Semasiographic Mercantile Script of the Indus Civilization'. International Sindhi Language Conference 2023. https://www.youtube.com/watch?v=ZOCNzAMxNYM

Mukhopadhyay, Bahata Ansumali. 2024. 'Did Indus Script Use Crucible-Blowpipe Based Symbols to Signify Gold, Precious Metals, and Goldsmithing? Script-Internal, Archaeological, Linguistic, and Historical Evidence'. Proceedings of the 2nd International Seminar in Commemoration of Padma Shri Iravatham Mahadevan, on Recent Advances in Archaeological Investigations of South India, Government of Tamil Nadu, Department of Archaeology. pp. 183–215

Munshi, Sadaf and Piar Karim. 2015. 'A Grammatical Sketch of Hunza Burushaski'. http://burushaskilanguage.com/wp-content/uploads/2015/05/grammatical_sketch.pdf

Narasimhan, Vagheesh, Nick Patterson, Priya Moorjani and 114 others. 2019. 'The Formation of Human Populations in South and Central Asia'. *Science* Vol. 365, No. 6457. https://www.ncbi.nlm.nih.gov/pmc/articles/PMC6822619/

Nehru, Jawaharlal. 1936 (1989). *An Autobiography*. Reprinted by the Jawaharlal Nehru Memorial Fund, distributed by Oxford University Press.

Newitt, Malyn D.D. 2010. *A history of Portuguese overseas expansion: 1400–1668*. London: Routledge.

Omvedt, Gail. 2003. *Buddhism in India: Challenging Brahmanism and Caste*. New Delhi: Sage Publications.

Osada, Toshiki. 2008. 'Mundari'. In Gregory D.S. Anderson (ed.), *The Munda Languages*. Routledge. https://www.routledgehandbooks.com/doi/10.4324/9781315822433.chThree (accessed 17 April 2023).

Pagani, Luca and Vicenza Colonna. 2017. 'An Ethnolinguistic and Genetic Perspective on the Origins of the Dravidian-Speaking

Brahui in Pakistan'. *Man India*: 97(1), pp. 267–78. https://www.ncbi.nlm.nih.gov/pmc/articles/PMC5378296/

Parpola, Asko. 2025. 'The Language of the Indus Civilization'. In *The Roots of Hinduism: The Early Aryans and The Indus Civilization*. Oxford Academic, pp. 163–72.

Penny, Mark, Joanna Penny and Pendur Durnath Rao. 2005. *Gondi Dictionary*. Utnoor, Andhra Pradesh: Integrated Tribal Development Agency.

Pirsig, Robert M. 1974. *Zen and the Art of Motorcycle Maintenance*. William Morrow and Company.

Poudel, Tikaram. 2017. 'The Semantics of the Ergative in Nepali'. *Gipan* 3(2). https://www.academia.edu/37799078/The_Semantics_of_the_Ergative_in_Nepali

Radloff, Carla F. and Henrik Liljegren. 2022. 'Ergativity and Gilgiti Shina'. In *Languages of Northern Pakistan: Essays in memory of Carla Radioff*. Oxford University Press, pp. 317–47. https://www.researchgate.net/publication/359452467_Ergativity_and_Gilgiti_Shina

Rahman, Syed Ubaidur. 2024. *Peaceful Expansion of Islam in India*. Delhi: Global Media Publications.

Rau, Felix and Paul Sidwell. 2019. 'The Munda Maritime Hypothesis'. *Journal of the Southeast Asian Linguistic Society*, *JSEALS* 12.2: 35–57. University of Hawaii Press. https://core.ac.uk/download/pdf/228160282.pdf

Riccio, Maria Eugenia, José Manuel Nunes, Melissa Rahal, Barbara Kervaire, Jean-Marie Tiercy, Alicia Sanchez-Mazas. 2011. 'The Austroasiatic Munda population from India and Its enigmatic origin: a HLA diversity study'. https://pubmed.ncbi.nlm.nih.gov/21740156/

Saikia, Pori and Maris Camilleri. 2019. 'Assamese Case Alignment Shifts in Progress'. *Proceedings of the LFG'19 Conference, Australian National University*. Miriam Butt, Tracy Holloway and Ida Toivonen (eds). Stanford CA: CSLI Publications, pp. 251–71. https://web.stanford.edu/group/cslipublications/cslipublications/LFG/LFG-2019/lfg2019-saikia-camilleri.pdf

Shahid, Sajjad and Shagufta Shaheen. 2017. 'The Unique Literary Traditions of Dakhnī'. In Kousar J. Azam (ed.), *Languages and Literary Cultures of Hyderabad.* Hyderabad: Manohar.

Shulman, David. 2016. *Tamil: A Biography.* Cambridge, Massachusetts: The Belknap Press of Harvard University Press.

Silva, Marina, Marisa Oliveira, Daniel Vieira et al. 2017. 'A Genetic Chronology for the Indian Subcontinent Points to Heavily Sex-Biased Dispersals'. *BMC Evolutionary Biology*, Vol. 17, Article No. 88.

Sinnemäki, Kaius. In press. 'Chapter 4—On the distribution and complexity of gender and numeral classifiers'. In Francesca Di Garbo and Bernhard Wälchli (eds), *Grammatical gender and linguistic complexity.* Berlin: Language Science Press. https://langsci-press.org/catalog/view/237/1856/1682-1 (accessed 23 April 2023).

Skilton, Amalia. 2021. 'Noun classes'. In *Introduction to Australian languages.* Chapter 19. https://bpb-us-e1.wpmucdn.com/blogs.cornell.edu/dist/3/9721/files/2021/09/Skilton_OGAL_NounClasses.pdf

Southworth, Franklin C. 1971. 'Detecting Prior Creolization: An Analysis of the Historical Origins of Marathi'. In Dell Hymes (ed.), *Pidginization and Creolization of Languages: Proceedings of a Conference Held at the University of the West Indies, Mona, Jamaica, April 1968*. Cambridge: Cambridge University Press.

Southworth, Franklin. 1979. 'Lexical Evidence for Early Contacts between Indo-Aryan and Dravidian'. In Madhav M. Deshpande and Peter Edwin Hook (eds), pp. 191–233.

Southworth, Franklin. 2005. Handout for 'SARVA: the South Asia Residual Vocabulary Assemblage Project'. http://ccat.sas.upenn.edu/~fsouth/SARVAProject2005.pdf

Srinivasan, Sharada. 2023. 'Ancient Nilgiri Metallurgy'. In *The Nilgiri Hills: A Kaleidoscope of People, Culture, and Nature.* Ed. Paul Hockings. Orient Blackswan, pp. 87–106.

Steever, Sanford B. 1978. *The Serial Verb Formation in the Dravidian Languages*. Delhi: Motilal Banarsidass.

Strońsky, Krzysztov. 2009. 'App.roaches to Ergativity in Indo-Aryan'. *Lingua Posnaniensis*: 78–118. https://sciendo.com/pdf/10.2478/v10122-009-0006-x

Subbarao, Karimuri V. and M. Kevichüsa. 1999. 'Internal relative clauses in Tenyidie (Angami): A case of hierarchical precedence vs. linear precedence'. *Linguistics of the Tibeto-Burman Area*, 22.1, pp. 149–81.

Subbarao, K.V. 2012. *South Asian Languages: A Syntactic Typology*. New York: Cambridge University Press.

Subbarao, K. V. Forthcoming. 'A Panorama of South Asian Relatives: A Case of Structural Convergence, Divergence, Innovation and Syntactic Change'. To appear in Pritha Chandra (ed.).

Tabasum, Saba. 2016. *Morphosyntactic study of Punjabi light verbs*. MPhil Thesis, University of Management and Technology, Lahore. http://escholar.umt.edu.pk:8080/jspui/handle/123456789/2090

Tätte, Kai, Luca Pagani, Ajai Pathak et al. 2019. 'The genetic legacy of continental scale admixture in Indian Austroasiatic speakers'. *Sci Rep*. 9: 3818. https://www.ncbi.nlm.nih.gov/pmc/articles/PMC6405872/

News Minute. 'Excavation findings show Iron Age in TN dates back 4,200 years'. 10 May 2022. https://www.thenewsminute.com/article/excavation-findings-show-iron-age-tn-dates-back-4200-years-all-you-need-know-163795

Vinson, Steve. 'Demotic: The History, Development and Techniques of Ancient Egypt's Popular Script'. In *ARCE (American Resource Center in Egypt)*. https://www.arce.org/resource/demotic-history-development-and-techniques-ancient-egypts-popular-script

Voorhoeve, Jan. 1971. 'Varieties of Creole in Suriname: Church Creole and Pagan Cult Languages'. In Hymes 1971, pp. 323–26.

Voorhoeve, Jan. 1971a. 'Varieties of Creole in Suriname: The Art of Reading Creole Poetry'. In Hymes 1971, pp. 323–26.

Voorhoeve, Jan. 1971b. 'Varieties of Creole in Suriname: Church Creole and Pagan Cult languages'. In Hymes 1971, pp. 305–15.

Weidert, Alfonso K. 1984. 'The classifier construction of Newari and its Southeast Asian background'. *Kailash* 11(3–4): 185–210.

Whinnom, Keith. 1965. 'The Origin of the European-Based Pidgins and Creoles'. *Orbis*. Vol. 14, pp. 509–27.

Witzel, Michael. 1999. 'Substrate Languages in Old Indo-Aryan (Ṛgvedic, Middle and Late Vedic'. *Electronic Journal of Vedic Studies (EJVS)* 5–1, pp. 1–67.

Witzel, Michael. 2000. 'The Languages of Harappa'. https://fid4sa-repository.ub.uni-heidelberg.de/120/1/LanguagesHarapp.a_1998.pdf

Witzel, Michael. 2005. 'Languages and Scripts of India'. In Stanley Wolpert (ed.), *Encyclopedia of India*. New York: Charles Scribner's Sons. https://www.academia.edu/43671585/Languages_and_scripts_of_India_

World Culture Encyclopedia. Vol. 4: People of India. (Updated 11 May 2018). https://www.encyclopedia.com/social-sciences-and-law/anthropology-and-archaeology/people/gond#:~:text=Gond%20society%20is%20divided%20into,release%20by%20the%20hero%20Lingal.

Yoshioka, Noburo. 2012. *A Reference Grammar of Eastern Burushaski*. Unpublished doctoral dissertation, Tokyo University of Foreign Studies. http://repository.tufs.ac.jp/bitstream/10108/72148/9/dt-ko-0158009.pdf.

Zehi, Mousa Mahmoud. 2006. 'The Morphology and Conjugation of Simple Verbs in Balochi and Their Comparison with Persian'. *Language and Linguistics: The Journal of the Linguistics Society of Iran*. https://lsi-linguistics.ihcs.ac.ir/article_1612.html?lang=en

Zide, Arlene R.K. and Norman H. Zide. 1976. 'Proto-Munda cultural vocabulary: evidence for early agriculture'. In Philip M. Jenner, Lawrence C. Thompson and Stanley Starosta (eds), *Austroasiatic Studies*. (Proceedings of the First International Conference on Austroasiatic Linguistics). Vol 2. Honolulu: University of Hawai'i Press, pp. 1295–334.

Notes

1 Alan Machado (Prabhu), *Discovering India Anew: Out of Africa to its Early History* (Hyderabad: Orient Blackswan, 2024), p. 40.
2 Suhrid Kumar Bhowmik, *Sã̄otāli choṭogalper bhūmikā* (Mecheda: Marang Book Press, 2000), quote from p. 13.

Ch. 1: The Road Within

1 'So Long, Frank Lloyd Wright' is a song written by Paul Simon and released on the 1970 Simon and Garfunkel album 1970 album *Bridge over Troubled Water*.
2 But my English was definitely Caribbean not British or American. I was not comfortable inverting for questions, and would always use, say, 'It's okay?' instead of 'Is it okay?' The inversion came into my repertoire years after when I was a student in the US. But, being a prakrit, my English was never 'wrong'.
3 The asterisk * before the example indicates that what follows is not a possible sentence, as it goes against the grammar of the language.
4 In my earlier book, *Wanderers, Kings, Merchants*, to show what I mean by this sort of radical mixture, I gave the example of a sentence in Jamaican creole, *mi go—but mi a com back; dat salt waata braad* (I went—but I am coming back; that salt water is too broad), and then the same sentence in two other English creoles, Trinidadian and Sranan Tongo from Suriname, a French Creole from Guadeloupe, and one West African language, Ewe. In all

these languages the grammar is exactly the same. The unmarked tense is the past, not the present: *go* means 'went'. The present tense needs to be specially marked: *mi* a *com*. And there is no verb 'to be' before the adjective. These are features that violate the rules of English and French in a way that the quaint sentences in Indian English examples do not. They are signs of mixture, of words from English and French put together with notions of grammar that come from West African languages.
Mohan 2021: 9–11, summarized in this table below.

mi	*go*		*m'*	*e kon*			*sootwatra*		-		*bradi*
mi	*go*	*but*	*mi*	*a com*	*back*	*dat*	*salt waata*		-		*braad*
ah	*go*	*but*	*ah*	*comin*	*back*	*dat*	*salt watah*		-	*too*	*broad*
mwen	*alé*		*an*	*ka viré*			*lanmè*	*-la*	-	*two*	*gran*
me	*-dzo*		*me-*	*gbɔ-na*			*atsiafu*	*la*	-		*keke*
I	*WENT*	*but*	*I*	*coming*	*back*	*that*	*salt water*	*the*	*IS*	*too*	*broad*

5 There is also a Spanish-based creole, Palenquero, spoken by a community descended from escaped African slaves, in Colombia, South America. And (I am reliably assured by a reviewer of *Wanderers, Kings, Merchants* in Manila) a few Spanish-based creoles in the Philippines.

6 This is explained in detail in Chapter 4 of my earlier book, *Wanderers, Kings, Merchants*.

7 Emanuel Drechsel (2014), however, speaks of Maritime Polynesian Pidgin, a link language not derived from any European language, which was spoken over the huge Pacific expanse from New Zealand to the west coast of Canada long before Europeans reached the Pacific. Over time, he says, this pidgin stabilized, but without developing into a creole (that is, without ever becoming the native language of any community).

8 There is a theory, promoted by linguists like Keith Whinnom (1965), that all pidgins trace back to a single pidgin, Sabir, spoken in slave and pirate times on the North African Barbary Coast, that *relexified*, taking on new vocabulary that matched new European players in the great game.

9 'Creole languages', Encyclopedia Britannica, https://www.britannica.com/topic/creole-languages (accessed 11 September 2022), p. 192.

10 Mufwene (2015: 136) cites Leonard Bloomfield (1933: 474) saying that 'when the jargon has become the only language of the subject group, it is a *creolized language*'. Bloomfield had worked on a number of Native American languages, and would have been familiar with Chinook Jargon, a pidgin used between different tribes for trade, and eventually between the tribes and European traders. Mufwene thinks that the word 'jargon' 'seems to have meant "pidgin" to [Bloomfield]'.

11 Mufwene 2020: 312.

12 Mufwene uses the term 'variety' in the sense that I use 'prakrit' here to mean something so close to the standard version of the language that, at times, speakers believe that they are actually speaking the standard language.

13 These features are discussed in detail in Chapter 4 of Mohan 2021.

14 Mufwene 2015: 135.

15 This is discussed in detail in Chapter 2 of *Wanderers, Kings, Merchants*: recent genetic studies of migrations into the Indian subcontinent after the first one out of Africa 70,000 years ago all show signs of the migrants essentially only in modern Y-DNA, which is passed from father to son, dating back to the times when specific migrations were known to have taken place. The female descent line in the subcontinent shows no hiccups of this sort.

16 Only the Munda languages, spoken in the forest areas of the eastern Māgadhan zone of north India, survive as examples of pre-Indo-Aryan languages, though even these are mixed (on account of male migrants from Southeast Asia about 4000 years ago, who left words and grammatical features in Munda that survive in newer Indo-Aryan languages of the area).

17 Mohan 1978, Chapter 1, and Mohan and Zador 1986.

18 Drechsel, Emanuel J. 2014. *Language Contact in the Early Colonial Pacific*. Cambridge UK: Cambridge University Press.

Fragments of this pidgin are found in the novels of nineteenth-century American writer Herman Melville, *Typee* and *Omoo*.

19 Mufwene 2020: 310.

20 Mohan 2021: 127.

21 Those who read Chapter 2 of my earlier book on Indian languages, *Wanderers, Kings, Merchants*, will remember how a series of retroflex sounds found their way into Sanskrit via these bilingual children, with even more of these sounds being there, and occurring more frequently, in the prakrits.

22 In Māgadhan and Munda languages numeral classifiers, like the *ekṭā* and *ekjon* in Bengali, come from Southeast Asian languages, and are a feature of most other Asian languages like Chinese, Japanese and Korean. Numeral classifiers would definitely count as a grammatical feature of the lexifier languages introduced by migrant men from Southeast Asia.

23 This is what Mufwene (2020: 311) calls 'speciation by basilectalization', to explain how Nigerian Pidgin English and Cameroon Pidgin English are actually *more* basilectal now (furthest from being like English) than they were when they started.

Ch. 2: The Deccan as a Twilight Zone

1 Literary Urdu, however, in the form of ghazals written in this previously colloquial language, did first appear in the Deccan. At that time it was called 'Hindi', not Urdu. But even before Hindi/Urdu was given importance as a written language, it was already being spoken in Delhi as early as the time of Amir Khusro in the thirteenth century.

2 Retroflexion is discussed in detail in *Wanderers, Kings, Merchants* as a major identifying feature of the South Asian linguistic zone. The dental-retroflex contrast in consonants is found all over South Asia, including Sri Lanka and the Andaman Islands (but not in Assam and the tribal languages of the North-east), and it exists nowhere else as a phonemic contrast, with the exception of First Australian languages and possibly the languages of central New Guinea. First Australians and New Guinea highlanders,

like First Indians, were both part of the first successful migration of Homo sapiens out of Africa.

3 The history of Urdu in north India is discussed in detail in Chapter 5 of *Wanderers, Kings, Merchants*. The following example, this *dohā* written by Amir Khusro in the late 1200s, shows how close early Dehlavi was to the Hindi/Urdu we speak now:
Khusro daryā prem kā, ulṭī wā kī dhār,
Jo utrā so ḍūb gayā, jo ḍūbā so pār.
Oh Khusro, love's river, it has a contrary flow,
Who wades in will drown, who drowns will cross below.

4 The dates here are all taken from Wikipedia, https://en.wikipedia.org/wiki/Alauddin_Khalji and https://en.wikipedia.org/wiki/Deccani_language (accessed 12 December 2022).

5 And not just Dehlavi. There are a number of words traceable to other northern dialects and languages, like Punjabi, in Dakkhini, which go back to the first migrants from the north.

6 For simplicity I use the term 'Dakkhini' here, even though its elite speakers almost all call it 'Dakhni'. This is because my first glimpse of the topic was from Subbarao's writings, and much of the data I refer to on the spoken variety that shows it as a mixed language is from linguists like Subbarao and Harbir K. Arora who call it 'Dakkhini'.

7 Think, for example, of the numeral classifiers in the Munda and Māgadhan languages of north-eastern India: the *ek-ṭā* and *ek-jon* of Bengali, for example, where *-jon* indicates that humans are being counted, while *-ṭā* is for non-human (but individual) entities. This goes back to a pattern in all the languages of East and Southeast Asia, from where there was a migration of men into the east of the subcontinent about 4000 years ago.

8 This is the same example I used in *Wanderers, Kings, Merchants* (Mohan 2021:200–01) to illustrate how Naga languages have recently started adopting an Indo-Aryan relative clause structure in place of their earlier pattern, which is essentially the same as the pattern in Dravidian languages. It was first reported in Subbarao and Kevichüsa 1999.

9 Subbarao (forthcoming). Note, in this example, the absence of the verb 'to be'.
10 *Ich* in Dakkhini is an emphatic: a particle that adds emphasis.
11 Arora 2004: 43.
12 Arora 2004: 97.
13 Subbarao (personal communication 12 February 2023).
14 Subbarao (forthcoming).
15 Subbarao (forthcoming):

Konkani:	*khanco mhāntāro pepar vaccat āssa ki to ḍākṭarunu āssa*
	which old man paper reading is (linker) he doctor is
Gujarati:	*kon beṭka avāya gi tena mora singati*
	which boy came (linker) he my friend

16 Arora 2004: 13.
17 Arora 2004: 103.
18 Balochi has no gender, but it does have ergativity in about half of its dialects. It is also an Iranian language, and not Indo-Aryan. Nepali, too, has an ergativity that goes back to Tibeto-Burman, not the IVC Periphery languages, and its gender is linked to natural gender.
19 In Urdu, *namāz*, prayers, are 'read', with the palms of the hands cupped to look like a book.
20 *paṛh liye* sounds a bit better.
21 BITS is an acronym for Birla Institute of Technology and Science, a university-level institute first set up in Pilani, Rajasthan (making Pilani part of the 'brand name').
22 Ravi Bhushan, PhD student in linguistics at BITS-Pilani, Hyderabad, 16 January 2023.
23 WhatsApp message, 21 January 2023. My take would be that *relgāṛī* also ends in *-ī*.
24 Note the Tamil *avan śāpaḍarān* (he eats), *avaḷ śāpaḍarā* (she eats) *adı śāpaḍadı* (it eats). These differing verb endings are linked only to natural gender. Inanimate nouns in Tamil are not masculine or feminine.
25 I have left out Malayalam, as it is unusual: it has no person markers on its finite verbs.
26 Mohan 2021: 150.
27 Shahid and Shaheen 2017: 91.

28 *Ibid.*: 98.
29 *Ibid.*: 98 (emphasis added).
30 Syed Ubaidur Rahman 2024: 115 (quoting Peter Hardy 1979: 85).
31 Shahid and Shaheen 2017: 99.
32 *Ibid.*: 99.
33 My (somewhat free) translation.
34 Arora 2004: 2.
35 *Ibid.*: 2–3.
36 Firas Alkhateeb. 2014.
37 'The demise of Buddhism in India', *Encyclopedia Britannica*, https://www.britannica.com (accessed 25 January 2023).
38 The term *nerey* was told to me by Sumanta Banerji, who writes about Bengali history, with the translation 'double-tonsured' provided by Tapan Bose, who has spent time studying the different caste groups in Bengal.
39 Mohan 2021: 129.
40 *Ibid.*: 183.
41 Basham 1954: 252.
42 Omvedt 2003: 122.
43 I found this out from Peer Mohammed, a journalist I met in Chennai, who is part of this community, and who spent time telling me about its antecedents and its differences from the Dakkhini-speaking Muslims in Tamil Nadu.
44 Dharurkar 2022.
45 *Ibid.*
46 *Ibid.*
47 Dharurkar (2022) gives *Kaa karlaalav*, in SE Marathi, and *Yen maadlikattiri*, in NE Kannada, both of which mean 'What are you doing?'. These, he says, differ from what you get in standard Marathi and standard Kannada, *kaay kari laaglaa aahat* and *Yen maadliki hattiri*, both of which mean 'What have you started doing?'. He calls this a 'contraction', where the SE Marathi and NE Kannada have 'come together' with a simpler set of morphemes to mean something slightly different. SE Marathi and NE Kannada seem to be totally in sync, while standard Marathi and standard Kannada are not.

48 Gumperz and Wilson 1971.
49 Kulkarni-Joshi 2016: 1.

Ch. 3: The Taming of the Ergative Dragon

1 I have made my dragon neuter, the way the Vritra was neuter in the Rig Veda.
2 While the modern Māgadhan languages are 'fiercely non-ergative', with none of the split ergativity found in the northwest, the northern Munda languages still have double marking: that is, finite verbs carry markers for both subject and object.
3 'Who coined the term 'ergativity' in Linguistics and when was it first used?', Quora, https://www.quora.com/Who-coined-the-term-ergativity-in-linguistics-and-when-was-it-first-used?top_ans=132683962 (accessed 18 October 2023).
4 'How did ergative languages evolve? Are there examples of transitions from ergative to nonergative languages?', Quora, https://www.quora.com/How-did-ergative-languages-evolveAre-there-examples-of-transitions-from-ergative-to-non-ergative-languages (accessed 18 October 2023).
5 See Mohan 2021: 109–16 for all the details.
6 Think of the Sanskrit phrase *satyameva jayate*. The active form would have to be *jayati*; *jayate* is an example of 'middle' voice. And it has a sort of reflexive sense to it. 'Truth prevails', or maybe even 'whatever prevails is truth'.
7 In English, it means using the verb 'have': I *have* broken, instead of I *am* broken. In Sanskrit it meant adding *-vat*, turning *khādita* into *khāditavat*.
8 Straightforward past tenses like *ate* and *did* do not exist in these languages. Instead, participles like *eaten* and *done* have become make-believe finite verbs.
9 Chandra 2017: 4. We say *he/she* without *it*, as Punjabi has a binary system of grammatical gender, where nouns can only be masculine or feminine, even if they are words for 'things'.
10 Examples elicited from Amita Paul, IAS.
11 Chandra and D'Alessandro (preprint pdf posted 2022). I'm guessing that what is 'optional' is ergative *marking*, not the alignment.

12 Grierson 1919 Vol. VIII: 23.

13 Chatterji 1926: 166.

14 This data is from Prof. Anwar Khairi, of Kandahar, Afghanistan, who teaches Pashto at Jawaharlal Nehru University, Delhi. He walked into our meeting already speaking about retroflexion and ergativity, as though reading my mind.

15 All the Iranian languages once had this feature, going back to the same time that it showed its face in the prakrits and Sanskrit. It has, however, been lost in modern Persian, though not in all its related languages.

16 Korn 2009: 60–61.

17 Yoshioka 2012: 32.

18 The Munda languages also put markers on the verb for both subject and object agreement, with the subject marker coming last of all. But the Māgadhan languages that have Munda as their substratum did not get ergativity at all.

19 According to Anvita Abbi, Great Andamanese too is a 'double-marking language with ergativity'. And it is strangely reminiscent of Burushaski in its marking of objects on verbs, and even the form of its ergative marker.

20 Abbi 2013: 65, 68.

21 See Chapter 5: p. 207.

22 Grierson 1906: 37 gives the Australian example *wākun-to minariṅ tatan*, crow-by what eats? What is the crow eating?

23 See this example from Kramer 2011: 48.

Almaz bet-u-n	*ayy-äćć-ɨ*w
Almaz house-DEF-ACC	see.PF-3FS-3MS.O

'Almaz saw the house'

24 Wikipedia gives this example:

Mtoto mdogo amekisoma

Child small SM-Perf-OM-verb stem

'The small child has read it [a book]'

Mtoto agrees with *mdogo*, both having the same prefix *m-*, a diminutive.

The subject marker is *a-*, the perfect tense marker is *-me-*, the object marker is *-ki-*, agreeing with the implicit *kitabu* 'book'.

'Bantu languages', Wikipedia, https://en.wikipedia.org/wiki/Bantu_languages (last accessed 9 December 2024).

25 Yoshioka 2012: 52.

26 ABS means 'absolutive'. In ergative-absolutive languages the absolutive is often unmarked, and similar in function to an object in nominative-accusative languages. The absolutive would also be the subject of an intransitive verb, as in 'he-ABS went'.

27 Radloff and Liljegren 2022: 330.

28 *Ibid.*: 321.

29 There are also, according to Chandra 2017 and 2022, Haryanvi dialects where there are no overt ergative markers at all, but still gender agreement in past sentences with the 'object', like Pashto.

30 The ergativity in Nepali and Assamese (and in Newari and Bodo/Meche) is not split ergativity with ergative realignment in the past perfect tense. It has a different source.

31 Abbi 2013: 80.

32 Skilton 2021.

33 'Amharic', Wikipedia, https://en.wikipedia.org/wiki/Amharic (last accessed 9 December 2024).

34 Stroński 2009: 105. Italics added.

35 See the poem by Kuraish Bidari in Chapter 2.

36 Deshpande, personal email communication (2 March 2023).

37 Not to forget the Dakkhini expression *mereku nakko*, where the verb analogous to *ćāhiye* or *vēṇum* is missing.

38 According to Wikipedia, the *Baudhayana Dharmasutra* (BDS) 1.1.2.10 (perhaps compiled in the eighth to sixth centuries BCE) declares that Āryāvarta is the land that lies west of the Kālakavana, east of Adarsana, south of the Himalayas and north of the Vindhyas, but in BDS 1.1.2.11 Āryāvarta is confined to the doab of the Ganges-Yamuna. BDS 1.1.2.13–15 considers the people from beyond this area to be 'of mixed origin, and hence not worthy of emulation by the Aryans'.
'Āryāvarta', Wikipedia, https://en.m.wikipedia.org/wiki/%C4%80ry%C4%81varta (accessed 14 March 2023).

39 Banerjee 2020: 57.

40 The quote from Banerjee 2020 is in a Bengali-influenced Sanskrit. I asked Madhav Deshpande for the original Sanskrit,

and he says that this quote is 'in the commentaries Balamanorama and Tattvabodhinī on Bhaṭṭoji's Siddhanta-Kaumudī on Pāṇini 3.2.114.' He added that he 'also finds this quotation in Nārāyaṇabhaṭṭa's Tristhalīsethu, a Dharmaśāstra work'. These works, he says, give 'only a generic reference to "a Smṛti"'... and that it is not in the verse index of the Manusmṛti.

41 Grierson (1906: 23) spells out in the Introduction to his volume on Munda languages that 'nouns do not differ for gender. The natural gender is distinguished by using different words or by adding words meaning "male," "female," respectively... Nouns, on the other hand, can be divided into two classes, *viz.*, those that denote animate beings, and those that denote inanimate objects respectively.' Numeral classifiers are discussed in Chapter 5.

42 Chatterji 1926: 174.

43 *Ibid.*: 177.

44 Delfarooz 2020: 103.

45 *Ibid.*: 97 clarifies that Brahui is a 'nominative-accusative language', and his texts and glossary are full of recent loanwords from Urdu, with no sign of influence from early prakrit times.

46 Bray 1909: 18–19.

Ch. 4: In Search of 'Language X'

1 This name was originally given by Colin Masica 1979: 134 who mentions a category he calls Unknown—31 per cent: 'the remainder—words of unknown origin—constitutes the largest category in our sample ... In addition, it should be remembered that a significant portion of the suggested Dravidian and Austro-Asiatic etymologies is uncertain.'

It is a neat term, so I have appropriated it here to mean the unidentified language that must have been the standard language in urban Harappa.

2 Witzel 2005.

3 Farmer, Sproat and Witzel 2004.

4 '$10,000 Prize Announced by Farmer, Sproat, and Witzel', Safarmer, https://www.safarmer.com/indus/prize.html (last accessed 9 December 2024).

5 Stefan Dige 2022. This article is the source of all the information cited here on the Rosetta Stone.
6 Steve Vinson in *ARCE* online.
7 Ansumali Mukhopadhyay 2019.
8 Ansumali Mukhopadhyay 2022: abstract.
9 Ansumali Mukhopadhyay 2023 (video).
10 Masica 1989.
11 Parpola 2015: 163.
12 Witzel 2000.
13 Joseph 2018: 44.
14 Joseph 2018: 65.
15 This is discussed in detail in Chapter 2 of Mohan 2021. It is also the subject of Deshpande 1979. The *ṣ* here is the retroflex 'sh' in words like *ūṣā*, Usha, the Goddess of the Dawn. And the *ḷ* is added as it occurs often in Prakrit, and in the first word-compound of the Rig Veda.
16 This is specifically about ergativity, where in the past tense the verb is transformed into a past participle, agreeing with what was otherwise the object: *food eaten (by me)*. This would be a gender agreement, and the earlier subject would be in the instrumental case. More on this as we go.
17 Balochi and Pashto are Iranian languages, but even they shared some of these features.
18 Brahui will be discussed separately, as it is possible that it represents a later migration from Dravidian territory in peninsular India.
19 The emergence of the modern Indo-Aryan languages is discussed in Chapter 4 of Mohan 2021.
20 More on this towards the end of Chapter 5, where we see how this happened in Bengal.
21 This is discussed briefly in Mohan 2021: 190.
22 Mohan 2021: 69. Paul Kiparsky, retired professor of Sanskrit and historical linguistics at Stanford University, and a native speaker of Finnish, told me in passing that he had interviewed this last speaker of Livonian.
23 'Latvian language', Wikipedia, https://en.m.wikipedia.org/wiki/Latvian_language (accessed 5 November 2023).

24 Krishnamurti 2003: 141.
25 Pagani and Colonna 2017: 1–2.
26 *Ibid.*: 7–8. '. . . the Brahui, the only Dravidian-speaking population of Pakistan, do not show higher genetic affinity with Dravidian Indians than any of their neighbouring Indo-European-speaking Pakistani populations. While this is still compatible with an ancient Dravidian genetic substrate . . . shared by all the Pakistani populations, this does not highlight a preferential link between Brahui and the other Dravidian-speaking populations.'
27 See Narasimhan et al. 2019, where the geneticists are unwilling to distinguish between the Dravidian heritage in modern south Indians and the Dravidian heritage that persists in present-day Indus Valley populations.
28 Grierson 1906, Volume IV: 646. 'Brahui is a distinctly Dravidian language. It seems to have more points of analogy with Kurukh and Malto than with other dialects belonging to the same family.'
29 When I recorded some of the last oral samples of my ethnic language, Trinidad Bhojpuri, back in the 1970s in Trinidad, I could only get data from the oldest and poorest Indians in villages in central Trinidad, in particular women who had not been to school, where the mainstream language, Creole English, would have pulled them away from the home language. While the old ones in my family knew this language, when they spoke they tuned it towards the Hindi they had learnt in school, and discouraged me from learning Bhojpuri. At the time I felt they were keeping me away from my heritage language. Now I see that they were actually doing what any upwardly mobile middle-class family would have done.
30 Grierson 1906: 642 notes that Brahui, unlike other Dravidian languages, has 'only one form of the plural in the first person', which means the distinction between the inclusive 'we' and the exclusive 'we' is not there. He also (1906: 643) says that 'Relative clauses are effected as in Balōchi. The Balōchi relative particle *ki* has been introduced into the language, and it is used in exactly the same way as in Balōchi and Persian.'
31 Bray 1909.

32 *Ibid.*: 3. 'An initial analysis based on microsatellite or short tandem repeats (STRs) showed that this language isolate group was genetically related to their neighbors and this has been borne out by several subsequent analyses.'

33 During the Indian migration to Trinidad between 1845 and 1919, attempts were made in the 1860s to include more women, so as to have 'natural increase' in the labour pool. The hope was that, with financial inducements, 40 per cent of the migrants might be women. But the numbers tended to stay at around 30 per cent. In a more fraught situation, of men moving on their own steam to a new land with no prospects, this number would certainly have been lower. Some groups, like the Ahom in Assam, do not seem to have included women at all.

34 Grierson 1906: 219.

35 Bhat 1973: 34, 35–36.

36 See Chapter 2 Note 8 of Mohan 2021, p. 286, which cites Anvita Abbi as saying that the sounds *t*, *d* and *ṭ*, *ḍ* are in phonemic contrast in Great Andamanese, citing the minimal pairs *thu*, 'to be born', and *ṭhu*, 'to be'.

37 See Chapter 5 of Mohan 2021.

38 The sound *ḷ* does occur at the very start of the Rig Veda, but this is a later addition, and is only a variant of *ḍ* that occurs between two vowels. Even Pāṇini, who wrote the *Aṣṭādhyāyī*, the definitive grammar of Sanskrit, does not list *ṛ* and *ḷ* as sounds of Sanskrit.

39 See note 21 above.

40 The use of an asterisk * before **phājī* indicates that that word does not exist.

41 This is a complicated swap: the *unaspirated* stops, *g j ḍ d b*, are pronounced implosively, while the voiced aspirates *gh jh ḍh dh bh* are simply pronounced without aspiration. In Grierson's *Linguistic Survey of India*, *Vol. VIII* on Sindhi, he writes these as *gg ḍḍ dd bb*.

42 Anderson 2006: 12 gives the words *khokṇḍo*, 'ill conditioned', and *oṭhŋgao*, 'to steady on' in Santali.

43 See, for example, Abbi 2021: 118, which lists *ṭh* and *kh*.

44 'Brahui language', Wikipedia, https://en.m.wikipedia.org/wiki/Brahui_language.
45 In Kālidāsa's *Abhijñānaśakuntalā*, Shakuntala, who as a woman speaks only in prakrit, tends to avoid voiced aspirates like *bh* and replace them with *h*, hearing the 'hiss' rather than the 'b' in *bh*.
46 Subbarao 2012: 20.
47 Munshi and Karim 2015: 11.
48 'Brahui', Mustgo.com, https://www.mustgo.com/worldlanguages/brahui/?amp (accessed 15 September 2023).
49 Starting Out: Learn Sanskrit Online. https://learnsanskrit.org
50 Southworth 1971: 263.
51 Munshi and Karim 2015: 17–22.
52 Bray 1909: 203–09.
53 *Balochi Dictionary*, section on adpositions.
54 Karim 2011.
55 Karim 2011: 73.
56 Zehi 2006: abstract.
57 Masood 2021, quoting Butt 2003: 1.
58 On light verbs in Hindi-Urdu, see Wikipedia: https://en.m.wikipedia.org/wiki/Light_verb
59 Saba, Tabasum 2016 (abstract).
60 Bray 1909: 181.
61 The asterisk * means that the example that follows is not an allowed form. Peter Hook, however, in an email (27 March 2023) added some clarifications: 'In speakers' minds and on their tongues such contradictions may find a happy home … in fact you ***can*** say it, especially after *to* or in questions … Indeed, there are contexts in which negated compound verbs are strongly preferred to non-compound verbs.'.
62 Mohan 2021: 199 gives the Nagamese sentence *moi tai nimite kitab ek-ta* kini di-se, 'I bought a book for ("gave") him', where *di-se*, from 'gave', is a vector with *kini*, 'buy'.
63 Mohan and Zador 1986: 299.
64 Steever 1987: 105.
65 *Ibid.*: 106.
66 Noburo Yoshioka, two emails sent on 1 March 2023.

67 Email on 28 February 2023.

68 Email sent on 25 March 2023.

69 'Pāṇini', Wikipedia, https://en.wikipedia.org/wiki/P%C4%81%E1%B9%87ini (accessed 27 March 2023).

70 WhatsApp from Nazir Shakir Brahui, 18 September 2023.

71 Yoshioka 2012: 108.

72 These examples are from *A Sanskrit Primer* by Madhav M. Deshpande, first published in 1997. When I told him the sentence sounded 'new', he admitted that he had written it, but added that such structures were not only endorsed by Pāṇini, but were even attested in Rig Vedic Sanskrit.

73 Yoshioka's 1 March 2023 email.

74 Yoshioka 2012: 166.

75 Abbi 2020: abstract.

76 Abbi 2018.

77 WhatsApp message from Nazir Shakir Brahui, 15 September 2023.

78 On 1 February 2024.

79 Grierson 1906: 642, writing about pronouns in Brahui, says: 'there is only one form of the plural of the first person'.

80 And maybe men too. I excluded Brahmin men from my study, though, as they tended to know just enough standard Hindi to make the Bhojpuri data unreliable. I suspected that if I were not there, they would be mixing in much less Hindi, and *that* was not the 'change' I was investigating.

81 Email received 30 March 2023.

82 *Ibid.*

83 Email received 29 March 2023.

84 This came in a footnote in Nehru 1989: 29–30.

85 Shulman 2016: 22 traces the *zh* in Tamil back to the Tamil Brahmi script, which 'if the newly proposed radiometric datings for Tamil Brāhmī inscriptions discovered at Porunthal and Kodumanal turn out to be correct, we would have to push the transition to protohistory back to the fourth or even fifth century B.C.' He is sceptical of this dating, however, as it would put Tamil Brāhmī as prior to Ashoka. And that is not even close to the time of the Indus Valley Civilization.

86 First Australians and people from central New Guinea, our fellow travellers out of Africa, also have retroflexion in their languages. It does seem to exist in Norwegian and Georgian, but that is another story.

87 Both the definition and the explanation are from Hook's email, 27 March 2023.

88 See, for example, this discussion thread: https://forum.wordreference.com/threads/punjabi-retroflex-l.899526/

Ch. 5: Across the Sangam

1 The story of Rani Saranga is one of the strands in my first book, *Jahajin* (Mohan 2007), which is based on the migration of indentured labourers from the Bhojpuri-speaking region of India to Trinidad between 1845 and 1919.

2 Bronkhorst 2007: 1.

3 *Ibid.*

4 Banerjee 2020: 57.

5 Abhay Tole Trivedi, history student at Ashoka University 2023.

6 Ashoka, as the grandson of Chandragupta Maurya, was a Kshatriya, and the Buddha was born as Prince Siddhartha. And all the Jain Tirthankaras were Kshatriyas. Prakrit was the language of the Kshatriyas, and their caste status would have been validated at some time by Brahmins from the Āryāvarta lands. See insightonindia.com for information about the Jain Tirthankaras, https://www.insightsonindia.com/indian-heritage-culture/religion/jainism/#:~:text=There%20are%20a%20total%20of,Tirthankaras%20were%20Kshatriyas%20by%20birth.

7 Unless they were from some other part of India, like Bengal. Bengali is a Māgadhan language too, as is Bhojpuri, but that does not help. It is a class difference, not a problem with communication. You do not 'out' yourself as a Māgadhan if you are elite.

8 Bronkhorst 2007: 15.

9 This is neatly summarized in Joseph 2018: 42–44.

10 'Direct Genetic Link between Australia and India Provides New Insight into the Origins of Australian Aboriginals', 23andMe, 24 July 2009, https://blog.23andme.com/articles/direct-genetic-

link-between-australia-and-india-provides-new-insight-into-the-origins-of-australian-aborigines (accessed 14 April 2023).

11 Seeing as we *all* seem to share mtDNA with these tribes, how different would the results have been had they taken DNA samples from just about any peninsular South Asian? And wouldn't the people of central New Guinea have shared these mtDNA mutations too?

12 This is based on Kumar, Reddy et al. 2009.

13 Mohan 2021: 22.

14 The tribal languages on the north-eastern fringe of South Asia do not have retroflexion, and the genetics of these populations are different, especially in terms of the maternal and paternal descent lines being essentially the same. Assamese, classed as an Indo-Aryan language, but located in the north-east, also does not have retroflexion.

15 See, for example, this YouTube video on indigenous Australian languages that demonstrates these retroflex sounds, https://m.youtube.com/watch?v=UumXjnt.Jjbl

16 'Baiga Tribe', IndiaNetzone, https://www.indianetzone.com/8/baiga.htm (accessed 15 April 2023).

17 'Birhor people', Wikipedia, https://en.m.wikipedia.org/wiki/Birhor_people (accessed 15 April 2023).

18 Grierson 1906 (2007): 2.

19 *Ibid.*: 3–4.

20 *Ibid.*: 5.

21 *Ibid.*: 1–2.

22 *Ibid.*: 1.

23 *Ibid.*: 5. Many conflate the much later migration of the Khasi, which had a large number of women, with the 4000-year-ago migration of the Austro-Asiatics, who were essentially only men. They were clearly two separate migrations, and the languages look nothing like each other (despite a few Mon-Khmer words in both). The Munda languages are mixed, Khasi is not.

24 'Indigenous Peoples in Malaysia'. https://www.iwgia.org/en/malaysia.html (accessed 28 April 2023).

25 Tätte, Pagani, Pathak et al. 2019: abstract. IBD stands for 'identical by descent'.

26 This is summarized in Mohan 2021: 209–10, based on Chaubey, Metspalu, Choi et al. 2011.

27 E. Kuhn, reported in Grierson 1906 (2007): 11.

28 I wonder if there is a genetic study on this. In Chapter 5 we will explore whether they are free of Austro-Asiatic influence in language.

29 This calls to mind the case of Saramacaans and Ndjuka, creole languages spoken in the interior of Suriname, which are classed as 'English-based', and which date back to a fifteen-year period in the 1600s when the English had control of the colony. The 'English' words in these languages feel like the Vietnamese words in the Munda languages: the resemblance clicks only after a linguist has pointed them out. The operating systems of Saramacaans and Ndjuka call to mind the general Caribbean pattern, seen in English-based and French-based creoles. But it's a huge stretch to call them varieties of English.

30 Grierson 1906 (2007): 18. Retyped exactly from the original.

31 Osada 2008: 106.

32 In fact, 'books' is not feminine in Sanskrit or the prakrits. It is neuter. It got assigned to the feminine gender at the time when the three-gender system in the prakrits was pared down to a two-gender system in all the western Indo-Aryan languages except Marathi, Gujarati and Konkani.

33 Tibetan alone in the whole of East and Southeast Asia does not have numeral classifiers.

34 Chatterji 1926: 778.

35 Emeneau 1956: 10.

36 *Ibid.*: 11.

37 *Ibid.*: 12.

38 Barz and Diller 1985.

39 *Ibid.*: 168.

40 Or, more likely, confuse me, as Grierson's data about Bhojpuri was as patchy as his data about the Munda languages. At least he had found a few in Bhojpuri.

41 Barz and Diller 1985: 164.

42 Going through Grierson's primary data in the Māgadhan as well as the Munda languages, I was amused to see 'fatted calf' uniformly

translated as 'fattened calf': it seems Grierson was not ready to explain that 'fatted' meant castrated, something that is certainly done in the Māgadhan area to animals meant to be eaten.

43 Barz and Diller: 157.

44 Chatterji 1926: 777–81.

45 Barz and Diller 1985: 169–71. I have changed the first three in Assamese to *jon*, *joni* and *jona*, in keeping with how they sound to me. In Chapter 7 I discuss how the large number of classifiers in Assamese links to a Tibeto-Burman language, Bodo, in its substratum, a close relative of Tibeto-Burman Newari in Nepal, which is the substratum of Nepali. All four languages, Assamese, Nepali, Bodo and Newari, have essentially the same classifiers, about fifteen in all.

46 *Ibid.*: 170.

47 Emeneau 1956: 11 (in a footnote).

48 See Wikipedia on Ahom language, the section on grammar. https://en.m.wikipedia.org/wiki/Ahom_language (accessed 30 April 2023).

49 In Assamese it is simply *ta*, with an alveolar *t* like in English. Assamese does not have retroflexion. These two options are based on information from Nilim Datta of Assam.

50 Barz and Diller 1985: 178. Barz and Diller say that 'the earliest Thai inscriptions show only a handful of classifiers of rather broad scope: *khon*, for humans; *tua*, for animals; and *'an*, for inanimate objects, and a few other shape-related forms. Comparative Tai evidence bears out postulating a reduced set for earlier stages of Tai. During the Ayudhya and early Bangkok eras (c. 1450-1850) several hundred classifiers came into use, at least in literate court and urban circles.'

51 The phonetic symbol *ʔ* represents a glottal stop, as in the cockney British pronunciation of 'bottle' as *boʔʔl*. It is produced by bringing the two vocal cords together to stop the airstream.

52 Osada 2008: 115.

53 Anderson 2008 and Ghosh 1994.

54 Ghosh 1994: 46.

55 Grierson 1906: 151.

56 *Ibid.*: 108.

57 Though, as we will see in Chapter 7, Assamese and Nepali also have a substratum of Bodo and Newar, which have a large amount of numeral classifiers, as well as a Tibeto-Burman form of ergativity.
58 See Witzel 1999.
59 Maria Eugenia Riccio et al., 'The Austroasiatic Munda population from India and Its enigmatic origin: a HLA diversity study', *Human Biology* Vol. 83,3 (2011): 405–35, https://pubmed.ncbi.nlm.nih.gov/21740156/; HLA stands for 'human leukocyte antigens': genes that help code for proteins that differentiate between self and non-self, part of the immune system defence.
60 Chaubey, Metspalu et al. 2019: abstract.
61 Rau and Sidwell 2019: 49.
62 Chaubey and van Driem 2020: 6.
63 Donegan and Stampe 2002: 111 quoting Grierson 1904: 2.
64 *Ibid.*
65 *Ibid.*: 113–14.
66 Bronkhorst 2007: 69–70.
67 Chatterji 1926: 43.
68 *Ibid.*: 46–47. The italics appear to be translations of quotes from the Vedic Brahmans.
69 Deshpande in an email on 6 May 2023.
70 This was first suggested by Anish Tore, my student at Ashoka University, and confirmed by Madhav Deshpande, in an email on 28 February 2024.
71 This was first suggested by Prachyadeep Dasgupta, my student at Ashoka University, and confirmed by Sumanta Banerjee, in an email on 28 February 2024.
72 This suggestion was made by Aditya Venkatesh Aiyar, my student at Ashoka University.
73 See Chapter 6 endnote 6, which quotes Narasimhan et al. 2019, where it does not seem possible to distinguish between the Dravidian ancestry in present-day south Indians and the old Indus Valley people.
74 *Ibid.*: 56–57.
75 *Ibid.*: 58.

76 Their names in earlier texts were spelled as Fa Hien and Hiuen Tsang.
77 S.K. Chatterji 1926 (1985, 1993, 2017): 77.
78 *Ibid.*: 100.
79 *Ibid.*: 78.
80 *Encyclopedia Britannica.* 'Buddhism: Historical Development'. https://www.britannica.com/topic/Buddhism/Historical-development (accessed 6 May 2023).
81 *Ibid.*: 101.
82 Banerjee 2020: 61.
83 *Ibid.*: 63.
84 *Ibid.*: 64.
85 *Ibid.*: 64. *Paighambar* means messenger (of Allah), *ghazi* is an honorific Muslim title, and *qazi* means a judge.
86 *Ibid.*: 63.
87 *Ibid.*: 65 quoting Shashibhusan Das Gupta 1962: 265.
88 *Ibid.*: 66.
89 The Bhojpuri sentence is from me, Maithili from my student Unnati Mishra of Ashoka University, Delhi, Bengali from Probal Dasgupta, Odia from Devdutt Pattanaik, Assamese from Nilim Datta, and Santali from Arun Ghosh.
90 The Mundari example is from Osada 2008: 121, and the other examples were sent to me by Arun Ghosh.
91 In Chapter 7, we will see this same enigma in the case of Nepali, where we will need to decide whether it is fundamentally a language with gender or one with numeral classifiers. And earlier in this chapter, when I introduce Probal Dasgupta, I mention that one thing that we talked about was the way languages were either gender languages or classifier languages, but not both.
92 This is a far cry from the Indo-Aryan languages, where *every* bit of vocabulary was replaced by forms from the prakrits.

Ch. 6: The Dravidian Dreamtime

1 Deshpande 2010. The *ḍ* ~ *ḷ* alternation is the *ḍ* in *īḍyaḥ* becoming *ḷ* in *īḷe* in the first line of the *Agnisuktaṁ*. This *ḍ* ~ *ḷ* alternation still exists, with the Arabic word *RamaDan*, where *D* is a

pharyngealized Arabic sound, becoming *Ramaḷan* in Tamil and Malayalam.

2 Madhav Deshpande in an email on 10 June 2023.

3 It is extremely difficult to get women to join migrations. Even when recruiters specifically wanted to include more women in the migration of Indian labour to the Caribbean in the nineteenth century, the best they could ever do was reach a 30 per cent proportion of female migrants on the ships. So while some women could have joined early migrations into South Asia, they are unlikely to have reached anything approaching equal representation.

4 Retroflexion is the series of consonants pronounced with the tip of the tongue curled backwards: *ṭ ḍ ṇ ḷ ṣ* (and others like *ṭṣ ḍẓ* that exist in north-western languages like Pashto and Burushaski). These retroflex consonants are in phonemic contrast with dental consonants, like *t d n l ś* (pronounced with the tip of the tongue behind the top front teeth). Like the contrast between *dānt* (tooth) and *ḍāṇṭ* (scolding), where all the consonants in the latter are retroflex.

5 Sanskrit, Persian and English would be the most striking exceptions to this pattern.

6 Narasimhan (and 116 others) 2019.

7 Chawla 1994: 2818.

8 Mohan 2021, Chapter 5.

9 See Chapter 3: pp. 73–74.

10 Abbi 2013:120–22.

11 Arun Ghosh, who works on Munda languages, sent me an email on 20 May 2023 with example sentences from all the Munda languages, and this summary:

'Of the northern Munda languages aside from Santali and Mundari, Ho and Birhor mark both subject (S) and object (O) on the verb. Korku of the north-western Munda marks object (O) on the verb.

'All the south Munda languages, like Sora, Gorum, Remo, Gutob and Gtaʔ mark subject (S) on the verb. Except Gorum all other languages of the group do not mark object (O) on the verb.

The intermediary Munda languages like Kharia and Juang mark subject (S) on the verb but not object (O).'

See, as an example, the object marker before the tense marker on the verb in the Santali example in the 'family photograph' of the Māgadhan languages in Chapter 5: pp. 207–10.

12 See Bibhu Dev Misra 2018.

13 Graeber and Wengrow 2021.

14 *Ibid.*: 89–90.

15 *Ibid.*: 105.

16 These examples were mentioned to me by Madhav Deshpande, and confirmed in an email on 30 July 2023.

17 See Note 6 above, a clear assertion from geneticists that they regard both the south Indian 'ASI' Dravidian populations and the 'Indus Periphery cline' as being of similar 'Dravidian stock': in fact, they have trouble telling both apart and distinguishing them as separate migrations: 'The strong correlation between *ASI* ancestry and present-day Dravidian languages suggests that the *ASI*, which we have shown formed as groups with ancestry typical of the *Indus Periphery Cline* moved south and east after the decline of the IVC to mix with groups with more *AASI* ancestry, most likely spoke an early Dravidian language.'

18 There are at least six different African communities in Trinidad and Tobago. The Africans brought by the Spanish in the 1500s and 1600s, the French-Creole-speaking Africans who came from Haiti, Martinique and Guadeloupe at the time of the French Revolution, the Ghanaians brought to Tobago, the Yoruba brought to Trinidad by the British, the 'Murricans', Afro-Americans settled in Trinidad after the American Civil War, and Africans who came from all the other islands and territories later on, as wages in Trinidad were higher.

19 The proportion of Indian women on the migrant ships to Trinidad never really went above 30 per cent, even with huge cash incentives offered to women in India to induce them to migrate. And most of the women on the ships were travelling without husbands, or with 'husbands' they had only just 'married' after an engagement ceremony in the Calcutta depot as they waited for the ship to arrive in Calcutta.

20 Bahata Ansumali Mukhopadhyay 2019.
21 Karan Pillai sent me a link to https://learnsangamtamil.com 201-400 that has the sources of these claims.
22 Sharada Srinivasan 2023.
23 *Ibid.*: 99.
24 'Excavation findings show iron age in TN dates back 4200 years', News Minute, 10 May 2022, https://www.thenewsminute.com/tamil-nadu/excavation-findings-show-iron-age-tn-dates-back-4200-years-all-you-need-know-163795#:~:text=Radiocarbon%20dating%20of%20excavations%20from,Assembly%20on%20Monday%2C%20May%209.
25 *Ibid.*
26 This was the 'Three-day 2nd International Seminar on *Reset Advances in Archaeological Investigations in South Asia* in commemoration of Padma Sri Iravatham Mahadevan's contribution to the Tamil Language and Tamil Society', organized by Tamil Nadu State Department of Archaeology, 10 to 12 March 2023.
27 Nazir Shakir Brahui, Director of the Brahui Research Institute, Shikarpur, Sindh, Pakistan, in a WhatsApp message sent on 7 September 2023.
28 Via WhatsApp message sent on 7 September 2023.
29 'Gonds', Encyclopedia.com, https://www.encyclopedia.com/social-sciences-and-law/anthropology-and-archaeology/people/gond#:~:text=Gond%20society%20is%20divided%20into,release%20by%20the%20hero%20Lingal (last accessed 9 December 2024).
30 Penny, Penny and Rao 2005: xiii.
31 Grierson 1906 (2017): 498–99.
32 K.V. Subbarao, a native speaker of Telugu, sent me a message on 3 September 2023 to tell me that Telugu, 'based on subject-verb agreement', has only two genders, masculine and non-masculine.
33 Penny, Penny and Rao 2005: xvii.
34 *Ibid.*: 500.
35 The final vowel *u* is an unrounded back vowel, written as *ı* in Turkish.

36 Grierson 1906 (2017): 301. The final vowel in the Tamil examples is an unrounded back vowel, written in Turkish as *ı*, though in the usual Romanization of Tamil it is written as *u*.

Ch. 7: A Chimera on the Northern Rim

1 Kilarsky and Tang 2018: 57.
2 *Ibid.*: abstract.
3 India Mapped: Languages of India.
4 'Prithvi Narayan Shah', Wikipedia, https://en.m.wikipedia.org/wiki/Prithvi_Narayan_Shah (accessed on 9 September 2023).
5 *Encyclopedia Britannica*: *Sino-Tibetan languages*. https://www.britannica.com/topic/Sino-Tibetan-languages?Use-of-noun-classifiers
6 The language is known as Newari (with a final –ī), and the speaker community is known as the Newar.
7 'History of Newar', Wikipedia, https://en.m.wikipedia.org/wiki/Newar_people (last accessed 9 December 2024).
8 *Ibid.*
9 Hyslop 2016: 17.
10 *Ibid.*
11 Meche is a Bodo-Garo language spoken in eastern Nepal, West Bengal and Assam, India.
12 Weidert 1984: 185.
13 Ebert 1994: 79–80.
14 Kansakar 2005: 110.
15 Kiryu 2009: 60.
16 *Ibid.*: 60–61.
17 *Ibid.*: 61–62.
18 *Ibid.*: 62.
19 See Chapter 5: pp. 179–80.
20 Assamese is an occasional exception, as both word orders are possible, the Māgadhan order with the numeral first, and the numeral following the noun, as was the pattern in Ahom.
21 See Chapter 5: p. 184.
22 Avtans 2022: 'Tibeto-Burman languages like Newari, Mizo, Galo, Rabha, Bodo, Garo, Karbi, and Kokborok are known to have an extensive set of classifiers but no grammatical gender.'

23 Masica 1991: 220–21.
24 Kilarski and Tang 2018: 59.
25 This is an example told to me by Ankit Wenju Shrestha, a native speaker of Newari and a student at Ashoka University, who sat in on a class discussion about the evolution of Nepali.
26 *Ibid.*
27 'Are Zebras White with Black Stripes or Black with White Stripes?' *Encyclopedia Britannica*: *Science & Tech.* https://www.britannica.com/story/are-zebras-white-with-black-stripes#:~:text=A%3A%20Azebra%20with%20A,revealing%20the%20rest%20as%20white.
28 This was Santosh Adhikari at Ashoka University, Delhi.
29 Poudel 2017: 2.
30 Li 2007: 172–73.
31 *Ibid.*: 181.
32 Kansākār 2005: 9-10.
33 See Chapter 3: pp. 73–75.
34 Bodo, like Newari, has no person agreement markers on verbs.
35 Amritavalli, R. and Sarma 2002: 1.
36 *Ibid.*
37 Saikia and Camilleri 2019: 264.
38 Bhandari 2008: 3.
39 *Ibid.*: 4.
40 *Ibid.*: 5.
41 Nagamese was discussed in detail in Chapter 6 of Mohan 2021.

Ch. 8: The Return of the Tiramisu Bear

1 The ones that weren't simply prakrits, like Nagamese.
2 Salikoko Mufwene's 2008 article in the *Encyclopedia Britannica* argues that the complex business dealings of the slave trade could not have been conducted in a 'broken language'.
3 Mufwene 2020: 312.
4 This is the retroflex ṣ in 'Usha', as distinct from the other ś in 'Asha'.
5 Tamil, because of the absence of Sanskrit/prakrit vocabulary, and Punjabi because it has all the retroflexes of Tamil, ***ṭ ḍ ṇ ḷ*** (*zh* is not actually retroflex, but retracted), avoids the voiced aspirates

gh jh ḍh dh bh, is full of geminate consonants like ***gg jj bb***, and is centred on modern-day Harappa.

6 'Retroflex Consonants', Wikipedia, https://en.wikipedia.org/wiki/Retroflex_consonant (last accessed 9 December 2024).

7 Kramer 2011: 48.

8 Donegan and Stampe 2002: 111 quoting Grierson 1904: 2.

9 Graeber and Wengrow 2021: 524.

Index

A

Abbi, Anvita 72, 325n19
Abhijñānaśakuntalaṁ 63
Aborigins, Grierson on 165
African/Africans 9, 12–15, 21, 23, 50, 162, 196, 245, 277; Muslims 245; slaves 2, 8, 11, 276–77, (*see also* slave plantations); women 15, 21–22, 276
Afro-Caribbean world 19
Agricultural vocabulary 192
Ajivikas 260, 197, 217
Aligarh 26–28
Aligarh Muslim University (AMU) 26
Amharic 72, 77, 286
Andamanese languages 135, 148, 210, 212
Andaman Islands 117, 228, 282–83
Andamans 72, 84, 120, 210, 212, 248
Ann Arbor 95
anti-Brahminism 204
Apabhraṁsas 80
Arab migration 245
Ardhamāgadhi 80, 159, 200, 217
Arora, Harbir Kaur 32–33, 35, 38–39, 45
Aryanization 201–2
Aryan language 201
Aryans 88, 95, 198, 200–201, 26
Āryāvarta 83, 86, 157, 159, 202–3, 217
Ashoka 63, 158–60, 174, 176, 200, 333n6; As Devānāmpiya Piyadasi 63; pillars 158
ASI (ancestral south Indians) 223–24
Assamese 172, 182–83, 187, 207–8, 260, 268–69, 271, 289; in the Indo-Aryan family 261; map 269
Atlantic slave trade 276

Australian(s): Aboriginal languages 77; Aborigines 162–63; First 116, 162–63, 188, 214; languages 72, 77; First 72, 77, 116, 212, 282–83; noun classes in languages 77
Austro-Asiatic 163, 165–66, 169, 172, 174, 183, 187–89, 191, 193, 195–97, 212, 215–16, 285; cognates 192; hybrids 207; languages 166, 195–96, 215; languages in Southeast Asia 172; language speakers 165, 190; lexifier languages 213; migration 87, 165, 187, 225; origins 189–90; people in Southeast Asia 167; populations 166; stamp 216; tribes 163
Avestan 64, 82, 102

B

Bahmani Sultanate 30, *see also* sultanates
Bahnar in Vietnam 170–71
Baiga tribes 162–63, 214
ballads 205, 218
Balochi 66, 70, 77, 79, 89, 91, 93, 110, 112–13, 117, 120, 122–24, 153; gender in 69
Balochistan 91, 101, 110–12, 114, 188, 222, 232, 241, 284
Baluchi 93
Banerjee, Sumanta 86, 88, 199, 203
Bangla 40, 85
Bantu languages 72, 77, 196, 245; of southern Africa 77
Barbadian 12
Barz, Richard 175–77, 179
Basham, A.L. 50
Bengal 48, 86, 199, 201–7, 213, 217–18
Bengali Language 87–88, 139, 172–73, 175, 182–83, 185, 199, 204–5, 218, 253–54, 260–61
Bhakti 48; cult 43; poets 105
Bhat, D.N.S. 116
Bhojpuri 39–41, 134, 136, 139, 146–47, 149–50, 159–60, 172–73, 177–78, 180–82, 186, 213–14, 253–54, 260–61; classifier 177–78; speakers 4; speaking migrants 177
Birhor 162–63, 209; as 'Munda' 163; tribes 163, 214
Bloch 182
Bodo 261, 268–69, 271, 289; map 269
Brahman: elite 218; and king nexus 205; Peshwas 206
brahmanism 160–61, 198
Brahman *śākhās* 7
Brahui (Dravidian language) 93, 112–13, 117, 123–24, 132, 141, 145–47, 149–50, 152–53, 281, 283–84; in

Balochistan 91, 110, 241, 281, 284; Caldwell and 92; conjunctive participles in 134; Kobayashi on 131; from IVC family 111, 149, 153; in Pakistan 91, 242; people 110, 242; reduplication in 138; as SOV languages 122; vocabulary 92; voiceless aspirates in 120
Brahui, Nazir Shakir 241–42
Braj 105, 176
Bray 92
Brazilian Portuguese 15
Bṛhadāraṇyaka Upaniṣad 198
Buddha 50, 159–60, 200
Buddhism 48, 51, 103, 159–60, 201, 203, 217, 257; in India 48, 201
Buddhism in India, Omvedt 50
Buddhists 48–51, 197–98, 200, 204, 257
Burmese 169, 174, 285, 290
Burushaski language 69–74, 76–77, 81–82, 89–90, 112–14, 117–18, 120, 122–23, 125–27, 129, 132, 134–37, 140–41, 145–50, 210–11, 228, 281–83; ergativity in 74; Hook, on 71; as IVC languages 70; in Karakorams 113; natural gender in 77; retroflexion in 118; verb agreement 126
Burusho 118, 137–38, 148, 282; in seclusion 289; wives 114

C

Caitanya Caritāmṛta, Gosvāmī 175
calques 28, 32, 106, 137, 280; modern 107
Cambodians 165
Caribbean: creoles 3, 8, 13, 28, 168; plantations 21–22; slave estates 12; sugar estates 9, 238
castes 47, 50, 140, 281; Brahmans 21, 81–82, 85, 87, 89, 126, 198, 203, 205–6, 218, 221; Draviḍa Brahmans 221; Kshatriyas 159–60, 198, 203; Namboodiri Brahmans 226; system 18, 47–49, 142–43, 160
cataclysms 202
Central Asia 89, 105, 223, 279, 311; male migrations 227
Central Asians 28, 144, 227, 280, 286
Champollion, Jean-Francois 99
Chao Li 266
Chatterji, Suniti Kumar 67, 88–89, 173–74, 198, 200–202
Chaubey, Gyaneshwer 189–90
Chinese 169, 172–74, 192
Chīshtī, Khwājā Muinuddin, (Sultan-é Hind, Gharīb Nawāz 1141-1236) 43
Christianity 49, 109
civilization 96, 99, 107, 142, 226

classifier languages 87, 211, 213, 216, 255, 264, 285, 288
Colonna, Vicenza 110, 113
conversion 47, 51, 53, 56–57, 280
Creole English 3–4, 12, 20, 22; Jamaican 3, 12; Trinidadian 3–4, 12, 22
'Creole Exceptionalism' 18
'Creole Languages' 14
creoles 2–4, 8–9, 11–15, 17–22, 24, 28, 41–42, 46, 54, 58, 101–2, 168, 170–71, 193–96, 215, 275–77, 279; backstory of 2; Dravidian 156; emergence of 12; English-based 168; in Gullah Islands 9; and homestead communities 14; as mixed languages 9; plantation 11, 18
creolisms 4

D

Dakhni /Dakni, Dakkhini or Dakkani 25, 27–28, 30, 32–39, 42–46, 51, 53–58, 78–79, 87, 152, 154, 250–51, 280–81; gender in 38; Hyderabadi Urdu as 27; literature 78; speakers 36, 52, 234; Telugu-flavoured 35; terrain (map) 29
Dardic language 74
Dasgupta, Probal 185, 187
Deccan 48; region 28, 30, 51; Sultanates 25, 32, 51–52, 56–57, 108
Dehlavi 29–30, 32, 43; dialect 42, 105, 280
Delhi Sultanate 28, 105, 227, 279
Demotic script 97–99
Deshpande, Madhav 79, 133, 142–43
Devanagari 48, 253
Dharurkar, Chinmay 53, 55, 139
diglossia 181
Diller, Anthony 175–77, 179
Dirr, Adolf 61
Donegan, Patricia Jane 191–93
Dravidian/Dravidians 33–35, 87–89, 91, 110, 112, 114, 151–52, 154–56, 163–65, 169, 171, 221–24, 236, 243, 251; civilization 228; culture 169, 250; first 249, 287; heritage 110–11; highway, map 229; migrants 236–37, 250–51; people 153, 219–20, 236, 249, 287, 290; saṁdhi rule 103, 118; settlement 235, 249; tribes 111, 163, 165
Dravidian languages 27–28, 32–34, 87, 90–91, 119, 127, 131–32, 135, 149–50, 152, 164, 223–24, 229–30, 243–44, 246–47, 249–51, 283–84, 287; first 251; gender in

39; mainstream 111, 243, 247, 250–51; mainstream, map 242; modern 78, 229; northern 132; southern 82, 129, 241; of south India 92, 112, 119, 228, 252; tribal 111, 242–43, 246, 250
Dreamtime 220–21, 247
Drechsel, Emanuel 20
Driem, George van 190

E

echo words 137–38, 145, 147
Egyptian hieroglyphics 97
Elamo-Dravidian 101
Emeneau, Murray B. 132, 174, 182, 184
English: grammar 5–6, 28; speakers 4, 7, 133; verb 6, 28, 81, *see also* Standard English
ergative: 'agent' 74; languages 36, 60–61, 266–67; marker 37, 45, 67–68, 73–74, 80–81, 265–67, 269, 271; realignment 61, 126, 129; variants in Extended Indus Valley Periphery (map) 75
ergativity 36–39, 53, 55, 58–74, 76–80, 83–86, 89–94, 112, 125, 129, 145–46, 149–50, 152–56, 210, 228, 234–35, 264–72, 282–89; Burushaski-style 146; in Dakkhini 154; and gender 115, 125–30, 149–50; in Nepali 265; split 58, 60, 66, 68, 71–72, 74, 76, 82–83, 90, 125–26, 129, 155–56, 269–70, 282–83; in western Balochi 69
Estonian 109
European languages 9, 11, 13, 15–16, 21, 24, 110, 172, 276–7, *see also* languages
Europeans 2, 9, 11, 13, 15–16, 20, 276–77

F

farmers 99, 114, 187, 222, 227, 232–33, 249
Farmer, Steve 96, 99
'father tongues' 114, 168, 193, 213
Faxian 200–201
Finnish 109
First Indian(s) 115–16, 137, 163, 165, 220, 222, 224, 236, 244, 246, 286–87; hunter-gatherers 249, 230, 232–33; languages of south 210, 223, 249–51; M haplogroup 164; population 231; tribes as 'Austro-Asiatic' 165, 183; wives 115, 235, 287–88; women 227
first migrants 19, 41, 58, 249

G

Ganga-Yamuna confluence 61, 86, 115, 217, 285; map 86

Garhwaḷi 116
Gauḍa Brahmans 221
gender agreement 36, 40–41, 66–67, 71, 73, 76–77, 79, 84, 150, 152, 159
gender system 38–41, 66–68, 71, 74, 76–78, 84, 87–88, 92, 125–27, 149–50, 171–72, 211–12, 216, 234–35, 253, 262–64, 271–72, 284–85; in Balochi 69; in Bhojpuri 40; in Dravidian languages 39; map of South Asia 128; markers 73, 93, 102, 126, 131, 146; in Pashto 68
Gésudarāz, *see* Hussaini, Khwaja Syed Mohammed 44
ghazals 42; literary Urdu in 320n1
Ghosh, Arun 185–86
Gilgiti Shina 74, 76
Göbelki Tepe 232–33
goldsmiths 49, 238–39
Gondi language 127, 243–44, 246–48
Gonds 243–44, 246; migrations 244
Gopālarājavaṃśavalī [GV] 259
Gorkhali language 255
Gorum 163, 209–10
Graeber, David 232–33, 293
grammar 2, 9–10, 13–14, 16–17, 24, 28, 31, 41–42, 98–99, 102, 110, 154–55, 277–79; accent 7, 16, 23, 102–3, 194, 273, 276–77; adjectives 36, 38–39, 41, 66, 71, 77, 84, 124, 126–27, 150, 156, 178, 272; adverbs 124, 130, 136; 'agent' 36, 60, 62, 65, 71, 74; compound verbs 115, 130–35, 145, 147–48, 150, 283; conjunctive participles 134–35, 145, 147; feminine 37–38, 40, 55, 62, 67–69, 77, 84, 234, 247, 262–63, 272; feminine nouns 38, 40, 172, 271; finite verbs 36, 62, 64–66, 80–83, 126, 129–32, 134–35, 139, 247; gender 38–41, 55, 58, 76–78, 85, 87–89, 104, 127, 155–56, 171, 195, 234–35, 254–55, 262–64, 270–72; 'green verbs' 4; natural gender 38, 40–41, 77–78, 84, 87, 90, 92, 127, 129, 171, 235, 247, 263–64, 272; nouns 10, 38–39, 41, 55, 66–67, 71, 88, 122–24, 126, 178, 182–83, 208, 257–58, 260, 262–63; 'object' 10, 36, 59–60, 65–69, 71–74, 76–78, 81–82, 84, 122, 126–27, 173, 209, 211–12, 228, 260, 264–65, 286; past participles 62–67, 74, 79–82, 85, 88, 90, 126, 129–30, 133, 142, 234; postpositions 5, 10, 60, 122–23, 145, 147; prepositions 122–24, 130; pronouns 35, 71, 87, 136, 152, 192, 247,

251; vector verb 131; verb endings 38–39, 41, 87, 152, 235; verb morphology 72, 85; verbs 36–40, 59–60, 62–63, 66–69, 71–74, 77, 79–81, 83–84, 122–24, 126–27, 129–30, 132–34, 150–52, 208–12, 228, 262–64, 266–67, 271–72
Great Andamanese 72, 81, 127; Abbi on 325n19; noun classes in 77
great disconnect 155, 159
Greek 50, 97–98, 102, 124, 293
Grierson, George 164–66, 173, 177–80, 182–83, 186, 192–93, 247, 249; language samples 197; Santali samples 202
Gujarat 36, 67, 238
Gujarati 77, 87, 104, 116, 121, 148
Gumperz, John 54
Guptas 201
Guyanese 12, 17

H

Harappa 58, 94, 106–7, 115, 118, 131, 146, 149–50, 152, 161, 239
Hawaii 9, 20, 190
Hawaiian: Pidgin English 20; sugar estates 20
Hindavi 45
Hindi 5, 28–29, 48, 62–63, 76–77, 79, 83–84, 130–31, 138–40, 151, 159–60, 214, 273; family 36, 104–5, 148
Hindi-Urdu 36, 78, 82, 87, 121, 124, 153; northern 35, 38, 45; north Indian 32–33, 35, 38, 45–46
Hinduism 47–49, 51, 201
Hinglish 152, 219
Ho 130, 163, 209
homestead farms 15, 21, 276
honorifics 115, 138–43, 145, 147, 149–50, 283
Hook, Peter 71, 131–32, 149
Hue in Vietnam 170
Huns 201
hunter-gatherers 101, 115, 210, 222, 230–32
Hunza Burushaski 123
Hussaini, Khwaja Syed Mohammed 44
hybridization 215, 235, 250
hybrid languages 25, 39, 213, 271
Hyderabad 26, 32, 37–38, 42, 47, 51, 162
Hyderabadi: Dakkhini 27; dialect 27

I

Indian English 5–6, 28, 81, 123, *see also* Standard English

Indian languages 6, 10, 28, 81, 123, 162, 253; First 81, 115, 127, 196, 210, 223, 249–51
Indian M haplogroup, First 164
Indian migration 12, 19, 237; to Caribbean 237; women in Indian migration to Trinidad 330n33, 341–41n19
Indo-Aryan (IA) 213, 217, 261; modern 80
Indo-Aryan languages 2–3, 5, 9–11, 16, 18, 21–22, 112, 121–22, 174, 184, 192, 211–13, 217, 251–52, 261–63, 267–68; dialects 277; hybrids 207; Māgadhan languages 172, 180, 184; Middle 80, 89, 174, 200, 202; modern 2, 5, 21, 70, 88–89, 92, 103–4, 112, 114, 134, 272; of South Asia 2; vocabularies 202, 235, 261; western 77–79, 90, 121, 158, 171, 212, 219, 262, 271–72, 287–88
Indo-European languages 109–10, 198
Indus Valley 68, 71, 77, 80, 90, 100–101, 104, 106–7, 113–14, 169, 171, 221–26, 229–31, 236, 238; Dravidians 229; languages 65, 70, 76, 107, 113, 127, 129, 141, 149, 228, 241, 251
Indus Valley Civilization (IVC) 97, 101, 107, 110, 112, 221–22, 224, 226–27, 231–32, 281, 283, 287, 290; fall of 226; old 143
Indus Valley Periphery 69–70, 91, 106, 109–10, 113, 117, 122–24, 147–48, 160, 228, 281; Extended 86, 88, 104, 106–7, 147, 150–51, 154–56, 158, 226, 228, 230–32, 249–50, 282; Extended, map 64; Extended, Modern gender in 84; Extended, languages 79, 104, 115, 156, 234–35, 285;map 52; modern 125, 269
interpreters 15–16, 24, 194, 276
Iranian languages 68, 70, 91, 120, 123, 148, 284, 325n15
Islam 31, 44–45, 47–48, 51–53, 56–57, 204, 245, 280

J

Jainism 103, 159–60, 217
Jains 197–98, 200
Jajolet, Michel 14
Jamaica 3, 54
Jamaicans 3–4, 17; migrants 50
Japanese 131, 152, 172–74, 183, 190

K

Kālidāsa 63
Kammalar community 242
Kannada 25, 30, 32–33, 41, 53–54, 144, 234–35, 243–44,

247, 250; grammar 31, 34; northern 53, 55; speakers 34; speakers (northern) 55; verbs 127
Karakorams 69, 74, 113, 125, 132, 135, 149, 210, 228, 281
Karim, Piar 123
Karnali-Seti river valley 255
Karnataka 51, 61
Karnataka Saraswat Konkani (Mangalore Konkani) 34
Kashmiri 122
Kathmandu Valley 256–57, 261, 270, 288
Khairi, Anwar 68
Khan, Changez 227
Khasas 255, 257, 261–63, 270, 288; migrants 270; vocabulary 261
Khasi 122, 165
Khaskura 255, 271
Khilji, Alauddin 30
Khmer 165, 174, 191, 290
Khusro, Amir 29, 105
Kiranti Languages 258
Kiryu, Kazuyuki 258, 260
Kiyaa, Peter 225
Kobayashi, Masato 131
Kōl tribes 202
Konkani 33–34, 55, 79, 104, 144, *see also* Karnataka Saraswat Konkani
Korean 172, 174, 190
Korku 116, 163, 191, 209–10
Kulkarni-Joshi, Sonal 54
Kumar, Satish 162
Kuraishi Bidari 45
Kuru kingdom 83, 111, 132, 284
Kurux/ Kurukh 111
Kushanas 51

L

labour force, contract labourers 20
languages: agglutinative 285; approximation of migrant men's 41; common 43, 45, 191, 290; ethnic 52, 54, 290; of First Indians 115; Indus Valley 16, 77, 81–84, 96, 100–101, 106, 109, 115, 120, 149, 184; of Indus Valley Periphery 69–70, 113, 120, 123–24, 147, 228, 281; local 24, 30, 118, 133, 159, 206, 218, 245, 277–78, 291; lexifier 24, 39, 122, 213; mainstream 91, 110, 112, 139, 248; mixed 3, 8–9, 11, 16–17, 19, 22, 25, 112, 114, 190, 193, 272, 275, 277–78, 280; mixed West African 11; modern Indian 8; native 8, 18, 24, 30, 101, 245; new 9, 58, 87, 89, 105, 155, 194–95, 213, 215, 217–18, 261, 264, 273, 280, 286; old 9, 13, 18–20, 90, 99, 101, 109–12, 155, 161, 164, 194–95, 278–79, 281; older local 16, 23, 215, 218, 279; old local 17;

of Pakistan (Punjabi, Sindhi, Balochi, Pashto) 36, 113, 115, 117, 137; Portuguese-based 14; of 'Saurashtra' 87; tribal 334n14
Latin 102, 109, 124, 134; 'ablative absolute' in 134
Light Verbs (LV) 115, 123–25, 145, 147; in Hindi-Urdu (Hindustani) 124; Pakistan 124
Lingala, in Democratic Republic of the Congo 72
linguistics 14, 49, 53–55, 104, 106, 110, 185, 187, 190, 192–93, 196, 213, 249, 251–52, 255, 272–73
Linguistic Survey of India (LSI) 72, 111, 116, 164, 170, 172–73, 176, 183, 186, 191–92, 197, 202
literature 13, 45, 99, 180, 204–5, 213–14, 218, 243
little people 11, 16, 18, 23–24, 39, 45–48, 56–57, 108, 154–55, 159–60, 176, 197, 204–6, 217–18, 279–80; languages 13, 24, 107, 217
localisms 7
local people 3, 16, 23, 30, 44, 107, 194, 203, 277, 280, 290

M

Madhya Pradesh 36, 163, 244
Magadha 85, 87, 160–61, 170, 197–98, 200–203, 205, 219; culture 217; dialects 286; forests 83; lands 115, 148, 182, 198, 228, 257, 284; region 104, 161, 174, 181, 207, 212–13, 218, 286
Māgadhan Apabhraṃśa 174
Māgadhan languages 154, 172–74, 183, 186, 207–8, 211, 215, 218, 253–54, 257, 260–61, 285, 288; map 158, 181; modern 85, 187; newest 131; as 'nonergative' 324n2
Māgadhan Prakrit 4, 64, 85, 159, 174, 200, 217
Māgadhans 86, 155, 158–59, 161, 173, 177, 186, 199, 219
Magahi 85, 104, 172, 178, 180–81, 213–14, 218
Maharashtra 27, 30, 36, 53, 61, 85–87, 230, 232, 234–35, 244, 249, 287–88
Mahārāshtri Prakrit 85
Mahavira 159–60, 200
Maithilī 85, 104, 172, 178–82, 207, 213, 218, 254, 260–61; Bengali 180; Bhojpurī 180; Brahmans 257, 260–61; Magadhī 180; northern 180; numeral classifiers 260; scribe 260
Malay 174; Peninsular tribes 165
Malayalam 83, 87, 119, 122, 139, 141, 148, 151–52, 241,

243, 247–48, 250, 296–98; Sanskrit words in 216
Malla 257–58
Malto 111
Marathi 30, 33–35, 53–55, 76–77, 79, 87, 119, 121, 144, 232, 234–35; Modern 67, 199, 234; southern 53, 55, 61; speaker 31, 34; Standard 31, 54, 234; territory (map) 52
Maritime Polynesian Pidgin (MPP) 20; Drechsel on 20
Markam, Santoshi 246
masculine 36–40, 55, 66–69, 77, 84, 126, 171, 234–35, 247, 262–63, 271–72; vs non-masculine 127
Masica, Colin P. 96, 101, 327n1
Masood, Talat 124
Mauryas 200
[Max] Müller, Friedrich 164, 192
Mayiladumparai 240
McAlpin, David 101
Mehrgarh (now Balochistan) 187, 222, 227
M haplogroup 161, 164, 188, 214
migrant labour 12, 41
migrants 19–21, 41–42, 70, 113–14, 187, 189–90, 194, 210–11, 215, 222–23, 231, 236–37, 249–50, 287–88; language 256; recruitment 20; Sultanate 46; from Zagros mountains 210
migration 19, 30, 114, 116, 153, 161–62, 166–67, 170, 187–88, 194, 214, 216, 231, 237–38, 241, 246, 251, 270, 285; First Peoples 166; as male-driven 225; marriage and 226; voluntary 50; from Zagros mountains 187, 222
Minhaj-i-Sirāj 202
modern languages 69–70, 82, 84–85, 91, 94, 104, 107, 109, 112–15, 146–47, 150, 155–56, 159, 205, 281–83; of north India 205
Mohenjo Daro 100, 107, 115, 239
Mon, from Thailand and Burma 170
Mon-Khmer languages 165, 191–92, 290
mother tongues 12, 16, 19, 22–23, 102, 237, 244
Mufwene, Salikoko 14–15, 17, 20, 24, 276–77
Mukhopadhyay, Bahata Ansumali 99–100, 104, 238
Munda 82, 87, 137, 161, 163–65, 167–70, 172–74, 180, 184–89, 191–97, 215–16; Gangetic 214; and Mon-Khmer languages 290; people/Muṇḍās 164, 187–89, 207, 215–16, 289; populations 190, 213, 284;

tribal language, (*See* Munda languages) tribes 163, 172, 212, 214, 284; vigesimal (old) 164
Munda-Austro-Asiatic Tiramisu bear 196
Munda languages: 87, 120, 164–66, 168–73, 183–85, 188, 190, 196–97, 207–8, 210–12, 215–16, 285–86, 327n41; as 'Austro-Asiatic' 196; as father tongues 190; North, map 208; northern 67, 81, 127, 209–11, 228–29, 285–86; old 161; Sora 116
Mundari 163, 184, 209
Muslims: early sultanates 205–6; rulers 205–6, 218; as rulers of Bengal 204; Tamil-speaking 52

N

Nagamese 131, 272–73, 291
Nancowry 165
native speakers 20, 23, 32, 42, 53, 55, 61, 123, 222, 234, 263; Marathi 32; of Telugu 28, 32, 246; of Trinidad Bhojpuri 131
Nawāz, Banda, *see* Hussaini, Khwaja Syed Mohammed
Ndjuka 196
Nehru, Jawaharlal 144
Nepali 252–55, 257–58, 261–66, 268–73, 283, 288–89
Nepal Mandala 257
Newari 257–58, 260–63, 266–71, 289; dialects of 257; Kiryu on 258; map 256; Modern 259–60; speakers 256, 270
Newitt, Malyn D.D. 15
Nigeria, indigenous languages of 18
Nigerian Pidgin English 17–18, *see also* Standard English
Nilgiris 239
non-native speaker 83, 131
non-Vedic Aryans 198
north Indian languages 8, 27, 32, 153, 290; modern 8, 11, 24, 121
numeral classifier systems 172–80, 182–87, 196–97, 207–8, 211–12, 215–17, 254–62, 264, 270–72, 285, 288–89
numerals 136, 182, 185, 192, 258–59

O

object marking 72, 77–78, 81–82, 209–10, 212, 216, 286
Odia 40, 85, 104, 172, 182–83, 218, 260
Omotic languages 286
Omvedt, Gail 50
onomatopoeic sounds 136
operating system 8, 56, 101, 170, 215, 223, 277

oral 7, 99, 103
'orang asli' 165–66, 193, 214

P

Pagani, Luca 110, 113
Pahari languages 255
Pakistan, Balochi and Brahui in, map 91
Pala dynasty 48, 201
Pālas of Bengal 202, 217
Pāli 80, 89, 133, 159, 200, 217
palm leaf manuscript 258–59
Pāṇini 100, 133, 142; grammar 81
Panjâbi 93
Para-Munda 101, *see also* Munda
Parpola, Asko 101
Pashto 66, 68–70, 76–77, 79, 113, 117–18, 120, 122–24, 148, 282; genders in 68
Pattanaik, Devdutt 138
Paÿol, Spanish-based language 14–15
Peaceful Expansion of Islam in India, Rahman 44
Persian 29–30, 42, 52, 56, 92–93, 110, 113, 123–24, 279, 286
pidgin-creole: model 8, 12, 42, 275; theory 9
pidgins 2–3, 8, 11–15, 17–20, 22, 42, 194, 231, 275–77; expanded 17–18; speakers 20; Whinnom, onKeith 318n8
plantations 14, 18–22, 24, 277; cocoa 14; colonial 11, 18, 20; economy 14, 21; settlement colonies 17
Pombeiros 15
Pontic Caspian Steppe 199
Portuguese 9, 15–16, 23, 169
Poudel, Tikaram 265
prakrit: languages 155; meaning of 5; speakers of 7, 23, 70
prakrits 3–7, 9–11, 15–16, 23–24, 56–58, 62–63, 65–66, 80–85, 103–6, 121–23, 125–27, 154–56, 158–60, 183–84, 194–95, 205–7, 213, 216–19, 276–79, 286–87; Indo-Aryan 16, 113, 216
Prasad, Venkat Kishan 246
Proto Indo-European 145
Proto-Munda 115, 187
Punjabi 66–67, 70, 76–77, 79, 113, 115–18, 120–24, 129, 131, 146–52, 282–83; Modern 66, 152

R

Rahman, Syed Ubaidur 44
Rajasthan 36, 67
Rajasthani 76, 79, 87, 104, 116, 121, 148

Rau, Felix 189
reduplication 115, 135–38, 145, 147
relative clauses 31–35, 45, 152–53; Dakkhini-style 153; Dravidian-style 153
'relative linker' 32–34
retroflex 68–69, 125, 145, 148, 162, 286; consonants 115–17, 163, 187; phonemes 116, 148; sounds 116, 118, 147, 151, 282
Rig Veda 7, 62, 82, 99–100, 108, 117, 142, 147; Sanskrit 146–47; story of Vritra in 225
rock inscriptions 63, 103, 158, *see also* Ashoka pillars
Rosetta Stone 98, 114
Rumi, Shah Sultan 204

S

Saba, Tabasum 124
saṁdhi rules 7, 10, 151
Sami 109
Sanskrit 2, 5–6, 16, 81, 133; as 'father tongue' 16; instrumental case ending 62, 65; native speakers of 23; as oral 103; oral nature 7; passives 65, 129–30; purists 7; speakers 7; verbs 65, 84, 89, 93, 155
Sanskrit-Prakrit-Brahmans-Kings formula 206
Santali 185–86, 207–9; speakers 163
Saramacaans 196
Saranga, Rani, story of 157
Satavahanas 51
Saurashtran Gujarati 34, 55
'Sayyid Muhammad Gesu Daraz' 44
Semitic 196
settlement colonies 18, 21–22
settlers 3, 16, 240, 277–79, 281, 289; in Kathmandu Valley 257; male 23; map 229
Shah, Prithvi Narayan 255
Shaheen, Shagufta 38, 43
Shahid, Baba Adam 43, 204
Shahid, Sajjad 36, 43
Shakespeare's *Macbeth* 22
Sherpa 258, 273
Shina languages 74, 89, 125, 132, 210, 267
Shivaji 206
Sidwell, Paul 189
Sindhi 66–67, 70–71, 77, 79, 92–93, 113, 115, 117, 120, 122–23, 129, 241
Sivakalai excavations 240
Skandapurāṇa 221
slave: plantations 2, 9, 196, 277; trade 15, 21, 50, *see also* plantations
slavery 9, 13, 21, 196, 245
Southeast Asian: classifier languages 212; japonica 167; languages 122–23, 130–31, 137, 164, 170, 173, 187

Southworth, Franklin 96, 101
'SOV' languages 122–23
Spanish 11, 14–15, 23
Sproat, Richard 96, 99
Srinivasan, Sharada 239–40, 242
Stampe, David 190–93
Standard English 3, 6, 27–29
standardization 181, 214
Steever, Sanford 131
steppe ancestry 200
Stieng in Vietnam 170
Subbarao, K.V. 28, 33–34, 55, 247
subjects 10, 36–37, 59–62, 65–66, 68–69, 74, 81–84, 102, 126–27, 211–12, 228, 234–35, 268–69, 282–83, 285–86
Sufiism 43
Sufis 43–44, 46–48, 51, 56, 78, 105, 204–5, 218
sugar estates 12, 49; plantations, Caribbean 12; of Hawaii 20, *see also* plantations; slave plantations
sultanates 30, 43–46, 51, 56, 204, 206, 279–80, *see also* Deccan sultanates;
Swahili 196, 245; in Tanzania 72
Syntactic Convergence, Arora 32

T

Ṭabaqāt-i-Nāṣirī 202
Tai 182
Tai-Ahom migration 182–83
Tamang 273
Tamil 137, 139, 141, 145–48, 150–52, 235, 241, 243–44, 246–48, 250, 283; Burushaski Brahui 145–56; civilization 240; verbs 127
Tamil Nadu 51, 139, 240, 242
Tangomaos 15
Tätte, Kai 165
Telugu 25, 30–33, 35, 39, 41, 54, 56–58, 78, 119, 122, 243–44, 246–47, 250; calques 28
'texts' 7, 35
Thai 174, 183
Tibetan languages 132, 271
Tibeto-Burman 261, 272, 288; languages 132, 256–58, 268, 270–71, 283; substratum 268, 272, 289; vocabularies 261
Tiramisu Bear 22, 156, 195, 207, 270, 273, 275, 277, 281, 284, 287–89
Tiramisu bear hybrids 223, 251
Tobagonian 17
trade: colonies 17; groups 163–64, 231, 244, 246, 250–51, 256; languages 116, 121–22, 137, 165, 228, 243, 251, 277, 291
tribal languages 116, 137, 165, 217, 228, 243, 277, 291, 320–21n2; of central India 122; as Dravidian 165, 251

Trinidad 3, 5, 19–20, 22, 134–35, 137, 141, 173, 177, 179; rural 22, 176; as Spanish colony 14
Trinidad Bhojpuri 131, 136
Trinidadian 17
bin Tughluq, Sultan Muhammad 30
Turks 202; Central Asia 30

U

Unravelling the Bengali Identity, Banerjee 203
urbanization 21, 240
Urdu 25, 28–29, 36, 54, 61, 92, 110, 113, 115, 117–18; Hyderabadi 27; northern 42, 250–51; Persian words in 216; speaking Aligarh 27
Uttar Pradesh 20, 26, 157
Uzbekistan 144, 286

V

Vedic: Ārya 198, 200; Brahmans 157, 160, 199–200; Hinduism 160; language 80; men 23, 70–71, 100–101, 103, 108, 117, 169, 188, 227; migration 16, 102, 108; Sanskrit 132, 141–42
vernaculars 80–81, 89, 141, 217; local 8
Vietnamese 165, 169, 174, 285, 290
voiced aspirates 119–21, 129–30, 145, 147; map of areas occur 121
voiceless aspirates 119–20, 122, 145, 147
Vrātyas 198–200

W

Wanderers, Kings, Merchants, Mohan 2, 11, 16, 49, 57, 109, 291
'Well' 276, 279
Wengrow, David 232–33, 293
West Africa 2, 12–13, 16, 21, 23–24, 196, 276; languages 9, 13, 16, 168
West Indies 3, 54, 168
WhatsApp 7, 38, 55, 138–39, 241
Whinnom, Keith 318n8
White: planters 23; traders 23, *see also* slave, trade
Wier, Thomas 61
Wilson, Robert 54
Winter, Paul 1, 26, 59, 95, 157, 220, 253, 275
Witzel, Michael 96, 99, 101
women 18–23, 47, 51, 70–71, 114, 193, 197, 225–27, 236–38, 287–88; Indian 20, 237; local 16, 19, 23, 107, 190, 194, 222, 226, 231, 237, 245, 251, 256
womenfolk 16, 19, 30, 227

word order 98, 115, 122–23, 191, 260
Wright, Frank Lloyd 1

X

Xhosa, Republic of South Africa 72
Xuanzang 200–201

Y

Yoshioka, Noburo 71, 132, 134, 136–37

Z

Zagros mountains 81, 101, 114, 153, 187, 210, 222, 227, 233, 236, 249
Zatalli 42
Zehi, Mousa Mahmoud 124
Zulu, Republic of South Africa 72

Scan QR code to access the
Penguin Random House India website